On Writing Well

BOOKS BY WILLIAM ZINSSER

Any Old Place With You

Seen Any Good Movies Lately?

The City Dwellers

Weekend Guests

The Haircurl Papers

Pop Goes America

The Paradise Bit

The Lunacy Boom

On Writing Well

Writing With a Word Processor

Willie and Dwike
(*republished as* Mitchell and Ruff)

Writing to Learn

Spring Training

American Places

Speaking of Journalism

Easy to Remember

AUDIO BOOKS BY WILLIAM ZINSSER

On Writing Well
How to Write a Memoir

BOOKS EDITED BY WILLIAM ZINSSER

Extraordinary Lives: The Art and Craft of American Biography

Inventing the Truth: The Art and Craft of Memoir

Spiritual Quests: The Art and Craft of Religious Writing

Paths of Resistance: The Art and Craft of the Political Novel

Worlds of Childhood: The Art and Craft of Writing for Children

They Went: The Art and Craft of Travel Writing

Going on Faith: Writing as a Spiritual Quest

On Writing Well

THE CLASSIC GUIDE TO WRITING NONFICTION

25th Anniversary Edition

William Zinsser

Quill
A HarperResource Book
An Imprint of HarperCollinsPublishers

HarperCollins books may be purchased for educational, business, or sales promotional use. For information, please write to: Special Markets Department, HarperCollins Publishers, Inc., 10 East 53rd Street, New York, NY 10022.

Designed by Alma Orenstein.

First HarperResource Quill edition published 2001.

Library of Congress Cataloging-in-Publication Data

Zinsser, William Knowlton.
    On writing well : the classic guide to writing nonfiction / William Zinsser. —
25th anniversary ed.
        p. cm.
    Includes bibliographical references.
    ISBN 0-06-000664-1
    1. English language—Rhetoric. 2. Exposition (Rhetoric) 3. Report writing.
        I. Title.

PE1429 .Z5 2001
808'.042—dc21   2001041623

ISBN 0-06-000664-1 (pbk.)

01 02 03 04 05 ❖/RRD 10 9 8 7 6 5 4 3

C O N T E N T S

PART IV   Attitudes

INTRODUCTION

When I first wrote this book, in 1976, the readers I had in mind were a relatively small segment of the population: students, writers, editors and people who wanted to learn to write. I wrote it on a typewriter, the highest technology then available. I had no inkling of the electronic marvels just around the corner that were about to revolutionize the act of writing. First came the word processor, in the 1980s, which made the computer an everyday tool for people who had never thought of themselves as writers. Then came the Internet and e-mail, in the 1990s, which completed the revolution. Today everybody in the world is writing to everybody else, keeping in touch and doing business across every border and time zone.

To me this is nothing less than a miracle, curing overnight what appeared to be a deep American disorder. I've been repeatedly told by people in nonwriting occupations—especially people in science, technology, medicine, business and finance—that they hate writing and can't write and don't want to be made to write. One thing they particularly didn't want to write was letters. Just getting started on a letter loomed as a chore with so many formalities—Where's the stationery? Where's the envelope? Where's the stamp?—that they would keep putting it off, and when they finally did sit down to write they would spend the entire first paragraph explaining why they hadn't written sooner.

In the second paragraph they would describe the weather in their part of the country—a subject of no interest anywhere else. Only in the third paragraph would they begin to relax and say what they wanted to say.

Then along came e-mail and all the formalities went away. E-mail has no etiquette. It doesn't require stationery, or neatness, or proper spelling, or preliminary chitchat. E-mail writers are like people who stop a friend on the sidewalk and say, "Did you see the game last night?" WHAP! No amenities. They just start typing at full speed. So here's the miracle: All those people who said they hate writing and can't write and don't want to write *can* write and *do* want to write. In fact, they can't be turned off. Never have so many Americans written so profusely and with so few inhibitions. Which means that it wasn't a cognitive problem after all. It was a cultural problem, rooted in that old bugaboo of American education: fear.

Fear of writing gets planted in American schoolchildren at an early age, especially children of scientific or technical or mechanical bent. They are led to believe that writing is a special language owned by the English teacher, available only to the humanistic few who have "a gift for words." But writing isn't a skill that some people are born with and others aren't, like a gift for art or music. Writing is talking to someone else on paper. Anybody who can think clearly can write clearly, about any subject at all. That has always been the central premise of this book.

On one level, therefore, the new fluency created by e-mail is terrific news. Any invention that eliminates the fear of writing is up there with air conditioning and the lightbulb. But, as always, there's a catch. Nobody told all the new e-mail writers that the essence of writing is rewriting. Just because they are writing with ease and enjoyment doesn't mean they are writing well.

That condition was first revealed in the 1980s, when people began writing on word processors. Two opposite things happened. The word processor made good writers better and bad writers worse. Good writers know that very few sentences come out right the first time, or even the third time or the fifth time. For them the word processor was a rare gift, enabling them to fuss endlessly with their sentences—cutting and revising and reshaping—without the drudgery of retyping. Bad writers became even more verbose because writing was suddenly so easy and their sentences looked so pretty on the screen. How could such beautiful sentences not be perfect?

E-mail pushed that verbosity to a new extreme: chatter unlimited. It's a spontaneous medium, not conducive to slowing down or looking back. That makes it ideal for the never-ending upkeep of personal life: maintaining contact with far-flung children and grandchildren and friends and long-lost classmates. If the writing is often garrulous or disorganized or not quite clear, no real harm is done.

But e-mail is also where much of the world's business is now conducted. Millions of e-mail messages every day give people the information they need to do their job, and a badly written message can cause a lot of damage. Employers have begun to realize that they literally cannot afford to hire men and women who can't write sentences that are tight and logical and clear. The new information age, for all its high-tech gadgetry, is, finally, writing-based. E-mail, the Internet and the fax are all forms of writing, and writing is, finally, a craft, with its own set of tools, which are words. Like all tools, they have to be used right.

On Writing Well is a craft book. That's what I set out to write 25 years ago—a book that would teach the craft of writing warmly and clearly—and its principles have never changed; they are as valid in the digital age as they were in the age of the typewriter. I don't mean that the book itself hasn't changed. I've revised and expanded it five times since 1976 to keep pace with new trends in the language and in society: a far greater interest in memoir-writing, for instance, and in writing about business and science and sports, and in nonfiction writing by women and by newcomers to the United States from other cultural traditions.

I'm also not the same person I was 25 years ago. Books that teach, if they have a long life, should reflect who the writer has become at later stages of his own long life—what he has been doing and thinking about. *On Writing Well* and I have grown older and wiser together. In each of the five new editions the new material consisted of things I had learned since the previous edition by continuing to wrestle with the craft as a writer. As a teacher, I've become far more preoccupied with the intangibles of the craft—the attitudes and values, like enjoyment and confidence and intention, that keep us going and produce our best work. But it wasn't until the sixth edition that I knew enough to write the two chapters (21 and 22) that deal at proper length with those attitudes and values.

Ultimately, however, good writing rests on craft and always will. I don't know what still newer electronic marvels are waiting just around the corner to make writing twice as easy and twice as fast in the next 25 years. But I do know they won't make writing twice as good. That will still require plain old hard work—clear thinking—and the plain old tools of the English language.

William Zinsser
September 2001

PART I

Principles

1

~~~
≈≈≈
~~~

The Transaction

A school in Connecticut once held "a day devoted to the arts," and I was asked if I would come and talk about writing as a vocation. When I arrived I found that a second speaker had been invited—Dr. Brock (as I'll call him), a surgeon who had recently begun to write and had sold some stories to magazines. He was going to talk about writing as an avocation. That made us a panel, and we sat down to face a crowd of students and teachers and parents, all eager to learn the secrets of our glamorous work.

Dr. Brock was dressed in a bright red jacket, looking vaguely bohemian, as authors are supposed to look, and the first question went to him. What was it like to be a writer?

He said it was tremendous fun. Coming home from an arduous day at the hospital, he would go straight to his yellow pad and write his tensions away. The words just flowed. It was easy. I then said that writing wasn't easy and wasn't fun. It was hard and lonely, and the words seldom just flowed.

Next Dr. Brock was asked if it was important to rewrite.

Absolutely not, he said. "Let it all hang out," he told us, and whatever form the sentences take will reflect the writer at his most natural. I then said that rewriting is the essence of writing. I pointed out that professional writers rewrite their sentences over and over and then rewrite what they have rewritten.

"What do you do on days when it isn't going well?" Dr. Brock was asked. He said he just stopped writing and put the work aside for a day when it would go better. I then said that the professional writer must establish a daily schedule and stick to it. I said that writing is a craft, not an art, and that the man who runs away from his craft because he lacks inspiration is fooling himself. He is also going broke.

"What if you're feeling depressed or unhappy?" a student asked. "Won't that affect your writing?"

Probably it will, Dr. Brock replied. Go fishing. Take a walk. Probably it won't, I said. If your job is to write every day, you learn to do it like any other job.

A student asked if we found it useful to circulate in the literary world. Dr. Brock said he was greatly enjoying his new life as a man of letters, and he told several stories of being taken to lunch by his publisher and his agent at Manhattan restaurants where writers and editors gather. I said that professional writers are solitary drudges who seldom see other writers.

"Do you put symbolism in your writing?" a student asked me.

"Not if I can help it," I replied. I have an unbroken record of missing the deeper meaning in any story, play or movie, and as for dance and mime, I have never had any idea of what is being conveyed.

"I *love* symbols!" Dr. Brock exclaimed, and he described with gusto the joys of weaving them through his work.

So the morning went, and it was a revelation to all of us. At the end Dr. Brock told me he was enormously interested in my answers—it had never occurred to him that writing could be hard. I told him I was just as interested in *his* answers—it had never occurred to me that writing could be easy. Maybe I should take up surgery on the side.

As for the students, anyone might think we left them bewildered. But in fact we gave them a broader glimpse of the writing process than if only one of us had talked. For there isn't any "right" way to do such personal work. There are all kinds of writers and all kinds of methods, and any method that helps you to say what you want to say is the right method for you. Some people write by day, others by night. Some people need silence, others turn on the radio. Some write by hand, some by word processor, some by talking into a tape recorder. Some people write their first draft in one long burst and then revise; others can't write the second paragraph until they have fiddled endlessly with the first.

But all of them are vulnerable and all of them are tense. They are driven by a compulsion to put some part of themselves on paper, and yet they don't just write what comes naturally. They sit down to commit an act of literature, and the self who emerges on paper is far stiffer than the person who sat down to write. The problem is to find the real man or woman behind the tension.

Ultimately the product that any writer has to sell is not the subject being written about, but who he or she is. I often find myself reading with interest about a topic I never thought would interest me—some scientific quest, perhaps. What holds me is the enthusiasm of the writer for his field. How was he drawn into it? What emotional baggage did he bring along? How did it change his life? It's not necessary to want to spend a year alone at Walden Pond to become involved with a writer who did.

This is the personal transaction that's at the heart of good nonfiction writing. Out of it come two of the most important qualities that this book will go in search of: humanity and warmth. Good writing has an aliveness that keeps the reader reading from one paragraph to the next, and it's not a question of gimmicks to "personalize" the author. It's a question of using the English language in a way that will achieve the greatest clarity and strength.

Can such principles be taught? Maybe not. But most of them can be learned.

2

—✖✖✖—

Simplicity

Clutter is the disease of American writing. We are a society strangling in unnecessary words, circular constructions, pompous frills and meaningless jargon.

Who can understand the clotted language of everyday American commerce: the memo, the corporation report, the business letter, the notice from the bank explaining its latest "simplified" statement? What member of an insurance or medical plan can decipher the brochure explaining his costs and benefits? What father or mother can put together a child's toy from the instructions on the box? Our national tendency is to inflate and thereby sound important. The airline pilot who announces that he is presently anticipating experiencing considerable precipitation wouldn't think of saying it may rain. The sentence is too simple—there must be something wrong with it.

But the secret of good writing is to strip every sentence to its cleanest components. Every word that serves no function, every long word that could be a short word, every adverb that carries the same meaning that's already in the verb, every passive con-

struction that leaves the reader unsure of who is doing what—
these are the thousand and one adulterants that weaken the
strength of a sentence. And they usually occur in proportion to
education and rank.

During the 1960s the president of my university wrote a letter to mollify the alumni after a spell of campus unrest. "You are
probably aware," he began, "that we have been experiencing
very considerable potentially explosive expressions of dissatisfaction on issues only partially related." He meant that the students
had been hassling them about different things. I was far more
upset by the president's English than by the students' potentially
explosive expressions of dissatisfaction. I would have preferred
the presidential approach taken by Franklin D. Roosevelt when
he tried to convert into English his own government's memos,
such as this blackout order of 1942:

> Such preparations shall be made as will completely
> obscure all Federal buildings and non-Federal buildings
> occupied by the Federal government during an air raid for
> any period of time from visibility by reason of internal or
> external illumination.

"Tell them," Roosevelt said, "that in buildings where they have
to keep the work going to put something across the windows."

Simplify, simplify. Thoreau said it, as we are so often
reminded, and no American writer more consistently practiced
what he preached. Open *Walden* to any page and you will find a
man saying in a plain and orderly way what is on his mind:

> I went to the woods because I wished to live deliberately,
> to front only the essential facts of life, and see if I could not
> learn what it had to teach, and not, when I came to die, dis-
> cover that I had not lived.

How can the rest of us achieve such enviable freedom from clutter? The answer is to clear our heads of clutter. Clear thinking becomes clear writing; one can't exist without the other. It's impossible for a muddy thinker to write good English. He may get away with it for a paragraph or two, but soon the reader will be lost, and there's no sin so grave, for the reader will not easily be lured back.

Who is this elusive creature, the reader? The reader is someone with an attention span of about 30 seconds—a person assailed by many forces competing for attention. At one time those forces were relatively few: newspapers, magazines, radio, spouse, children, pets. Today they also include a "home entertainment center" (television, VCR, tapes, CDs), e-mail, the Internet, the cellular phone, the fax machine, a fitness program, a pool, a lawn, and that most potent of competitors, sleep. The man or woman snoozing in a chair with a magazine or a book is a person who was being given too much unnecessary trouble by the writer.

It won't do to say that the reader is too dumb or too lazy to keep pace with the train of thought. If the reader is lost, it's usually because the writer hasn't been careful enough. That carelessness can take any number of forms. Perhaps a sentence is so excessively cluttered that the reader, hacking through the verbiage, simply doesn't know what it means. Perhaps a sentence has been so shoddily constructed that the reader could read it in several ways. Perhaps the writer has switched pronouns in mid-sentence, or has switched tenses, so the reader loses track of who is talking or when the action took place. Perhaps Sentence B is not a logical sequel to Sentence A; the writer, in whose head the connection is clear, hasn't bothered to provide the missing link. Perhaps the writer has used a word incorrectly by not taking the trouble to look it up. He or she may think "sanguine" and "sanguinary" mean the same thing, but the difference is a bloody big one. The reader can only infer (speaking of big differences) what the writer is trying to imply.

5 --

is too dumb or too lazy to keep pace with the ~~writer's~~ train of thought. My sympathies are ~~entirely~~ with him.) ~~He's not so dumb.~~ (If the reader is lost, it is generally because the writer ~~of the article~~ has not been careful enough to keep him on the ~~proper~~ path.

This carelessness can take any number of ~~different~~ forms. Perhaps a sentence is so excessively ~~long and~~ cluttered that the reader, hacking his way through ~~all~~ the verbiage, simply doesn't know what *it* ~~the writer~~ means. Perhaps a sentence has been so shoddily constructed that the reader could read it in any of *several* ~~two or three different~~ ways. ~~He thinks he knows what the writer is trying to say, but he's not sure.~~ Perhaps the writer has switched pronouns in mid-sentence, or ~~perhaps he~~ has switched tenses, so the reader loses track of who is talking ~~to whom,~~ or ~~exactly~~ when the action took place. Perhaps Sentence B is not a logical sequel to Sentence A -- the writer, in whose head the connection is ~~perfectly~~ clear, has not *bothered to provide* ~~given enough thought to providing~~ the missing link. Perhaps the writer has used an important word incorrectly by not taking the trouble to look it up ~~and make sure.~~ He may think that "sanguine" and "sanguinary" mean the same thing, but) ~~I can assure you that~~ (the difference is a bloody big one ~~to the reader.~~ *The reader* ~~He~~ can only ~~try to~~ infer ~~what~~ (speaking of big differences) what the writer is trying to imply.

Faced with *these* ~~such a variety of~~ obstacles, the reader is at first a remarkably tenacious bird. He ~~tends to~~ blame*s* himself. ~~He~~ obviously missed something, ~~he thinks,~~ and he goes back over the mystifying sentence, or over the whole paragraph,

6 --

piecing it out like an ancient rune, making guesses and moving

on. But he won't do this for long. ~~He will soon run out of~~

~~patience.~~ The writer is making him work too hard ~~→harder~~

~~than he should have to work~~ and the reader will look for

~~a writer~~ who is better at his craft.
       one

     The writer must therefore constantly ask himself: What am

I trying to say? ~~in this sentence?~~ Surprisingly often, he

doesn't know. ~~And~~ Then he must look at what he has ~~just~~

written and ask: Have I said it? Is it clear to someone
       encountering
~~who is coming upon~~ the subject for the first time? If it's

not, ~~clear,~~ it is because some fuzz has worked its way into the

machinery. The clear writer is a person ~~who is~~ clear-headed

enough to see this stuff for what it is: fuzz.

     I don't mean ~~to suggest~~ that some people are born

clear-headed and are therefore natural writers, whereas
others
~~other people~~ are naturally fuzzy and will ~~therefore~~ never write

well. Thinking clearly is ~~an entirely~~ conscious act that the
                 force
writer must ~~keep forcing~~ upon himself, just as if he were
embarking
~~starting out~~ on any other ~~kind of~~ project that ~~calls for~~ logic:
                                              requires
adding up a laundry list or doing an algebra problem ~~or playing~~

~~chess.~~ Good writing doesn't ~~just~~ come naturally, though most
                               it does.
people obviously think ~~it's as easy as walking.~~ The professional

Two pages of the final manuscript of this chapter from the First Edition
of *On Writing Well*. Although they look like a first draft, they had
already been rewritten and retyped—like almost every other page—
four or five times. With each rewrite I try to make what I have written
tighter, stronger and more precise, eliminating every element that's not
doing useful work. Then I go over it once more, reading it aloud, and
am always amazed at how much clutter can still be cut. (In later editions I eliminated the sexist pronoun "he" denoting "the writer" and
"the reader.")

Faced with such obstacles, readers are at first tenacious. They blame themselves—they obviously missed something, and they go back over the mystifying sentence, or over the whole paragraph, piecing it out like an ancient rune, making guesses and moving on. But they won't do that for long. The writer is making them work too hard, and they will look for one who is better at the craft.

Writers must therefore constantly ask: what am I trying to say? Surprisingly often they don't know. Then they must look at what they have written and ask: have I said it? Is it clear to someone encountering the subject for the first time? If it's not, some fuzz has worked its way into the machinery. The clear writer is someone clearheaded enough to see this stuff for what it is: fuzz.

I don't mean that some people are born clearheaded and are therefore natural writers, whereas others are naturally fuzzy and will never write well. Thinking clearly is a conscious act that writers must force on themselves, as if they were working on any other project that requires logic: making a shopping list or doing an algebra problem. Good writing doesn't come naturally, though most people seem to think it does. Professional writers are constantly bearded by people who say they'd like to "try a little writing sometime"—meaning when they retire from their real profession, like insurance or real estate, which is hard. Or they say, "I could write a book about that." I doubt it.

Writing is hard work. A clear sentence is no accident. Very few sentences come out right the first time, or even the third time. Remember this in moments of despair. If you find that writing is hard, it's because it *is* hard.

3

Clutter

Fighting clutter is like fighting weeds—the writer is always slightly behind. New varieties sprout overnight, and by noon they are part of American speech. Consider what President Nixon's aide John Dean accomplished in just one day of testimony on television during the Watergate hearings. The next day everyone in America was saying "at this point in time" instead of "now."

Consider all the prepositions that are draped onto verbs that don't need any help. We no longer head committees. We head them up. We don't face problems anymore. We face up to them when we can free up a few minutes. A small detail, you may say—not worth bothering about. It *is* worth bothering about. Writing improves in direct ratio to the number of things we can keep out of it that shouldn't be there. "Up" in "free up" shouldn't be there. Examine every word you put on paper. You'll find a surprising number that don't serve any purpose.

Take the adjective "personal," as in "a personal friend of mine," "his personal feeling" or "her personal physician." It's typical of hundreds of words that can be eliminated. The personal friend has come into the language to distinguish him or her from the business friend, thereby debasing both language and friendship. Someone's feeling *is* that person's personal feeling—that's what "his" means. As for the personal physician, that's the man or woman summoned to the dressing room of a stricken actress so she won't have to be treated by the impersonal physician assigned to the theater. Someday I'd like to see that person identified as "her doctor." Physicians are physicians, friends are friends. The rest is clutter.

Clutter is the laborious phrase that has pushed out the short word that means the same thing. Even before John Dean, people and businesses had stopped saying "now." They were saying "currently" ("all our operators are currently busy"), or "at the present time," or "presently" (which means "soon"). Yet the idea can always be expressed by "now" to mean the immediate moment ("Now I can see him"), or by "today" to mean the historical present ("Today prices are high"), or simply by the verb "to be" ("It is raining"). There's no need to say, "At the present time we are experiencing precipitation."

"Experiencing" is one of the ultimate clutterers. Even your dentist will ask if you are experiencing any pain. If he had his own kid in the chair he would say, "Does it hurt?" He would, in short, be himself. By using a more pompous phrase in his professional role he not only sounds more important; he blunts the painful edge of truth. It's the language of the flight attendant demonstrating the oxygen mask that will drop down if the plane should run out of air. "In the unlikely possibility that the aircraft should experience such an eventuality," she begins—a phrase so oxygen-depriving in itself that we are prepared for any disaster.

Clutter is the ponderous euphemism that turns a slum into a depressed socioeconomic area, garbage collectors into waste-disposal personnel and the town dump into the volume reduction unit. I think of Bill Mauldin's cartoon of two hoboes riding a freight car. One of them says, "I started as a simple bum, but now I'm hard-core unemployed." Clutter is political correctness gone amok. I saw an ad for a boys' camp designed to provide "individual attention for the minimally exceptional."

Clutter is the official language used by corporations to hide their mistakes. When the Digital Equipment Corporation eliminated 3,000 jobs its statement didn't mention layoffs; those were "involuntary methodologies." When an Air Force missile crashed, it "impacted with the ground prematurely." When General Motors had a plant shutdown, that was a "volume-related production-schedule adjustment." Companies that go belly-up have "a negative cash-flow position."

Clutter is the language of the Pentagon calling an invasion a "reinforced protective reaction strike" and justifying its vast budgets on the need for "counterforce deterrence." As George Orwell pointed out in "Politics and the English Language," an essay written in 1946 but often cited during the Vietnam and Cambodia years of Presidents Johnson and Nixon, "political speech and writing are largely the defense of the indefensible. . . . Thus political language has to consist largely of euphemism, question-begging and sheer cloudy vagueness." Orwell's warning that clutter is not just a nuisance but a deadly tool has come true in the recent decades of American military adventurism in Southeast Asia and other parts of the world.

Verbal camouflage reached new heights during General Alexander Haig's tenure as President Reagan's secretary of state. Before Haig nobody had thought of saying "at this juncture of maturization" to mean "now." He told the American people that terrorism could be fought with "meaningful sanctionary teeth" and that intermediate nuclear missiles were "at the vortex of cruciality." As for any worries that the public might harbor, his message was "leave it to Al," though what he actually said was: "We must push this to a lower decibel of public fixation. I don't think there's much of a learning curve to be achieved in this area of content."

I could go on quoting examples from various fields—every profession has its growing arsenal of jargon to throw dust in the eyes of the populace. But the list would be tedious. The point of raising it now is to serve notice that clutter is the enemy. Beware, then, of the long word that's no better than the short word: "assistance" (help), "numerous" (many), "facilitate" (ease), "individual" (man or woman), "remainder" (rest), "initial" (first), "implement" (do), "sufficient" (enough), "attempt" (try), "referred to as" (called) and hundreds more. Beware of all the slippery new fad words: paradigm and parameter, prioritize and potentialize. They are all weeds that will smother what you write. Don't dialogue with someone you can talk to. Don't interface with anybody.

Just as insidious are all the word clusters with which we explain how we propose to go about our explaining: "I might add," "It should be pointed out," "It is interesting to note." If you might add, add it. If it should be pointed out, point it out. If it is interesting to note, *make* it interesting; are we not all stupefied by what follows when someone says, "This will interest you"? Don't inflate what needs no inflating: "with the possible exception of" (except), "due to the fact that" (because), "he totally lacked the ability to" (he couldn't), "until such time as" (until), "for the purpose of" (for).

Is there any way to recognize clutter at a glance? Here's a device my students at Yale found helpful. I would put brackets around every component in a piece of writing that wasn't doing useful work. Often just one word got bracketed: the unnecessary preposition appended to a verb ("order up"), or the adverb that carries the same meaning as the verb ("smile happily"), or the adjective that states a known fact ("tall skyscraper"). Often my brackets surrounded the little qualifiers that weaken any sentence they inhabit ("a bit," "sort of"), or phrases like "in a sense," which don't mean anything. Sometimes my brackets surrounded an entire sentence—the one that essentially repeats what the previous sentence said, or that says something readers don't need to know or can figure out for themselves. Most first drafts can be cut by 50 percent without losing any information or losing the author's voice.

My reason for bracketing the students' superfluous words, instead of crossing them out, was to avoid violating their sacred prose. I wanted to leave the sentence intact for them to analyze. I was saying, "I may be wrong, but I think this can be deleted and the meaning won't be affected. But *you* decide. Read the sentence without the bracketed material and see if it works." In the early weeks of the term I handed back papers that were festooned with brackets. Entire paragraphs were bracketed. But soon the students learned to put mental brackets around their own clutter, and by the end of the term their papers were almost clean. Today many of those students are professional writers, and they tell me, "I still see your brackets—they're following me through life."

You can develop the same eye. Look for the clutter in your writing and prune it ruthlessly. Be grateful for everything you can throw away. Reexamine each sentence you put on paper. Is every word doing new work? Can any thought be expressed with more economy? Is anything pompous or pretentious or faddish? Are you hanging on to something useless just because you think it's beautiful?

Simplify, simplify.

4

Style

So much for early warnings about the bloated monsters that lie in ambush for the writer trying to put together a clean English sentence.

"But," you may say, "if I eliminate everything you think is clutter and if I strip every sentence to its barest bones, will there be anything left of me?" The question is a fair one; simplicity carried to an extreme might seem to point to a style little more sophisticated than "Dick likes Jane" and "See Spot run."

I'll answer the question first on the level of carpentry. Then I'll get to the larger issue of who the writer is and how to preserve his or her identity.

Few people realize how badly they write. Nobody has shown them how much excess or murkiness has crept into their style and how it obstructs what they are trying to say. If you give me an eight-page article and I tell you to cut it to four pages, you'll howl and say it can't be done. Then you'll go home and do it, and it will be much better. After that comes the hard part: cutting it to three.

The point is that you have to strip your writing down before you can build it back up. You must know what the essential tools are and what job they were designed to do. Extending the metaphor of carpentry, it's first necessary to be able to saw wood neatly and to drive nails. Later you can bevel the edges or add elegant finials, if that's your taste. But you can never forget that you are practicing a craft that's based on certain principles. If the nails are weak, your house will collapse. If your verbs are weak and your syntax is rickety, your sentences will fall apart.

I'll admit that certain nonfiction writers, like Tom Wolfe and Norman Mailer, have built some remarkable houses. But these are writers who spent years learning their craft, and when at last they raised their fanciful turrets and hanging gardens, to the surprise of all of us who never dreamed of such ornamentation, they knew what they were doing. Nobody becomes Tom Wolfe overnight, not even Tom Wolfe.

First, then, learn to hammer the nails, and if what you build is sturdy and serviceable, take satisfaction in its plain strength.

But you will be impatient to find a "style"—to embellish the plain words so that readers will recognize you as someone special. You will reach for gaudy similes and tinseled adjectives, as if "style" were something you could buy at the style store and drape onto your words in bright decorator colors. (Decorator colors are the colors that decorators come in.) There is no style store; style is organic to the person doing the writing, as much a part of him as his hair, or, if he is bald, his lack of it. Trying to add style is like adding a toupee. At first glance the formerly bald man looks young and even handsome. But at second glance—and with a toupee there's always a second glance—he doesn't look quite right. The problem is not that he doesn't look well groomed; he does, and we can only admire the wigmaker's skill. The point is that he doesn't look like himself.

This is the problem of writers who set out deliberately to garnish their prose. You lose whatever it is that makes you unique. The reader will notice if you are putting on airs. Readers want the person who is talking to them to sound genuine. Therefore a fundamental rule is: be yourself.

No rule, however, is harder to follow. It requires writers to do two things that by their metabolism are impossible. They must relax, and they must have confidence.

Telling a writer to relax is like telling a man to relax while being examined for a hernia, and as for confidence, see how stiffly he sits, glaring at the screen that awaits his words. See how often he gets up to look for something to eat or drink. A writer will do anything to avoid the act of writing. I can testify from my newspaper days that the number of trips to the water cooler per reporter-hour far exceeds the body's need for fluids.

What can be done to put the writer out of these miseries? Unfortunately, no cure has been found. I can only offer the consoling thought that you are not alone. Some days will go better than others. Some will go so badly that you'll despair of ever writing again. We have all had many of those days and will have many more.

Still, it would be nice to keep the bad days to a minimum, which brings me back to the problem of trying to relax.

Assume that you are the writer sitting down to write. You think your article must be of a certain length or it won't seem important. You think how august it will look in print. You think of all the people who will read it. You think that it must have the solid weight of authority. You think that its style must dazzle. No wonder you tighten; you are so busy thinking of your awesome responsibility to the finished article that you can't even start. Yet you vow to be worthy of the task, and, casting about for grand phrases that wouldn't occur to you if you weren't trying so hard to make an impression, you plunge in.

Paragraph 1 is a disaster—a tissue of generalities that seem to have come out of a machine. No *person* could have written them. Paragraph 2 isn't much better. But Paragraph 3 begins to have a somewhat human quality, and by Paragraph 4 you begin to sound like yourself. You've started to relax. It's amazing how often an editor can throw away the first three or four paragraphs of an article, or even the first few pages, and start with the paragraph where the writer begins to sound like himself or herself. Not only are those first paragraphs impersonal and ornate; they don't say anything—they are a self-conscious attempt at a fancy introduction. What I'm always looking for as an editor is a sentence that says something like "I'll never forget the day when I . . ." I think, "Aha! A person!"

Writers are obviously at their most natural when they write in the first person. Writing is an intimate transaction between two people, conducted on paper, and it will go well to the extent that it retains its humanity. Therefore I urge people to write in the first person: to use "I" and "me" and "we" and "us." They put up a fight.

"Who am I to say what *I* think?" they ask. "Or what *I* feel?"

"Who are you *not* to say what you think?" I tell them. "There's only one you. Nobody else thinks or feels in exactly the same way."

"But nobody cares about my opinions," they say. "It would make me feel conspicuous."

"They'll care if you tell them something interesting," I say, "and tell them in words that come naturally."

Nevertheless, getting writers to use "I" is seldom easy. They think they must earn the right to reveal their emotions or their thoughts. Or that it's egotistical. Or that it's undignified—a fear that afflicts the academic world. Hence the professorial use of "one" ("One finds oneself not wholly in accord with Dr. Maltby's view of the human condition"), or of the impersonal "it is" ("It is to be hoped that Professor Felt's monograph will find the wider audience it most assuredly deserves"). I don't want to meet "one"—he's a boring guy. I want a professor with a passion for his subject to tell me why it fascinates *him*.

I realize that there are vast regions of writing where "I" isn't allowed. Newspapers don't want "I" in their news stories; many magazines don't want it in their articles; businesses and institutions don't want it in the reports they send so profusely into the American home; colleges don't want "I" in their term papers or dissertations, and English teachers discourage any first-person pronoun except the literary "we" ("We see in Melville's symbolic use of the white whale. . . "). Many of those prohibitions are valid. Newspaper articles should consist of news, reported objectively. I also sympathize with teachers who don't want to give students an easy escape into opinion—"I think Hamlet was stupid"—before they have grappled with the discipline of assessing a work on its merits and on external sources. "I" can be a self-indulgence and a cop-out.

Still, we have become a society fearful of revealing who we are. The institutions that seek our support by sending us their brochures sound remarkably alike, though surely all of them—hospitals, schools, libraries, museums, zoos—were founded and are still sustained by men and women with different dreams and visions. Where are these people? It's hard to glimpse them among all the impersonal passive sentences that say "initiatives were undertaken" and "priorities have been identified."

Even when "I" isn't permitted, it's still possible to convey a sense of I-ness. The political columnist James Reston didn't use "I" in his columns; yet I had a good idea of what kind of person he was, and I could say the same of many other essayists and reporters. Good writers are visible just behind their words. If you aren't allowed to use "I," at least think "I" while you write, or write the first draft in the first person and then take the "I"s out. It will warm up your impersonal style.

Style is tied to the psyche, and writing has deep psychological roots. The reasons why we express ourselves as we do, or fail to express ourselves because of "writer's block," are partly buried in the subconscious mind. There are as many kinds of writer's block as there are kinds of writers, and I have no intention of trying to untangle them. This is a short book, and my name isn't Sigmund Freud.

But I've also noticed a new reason for avoiding "I": Americans are unwilling to go out on a limb. A generation ago our leaders told us where they stood and what they believed. Today they perform strenuous verbal feats to escape that fate. Watch them wriggle through TV interviews without committing themselves. I remember President Ford assuring a group of visiting businessmen that his fiscal policies would work. He said: "We see nothing but increasingly brighter clouds every month." I took this to mean that the clouds were still fairly dark. Ford's sentence was just vague enough to say nothing and still sedate his constituents.

Later administrations brought no relief. Defense Secretary Caspar Weinberger, assessing a Polish crisis in 1984, said: "There's continuing ground for serious concern and the situation remains serious. The longer it remains serious, the more ground there is for serious concern." President Bush, questioned about his stand on assault rifles in 1989, said: "There are various groups that think you can ban certain kinds of guns. I am not in that mode. I am in the mode of being deeply concerned."

But my all-time champ is Elliot Richardson, who held four major cabinet positions in the 1970s. It's hard to know where to begin picking from his trove of equivocal statements, but consider this one: "And yet, on balance, affirmative action has, I think, been a qualified success." A 13-word sentence with five hedging words. I give it first prize as the most wishy-washy sentence in modern public discourse, though a rival would be his analysis of how to ease boredom among assembly-line workers: "And so, at last, I come to the one firm conviction that I mentioned at the beginning: it is that the subject is too new for final judgments."

That's a firm conviction? Leaders who bob and weave like

aging boxers don't inspire confidence—or deserve it. The same thing is true of writers. Sell yourself, and your subject will exert its own appeal. Believe in your own identity and your own opinions. Writing is an act of ego, and you might as well admit it. Use its energy to keep yourself going.

5

The Audience

Soon after you confront the matter of preserving your identity, another question will occur to you: "Who am I writing for?"

It's a fundamental question, and it has a fundamental answer: You are writing for yourself. Don't try to visualize the great mass audience. There is no such audience—every reader is a different person. Don't try to guess what sort of thing editors want to publish or what you think the country is in a mood to read. Editors and readers don't know what they want to read until they read it. Besides, they're always looking for something new.

Don't worry about whether the reader will "get it" if you indulge a sudden impulse for humor. If it amuses you in the act of writing, put it in. (It can always be taken out, but only you can put it in.) You are writing primarily to please yourself, and if you go about it with enjoyment you will also entertain the readers who are worth writing for. If you lose the dullards back in the dust, you don't want them anyway.

This may seem to be a paradox. Earlier I warned that the reader is an impatient bird, perched on the thin edge of distraction or sleep. Now I'm saying you must write for yourself and not be gnawed by worry over whether the reader is tagging along.

I'm talking about two different issues. One is craft, the other is attitude. The first is a question of mastering a precise skill. The second is a question of how you use that skill to express your personality.

In terms of craft, there's no excuse for losing readers through sloppy workmanship. If they doze off in the middle of your article because you have been careless about a technical detail, the fault is yours. But on the larger issue of whether the reader likes you, or likes what you are saying or how you are saying it, or agrees with it, or feels an affinity for your sense of humor or your vision of life, don't give him a moment's worry. You are who you are, he is who he is, and either you'll get along or you won't.

Perhaps this still seems like a paradox. How can you think carefully about not losing the reader and still be carefree about his opinion? I assure you that they are separate processes.

First, work hard to master the tools. Simplify, prune and strive for order. Think of this as a mechanical act, and soon your sentences will become cleaner. The act will never become as mechanical as, say, shaving or shampooing—you will always have to think about the various ways in which the tools can be used. But at least your sentences will be grounded in solid principles, and your chances of losing the reader will be smaller.

Think of the other as a creative act: the expressing of who you are. Relax and say what you want to say. And since style is who you are, you only need to be true to yourself to find it gradually emerging from under the accumulated clutter and debris, growing more distinctive every day. Perhaps the style won't solidify for years as *your* style, *your* voice. Just as it takes time to find yourself as a person, it takes time to find yourself as a stylist, and even then your style will change as you grow older.

But whatever your age, be yourself when you write. Many old men still write with the zest they had in their twenties or thirties; obviously their ideas are still young. Other old writers ramble and repeat themselves; their style is the tip-off that they have turned into garrulous bores. Many college students write as if they were desiccated alumni 30 years out. Never say anything in writing that you wouldn't comfortably say in conversation. If you're not a person who says "indeed" or "moreover," or who calls someone an individual ("he's a fine individual"), *please* don't write it.

Let's look at a few writers to see the pleasure with which they put on paper their passions and their crotchets, not caring whether the reader shares them or not. The first excerpt is from "The Hen (An Appreciation)," written by E. B. White in 1944, at the height of World War II:

> Chickens do not always enjoy an honorable position among city-bred people, although the egg, I notice, goes on and on. Right now the hen is in favor. The war has deified her and she is the darling of the home front, feted at conference tables, praised in every smoking car, her girlish ways and curious habits the topic of many an excited husbandryman to whom yesterday she was a stranger without honor or allure.
>
> My own attachment to the hen dates from 1907, and I have been faithful to her in good times and bad. Ours has not always been an easy relationship to maintain. At first, as a boy in a carefully zoned suburb, I had neighbors and police to reckon with; my chickens had to be as closely guarded as an underground newspaper. Later, as a man in the country, I had my old friends in town to reckon with, most of whom regarded the hen as a comic prop straight out of vaudeville. . . . Their scorn only increased my devotion to the hen. I remained loyal, as a man would to a bride whom his family received with open ridicule. Now it is my turn to wear the smile, as I listen to the enthusiastic cackling of urbanites, who have suddenly taken up the hen socially and

who fill the air with their newfound ecstasy and knowledge
and the relative charms of the New Hampshire Red and the
Laced Wyandotte. You would think, from their nervous cries
of wonder and praise, that the hen was hatched yesterday in
the suburbs of New York, instead of in the remote past in the
jungles of India.

To a man who keeps hens, all poultry lore is exciting and
endlessly fascinating. Every spring I settle down with my farm
journal and read, with the same glazed expression on my face,
the age-old story of how to prepare a brooder house. . . .

There's a man writing about a subject I have absolutely no
interest in. Yet I enjoy this piece thoroughly. I like the simple
beauty of its style. I like the rhythms, the unexpected but
refreshing words ("deified," "allure," "cackling"), the specific
details like the Laced Wyandotte and the brooder house. But
mainly what I like is that this is a man telling me unabashedly
about a love affair with poultry that goes back to 1907. It's written with humanity and warmth, and after three paragraphs I
know quite a lot about what sort of man this hen-lover is.

Or take a writer who is almost White's opposite in terms of
style, who relishes the opulent word for its opulence and doesn't
deify the simple sentence. Yet they are brothers in holding firm
opinions and saying what they think. This is H. L. Mencken
reporting on the notorious "Monkey Trial"—the trial of John
Scopes, a young teacher who taught the theory of evolution in
his Tennessee classroom—in the summer of 1925:

It was hot weather when they tried the infidel Scopes at
Dayton, Tenn., but I went down there very willingly, for I was
eager to see something of evangelical Christianity as a going
concern. In the big cities of the Republic, despite the endless
efforts of consecrated men, it is laid up with a wasting disease.
The very Sunday-school superintendents, taking jazz from the

stealthy radio, shake their fire-proof legs; their pupils, moving into adolescence, no longer respond to the proliferating hormones by enlisting for missionary service in Africa, but resort to necking instead. Even in Dayton, I found, though the mob was up to do execution on Scopes, there was a strong smell of antinomianism. The nine churches of the village were all half empty on Sunday, and weeds choked their yards. Only two or three of the resident pastors managed to sustain themselves by their ghostly science; the rest had to take orders for mail-order pantaloons or work in the adjacent strawberry fields; one, I heard, was a barber. . . . Exactly twelve minutes after I reached the village I was taken in tow by a Christian man and introduced to the favorite tipple of the Cumberland Range; half corn liquor and half Coca-Cola. It seemed a dreadful dose to me, but I found that the Dayton illuminati got it down with gusto, rubbing their tummies and rolling their eyes. They were all hot for Genesis, but their faces were too florid to belong to teetotalers, and when a pretty girl came tripping down the main street, they reached for the places where their neckties should have been with all the amorous enterprise of movie stars. . . .

This is pure Mencken in its surging momentum and its irreverence. At almost any page where you open his books he is saying something sure to outrage the professed pieties of his countrymen. The sanctity in which Americans bathed their heroes, their churches and their edifying laws—especially Prohibition—was a well of hypocrisy for him that never dried up. Some of his heaviest ammunition he hurled at politicians and Presidents—his portrait of "The Archangel Woodrow" still scorches the pages—and as for Christian believers and clerical folk, they turn up unfailingly as mountebanks and boobs.

It may seem a miracle that Mencken could get away with such heresies in the 1920s, when hero worship was an American religion and the self-righteous wrath of the Bible Belt oozed from coast to coast. Not only did he get away with it; he was the most revered and influential journalist of his generation. The impact he made on subsequent writers of nonfiction is beyond measuring, and even now his topical pieces seem as fresh as if they were written yesterday.

The secret of his popularity—aside from his pyrotechnical use of the American language—was that he was writing for himself and didn't give a damn what the reader might think. It wasn't necessary to share his prejudices to enjoy seeing them expressed with such mirthful abandon. Mencken was never timid or evasive; he didn't kowtow to the reader or curry anyone's favor. It takes courage to be such a writer, but it is out of such courage that revered and influential journalists are born.

Moving forward to our own time, here's an excerpt from *How to Survive in Your Native Land*, a book by James Herndon describing his experiences as a teacher in a California junior high school. Of all the earnest books on education that have sprouted in America, Herndon's is—for me—the one that best captures how it really is in the classroom. His style is not quite like anybody else's, but his voice is true. Here's how the book starts:

> I might as well begin with Piston. Piston was, as a matter of description, a red-headed medium-sized chubby eighth-grader; his definitive characteristic was, however, stubbornness. Without going into a lot of detail, it became clear right away that what Piston didn't want to do, Piston didn't do; what Piston wanted to do, Piston did.
>
> It really wasn't much of a problem. Piston wanted mainly to paint, draw monsters, scratch designs on mimeograph blanks and print them up, write an occasional horror story—some kids referred to him as The Ghoul—and when he didn't want to do any of those, he wanted to roam the halls and on occasion (we heard) investigate the girls' bathrooms.

We had minor confrontations. Once I wanted everyone to sit down and listen to what I had to say—something about the way they had been acting in the halls. I was letting them come and go freely and it was up to them (I planned to point out) not to raise hell so that I had to hear about it from other teachers. Sitting down was the issue—I was determined everyone was going to do it first, then I'd talk. Piston remained standing. I reordered. He paid no attention. I pointed out that I was talking to him. He indicated he heard me. I inquired then why in hell didn't he sit down. He said he didn't want to. I said I did want him to. He said that didn't matter to him. I said do it anyway. He said why? I said because I said so. He said he wouldn't. I said Look I want you to sit down and listen to what I'm going to say. He said he *was* listening. I'll listen but I won't sit down.

Well, that's the way it goes sometimes in schools. You as teacher become obsessed with an issue—I was the injured party, conferring, as usual, unheard-of freedoms, and here they were as usual taking advantage. It ain't pleasant coming in the teachers' room for coffee and having to hear somebody say that so-and-so and so-and-so from *your* class were out in the halls *without a pass* and *making faces* and *giving the finger* to kids in *my* class during the most *important* part of *my* lesson about *Egypt*—and you ought to be allowed your tendentious speech, and most everyone will allow it, sit down for it, but occasionally someone wises you up by refusing to submit where it isn't necessary. . . . How did any of us get into this? we ought to be asking ourselves.

Any writer who uses "ain't" and "tendentious" in the same sentence, who quotes without using quotation marks, knows what he's doing. This seemingly artless style, so full of art, is ideal for Herndon's purpose. It avoids the pretentiousness that infects so much writing by people who are doing worthy work, and it allows for a rich vein of humor and common sense. Herndon sounds like a good teacher and a man whose company I would enjoy. But ultimately he is writing for himself: an audience of one.

"Who am I writing for?" The question that begins this chapter has irked some readers. They want me to say "Whom am I writing for?" But I can't bring myself to say it. It's just not me.

6

❧❧❧

Words

There is a kind of writing that might be called journalese, and it's the death of freshness in anybody's style. It's the common currency of newspapers and of magazines like *People*—a mixture of cheap words, made-up words and clichés that have become so pervasive that a writer can hardly help using them. You must fight these phrases or you'll sound like every hack. You'll never make your mark as a writer unless you develop a respect for words and a curiosity about their shades of meaning that is almost obsessive. The English language is rich in strong and supple words. Take the time to root around and find the ones you want.

What is "journalese"? It's a quilt of instant words patched together out of other parts of speech. Adjectives are used as nouns ("greats," "notables"). Nouns are used as verbs ("to host"), or they are chopped off to form verbs ("enthuse," "emote"), or they are padded to form verbs ("beef up," "put teeth into"). This is a world where eminent people are "famed" and their associates are "staffers," where the future is always "upcoming" and

someone is forever "firing off" a note. Nobody in America has
sent a note or a memo or a telegram in years. Famed diplomat
Henry Kissinger, who hosted foreign notables to beef up the
morale of top State Department staffers, sat down and fired off
a lot of notes. Notes that are fired off are always fired in anger
and from a sitting position. What the weapon is I've never found
out.

Here's an article from a famed newsmagazine that is hard to
match for fatigue:

> Last February, Plainclothes Patrolman Frank Serpico
> knocked at the door of a suspected Brooklyn heroin pusher.
> When the door opened a crack, Serpico shouldered his way in
> only to be met by a .22-cal. pistol slug crashing into his face.
> Somehow he survived, although there are still buzzing frag-
> ments in his head, causing dizziness and permanent deafness
> in his left ear. Almost as painful is the suspicion that he may
> well have been set up for the shooting by other policemen.
> For Serpico, 35, has been waging a lonely, four-year war
> against the routine and endemic corruption that he and others
> claim is rife in the New York City police department. His
> efforts are now sending shock waves through the ranks of New
> York's finest. . . . Though the impact of the commission's
> upcoming report has yet to be felt, Serpico has little hope
> that. . .

The upcoming report has yet to be felt because it's still
upcoming, and as for the permanent deafness, it's a little early to
tell. And what makes those buzzing fragments buzz? By now
only Serpico's head should be buzzing. But apart from these
lazinesses of logic, what makes the story so tired is the failure of
the writer to reach for anything but the nearest cliché. "Shoul-
dered his way," "only to be met," "crashing into his face," "wag-
ing a lonely war," "corruption that is rife," "sending shock

waves," "New York's finest"—these dreary phrases constitute writing at its most banal. We know just what to expect. No surprise awaits us in the form of an unusual word, an oblique look. We are in the hands of a hack, and we know it right away. We stop reading.

Don't let yourself get in this position. The only way to avoid it is to care deeply about words. If you find yourself writing that someone recently enjoyed a spell of illness, or that a business has been enjoying a slump, ask yourself how much they enjoyed it. Notice the decisions that other writers make in their choice of words and be finicky about the ones you select from the vast supply. The race in writing is not to the swift but to the original.

Make a habit of reading what is being written today and what has been written by earlier masters. Writing is learned by imitation. If anyone asked me how I learned to write, I'd say I learned by reading the men and women who were doing the kind of writing *I* wanted to do and trying to figure out how they did it. But cultivate the best models. Don't assume that because an article is in a newspaper or a magazine it must be good. Sloppy editing is common in newspapers, often for lack of time, and writers who use clichés often work for editors who have seen so many clichés that they no longer even recognize them.

Also get in the habit of using dictionaries. My favorite for handy use is *Webster's New World Dictionary,* Second College Edition, although, like all word freaks, I own bigger dictionaries that will reward me when I'm on some more specialized search. If you have any doubt of what a word means, look it up. Learn its etymology and notice what curious branches its original root has put forth. See if it has any meanings you didn't know it had. Master the small gradations between words that seem to be synonyms. What's the difference between "cajole," "wheedle," "blandish" and "coax"? Get yourself a dictionary of synonyms.

And don't scorn that bulging grab bag *Roget's Thesaurus.* It's easy to regard the book as hilarious. Look up "villain," for instance, and you'll be awash in such rascality as only a lexicographer could conjure back from centuries of iniquity, obliquity, depravity, knavery, profligacy, frailty, flagrancy, infamy, immorality, corruption, wickedness, wrongdoing, backsliding and sin. You'll find ruffians and riffraff, miscreants and malefactors, reprobates and rapscallions, hooligans and hoodlums, scamps and scapegraces, scoundrels and scalawags, jezebels and jades. You'll find adjectives to fit them all (foul and fiendish, devilish and diabolical), and adverbs and verbs to describe how the wrongdoers do their wrong, and cross-references leading to still other thickets of venality and vice. Still, there's no better friend to have around to nudge the memory than *Roget*. It saves you the time of rummaging in your brain—that network of overloaded grooves—to find the word that's right on the tip of your tongue, where it doesn't do you any good. The *Thesaurus* is to the writer what a rhyming dictionary is to the songwriter—a reminder of all the choices—and you should use it with gratitude. If, having found the scalawag and the scapegrace, you want to know how they differ, *then* go to the dictionary.

Also bear in mind, when you're choosing words and stringing them together, how they sound. This may seem absurd: readers read with their eyes. But in fact they hear what they are reading far more than you realize. Therefore such matters as rhythm and alliteration are vital to every sentence. A typical example— maybe not the best, but undeniably the nearest—is the preceding paragraph. Obviously I enjoyed making a certain arrangement of my ruffians and riffraff, my hooligans and hoodlums, and my readers enjoyed it too—far more than if I had provided a mere list. They enjoyed not only the arrangement but the effort to entertain them. They weren't enjoying it, however, with their eyes. They were hearing the words in their inner ear.

E. B. White makes the case cogently in *The Elements of Style*, a book every writer should read once a year, when he suggests trying to rearrange any phrase that has survived for a century or two, such as Thomas Paine's "These are the times that try men's souls":

> Times like these try men's souls.
> How trying it is to live in these times!
> These are trying times for men's souls.
> Soulwise, these are trying times.

Paine's phrase is like poetry and the other four are like oatmeal—which is the divine mystery of the creative process. Good writers of prose must be part poet, always listening to what they write. E. B. White is one of my favorite stylists because I'm conscious of being with a man who cares about the cadences and sonorities of the language. I relish (in my ear) the pattern his words make as they fall into a sentence. I try to surmise how in rewriting the sentence he reassembled it to end with a phrase that will momentarily linger, or how he chose one word over another because he was after a certain emotional weight. It's the difference between, say, "serene" and "tranquil"—one so soft, the other strangely disturbing because of the unusual n and q.

Such considerations of sound and rhythm should be woven through everything you write. If all your sentences move at the same plodding gait, which even you recognize as deadly but don't know how to cure, read them aloud. (I write entirely by ear and read everything aloud before letting it go out into the world.) You'll begin to hear where the trouble lies. See if you can gain variety by reversing the order of a sentence, or by substituting a word that has freshness or oddity, or by altering the length of your sentences so they don't all sound as if they came out of the same mold. An occasional short sentence can carry a tremendous punch. It stays in the reader's ear.

Remember that words are the only tools you've got. Learn to use them with originality and care. And also remember: somebody out there is listening.

7

Usage

All this talk about good words and bad words brings us to a gray but important area called "usage." What is good usage? What is good English? What newly minted words is it O.K. to use, and who is to be the judge? Is it O.K. to use "O.K."?

Earlier I mentioned an incident of college students hassling the administration, and in the last chapter I described myself as a word freak. Here are two fairly recent arrivals. "Hassle" is both a verb and a noun, meaning to give somebody a hard time, or the act of being given a hard time, and anyone who has ever been hassled for not properly filling out Form 35-BX will agree that the word sounds exactly right. "Freak" means an enthusiast, and there's no missing the aura of obsession that goes with calling someone a jazz freak, or a chess freak, or a sun freak, though it would probably be pushing my luck to describe a man who compulsively visits circus sideshows as a freak freak.

Anyway, I accept these two usages gladly. I don't consider them slang, or put quotation marks around them to show that I'm mucking about in the argot of the youth culture and really know better. They're good words and we need them. But I won't accept "notables" and "greats" and "upcoming" and many other newcomers. They are cheap words and we *don't* need them.

Why is one word good and another word cheap? I can't give you an answer, because usage has no fixed boundaries. Language is a fabric that changes from one week to another, adding new strands and dropping old ones, and even word freaks fight over what is allowable, often reaching their decision on a wholly subjective basis such as taste ("notables" is sleazy). Which still leaves the question of who our tastemakers are.

The question was confronted by the editors of a brand-new dictionary, *The American Heritage Dictionary*, at the outset of their task in the mid–1960s. They assembled a "Usage Panel" to help them appraise the new words and dubious constructions that had come knocking at the door. Which ones should be ushered in, which thrown out on their ear? The panel consisted of 104 men and women—mostly writers, poets, editors and teachers—who were known for caring about the language and trying to use it well. I was a member of the panel, and over the next few years I kept getting questionnaires. Would I accept "finalize" and "escalate"? How did I feel about "It's me"? Would I allow "like" to be used as a conjunction—like so many people do? How about "mighty," as in "mighty fine"?

We were told that in the dictionary our opinions would be tabulated in a separate "Usage Note," so that readers could see how we voted. The questionnaire also left room for any comments we might feel impelled to make—a chance that the panelists seized avidly, as we found when the dictionary was published and our comments were released to the press. Passions ran high. "Good God, no! Never!" cried Barbara W. Tuchman, asked about the verb "to author." Scholarship hath no fury like that of a language purist faced with sludge, and I shared Tuchman's vow that "author" should never be authorized, just as I agreed with Lewis

Mumford that the adverb "good" should be "left as the exclusive property of Ernest Hemingway."

But guardians of usage are doing only half their job if they merely keep the language from becoming sloppy. Any dolt can rule that the suffix "wise," as in "healthwise," is doltwise, or that being "rather unique" is no more possible than being rather pregnant. The other half of the job is to help the language grow by welcoming any immigrant that will bring strength or color. Therefore I was glad that 97 percent of us voted to admit "dropout," which is clean and vivid, but that only 47 percent would accept "senior citizen," which is typical of the pudgy new intruders from the land of sociology, where an illegal alien is now an undocumented resident. I'm glad we accepted "escalate," the kind of verbal contraption I generally dislike but which the Vietnam war endowed with a precise meaning, complete with overtones of blunder.

I'm glad we took into full membership all sorts of robust words that previous dictionaries derided as "colloquial": adjectives like "rambunctious," verbs like "trigger" and "rile," nouns like "shambles" and "tycoon" and "trek," the latter approved by 78 percent to mean any difficult trip, as in "the commuter's daily trek to Manhattan." Originally it was a Cape Dutch word applied to the Boers' arduous journey by ox wagon. But our panel evidently felt that the Manhattan commuter's daily trek is no less arduous.

Still, 22 percent were unwilling to let "trek" slip into general usage. That was the virtue of revealing how our panel voted— it put our opinions on display, and writers in doubt can conduct themselves accordingly. Thus our 95 percent vote against "myself," as in "He invited Mary and myself to dinner," a word condemned as "prissy," "horrible" and "a genteelism," ought to warn off anyone who doesn't want to be prissy, horrible and genteel. As Red Smith put it, "'Myself' is the refuge of idiots taught early that 'me' is a dirty word."

On the other hand, only 66 percent of our panel rejected the verb "to contact," once regarded as tacky, and only half opposed the split infinitive and the verbs "to fault" and "to bus." So only 50 percent of your readers will fault you if you decide to voluntarily call your school board and to bus your children to another town. If you contact your school board you risk your reputation by another 16 percent. Our apparent rule of thumb was stated by Theodore M. Bernstein, author of the excellent *The Careful Writer:* "We should apply the test of convenience. Does the word fill a real need? If it does, let's give it a franchise."

All of this confirms what lexicographers have always known: that the laws of usage are relative, bending with the taste of the lawmaker. One of our panelists, Katherine Anne Porter, called "O.K." a "detestable vulgarity" and claimed she had never spoken the word in her life, whereas I freely admit that I have spoken the word "O.K." "Most," as in "most everyone," was scorned as "cute farmer talk" by Isaac Asimov and embraced as a "good English idiom" by Virgil Thomson. "Regime," meaning any administration, as in "the Truman regime," drew the approval of most everyone on the panel, as did "dynasty." But they drew the wrath of Jacques Barzun, who said, "These are technical terms, you blasted non-historians!" Probably I gave my O.K. to "regime." Now, chided by Barzun for imprecision, I think it looks like journalese. One of the words *I* railed against was "personality," as in a "TV personality." But now I wonder if it isn't the only word for that vast swarm of people who are famous for being famous—and possibly nothing else. What do the Gabor sisters *do?*

In the end it comes down to what is "correct" usage. We have no king to establish the King's English; we only have the President's English, which we don't want. *Webster,* long a defender of the faith, muddied the waters in 1961 with its permissive Third Edition, which argued that almost anything goes as long as somebody uses it, noting that "ain't" is "used orally in most parts of the U.S. by many cultivated speakers."

Just where *Webster* cultivated those speakers I ain't sure. Nevertheless it's true that the spoken language is looser than the written language, and *The American Heritage Dictionary* properly put its question to us in both forms. Often we allowed an oral idiom that we forbade in print as too informal, fully realizing, however, that "the pen must at length comply with the tongue," as Samuel Johnson said, and that today's spoken garbage may be tomorrow's written gold. The growing acceptance of the split infinitive, or of the preposition at the end of a sentence, proves that formal syntax can't hold the fort forever against a speaker's more comfortable way of getting the same thing said—and shouldn't. I think a sentence is a fine thing to put a preposition at the end of.

Our panel recognized that correctness can even vary within a word. We voted heavily against "cohort" as a synonym for "colleague," except where the tone was jocular. Thus a professor would not be among his cohorts at a faculty meeting, but they would abound at his college reunion, wearing funny hats. We rejected "too" as a synonym for "very," as in "His health is not too good." Whose health is? But we approved it in sardonic or humorous use, as in "He was not too happy when she ignored him."

These may seem like picayune distinctions. They're not. They are signals to the reader that you are sensitive to the shadings of usage. "Too" when substituted for "very" is clutter—"He didn't feel too much like going shopping." But the wry example in the previous paragraph is worthy of Ring Lardner. It adds a tinge of sarcasm that otherwise wouldn't be there.

Luckily, a pattern emerged from the deliberations of our panel, and it offers a guideline that is still useful. We turned out to be liberal in accepting new words and phrases, but conservative in grammar.

It would be foolish to reject a word as perfect as "dropout," or to pretend that countless words and phrases are not entering the gates of correct usage every day, borne on the winds of science and technology, fad and fashion and social change: "cyberspace," "meltdown," "skyjacker," "wetlands," "software," "fax," "macho," "yuppie," "gentrify" and hundreds of others. Nor should we forget all the short words invented by the counterculture in the 1960s as a way of lashing back at the self-important verbiage of the Establishment: "trip," "rap," "crash," "trash," "funky," "split," "rip-off," "vibes," "downer," "bummer" and many more. If brevity is a prize, these were winners. The only trouble with accepting words that entered the language overnight is that they often leave just as abruptly. The "happenings" of the late 1960s no longer happen, "out of sight" is out of sight, and even "awesome" has begun to chill out. The writer who cares about usage must always know the quick from the dead.

As for the area where our Usage Panel was conservative, we upheld most of the classic distinctions in grammar—"can" and "may," "fewer" and "less," "eldest" and "oldest," etc.—and decried the classic errors, insisting that "flout" still doesn't mean "flaunt," no matter how many writers flaunt their ignorance by flouting the rule, and that "fortuitous" still means "accidental," "disinterested" still means "impartial," and "infer" doesn't mean "imply." Here we were motivated by our love of the language's beautiful precision. Incorrect usage will lose you the readers you would most like to win. Know the difference between a "reference" and an "allusion," between "connive" and "conspire," between "compare with" and "compare to." If you must use "comprise," use it right. It means "include"; dinner comprises meat, potatoes, salad and dessert.

"I choose always the grammatical form unless it sounds affected," Marianne Moore explained, and that's finally where our panel took its stand. We were not pedants, so hung up on correctness that we didn't want the language to keep refreshing itself with phrases like "hung up." But that didn't mean we had to accept every atrocity that comes stumbling in.

Meanwhile the battle continues. In 1980 the Usage Panel was reconstituted, and today I still receive ballots soliciting my opinion on new locutions: verbs like "definitize" ("Congress definitized a proposal"), nouns like "affordables," colloquialisms like "the bottom line" and strays like "into" ("He's into backgammon and she's into jogging").

It no longer takes a panel of experts to notice that jargon is flooding our daily life and language. President Carter signed an executive order directing that federal regulations be written "simply and clearly." President Clinton's attorney general, Janet Reno, urged the nation's lawyers to replace "a lot of legalese" with "small, old words that all people understand"—words like "right" and "wrong" and "justice." Corporations have hired consultants to make their prose less opaque, and even the insurance industry is trying to rewrite its policies to tell us in less disastrous English what redress will be ours when disaster strikes. Whether these efforts will do much good I wouldn't want to bet. Still, there's comfort in the sight of so many watchdogs standing Canute-like on the beach, trying to hold back the tide. That's where all careful writers ought to be—looking at every new piece of flotsam that washes up and asking "Do we need it?"

I remember the first time somebody asked me, "How does that impact you?" I always thought "impact" was a noun, except in dentistry. Then I began to meet "de-impact," usually in connection with programs to de-impact the effects of some adversity. Nouns now turn overnight into verbs. We target goals and we access facts. Train conductors announce that the train won't platform. A sign on an airport door tells me that the door is alarmed. Companies are downsizing. It's part of an ongoing effort to grow the business. "Ongoing" is a jargon word whose main use is to raise morale. We face our daily job with more zest if the boss tells us it's an ongoing project; we give more willingly to institutions if they have targeted our funds for ongoing needs. Otherwise we might fall prey to disin-centivization.

I could go on; I have enough examples to fill a book, but it's not a book I would want anyone to read. We're still left with the question: What is good usage? One helpful approach is to try to separate usage from jargon.

I would say, for example, that "prioritize" is jargon—a pompous new verb that sounds more important than "rank"—and that "bottom line" is usage, a metaphor borrowed from the world of bookkeeping that conveys an image we can picture. As every businessman knows, the bottom line is the one that matters. If someone says, "The bottom line is that we just can't work together," we know what he means. I don't much like the phrase, but the bottom line is that it's here to stay.

New usages also arrive with new political events. Just as Vietnam gave us "escalate," Watergate gave us a whole lexicon of words connoting obstruction and deceit, including "stonewall," "deep-six," "launder," "enemies list" and other "gate"-suffix scandals ("Irangate"). It's a fitting irony that under Richard Nixon "launder" became a dirty word. Today when we hear that someone laundered his funds to hide the origin of the money and the route it took, the word has a precise meaning. It's short, it's vivid, and we need it. I accept "launder" and "stonewall"; I don't accept "prioritize" and "disincentive."

I would suggest a similar guideline for separating good English from technical English. It's the difference between, say, "printout" and "input." A printout is a specific object that a computer emits. Before the advent of computers it wasn't needed; now it is. But it has stayed where it belongs. Not so with "input," which was coined to describe the information that's fed to a computer. Our input is sought on every subject, from diets to philosophical discourse ("I'd like your input on whether God really exists").

I don't want to give somebody my input and get his feedback, though I'd be glad to offer my ideas and hear what he thinks of them. Good usage, to me, consists of using good words if they already exist—as they almost always do—to express myself clearly and simply to someone else. You might say it's how I verbalize the interpersonal.

PART II

Methods

8

————— ∞ —————

Unity

You learn to write by writing. It's a truism, but what makes it a truism is that it's true. The only way to learn to write is to force yourself to produce a certain number of words on a regular basis.

If you went to work for a newspaper that required you to write two or three articles every day, you would be a better writer after six months. You wouldn't necessarily be writing well—your style might still be full of clutter and clichés. But you would be exercising your powers of putting the English language on paper, gaining confidence and identifying the most common problems.

All writing is ultimately a question of solving a problem. It may be a problem of where to obtain the facts or how to organize the material. It may be a problem of approach or attitude, tone or style. Whatever it is, it has to be confronted and solved. Sometimes you will despair of finding the right solution—or any solution. You'll think, "If I live to be ninety I'll never get out of this mess." I've often thought it myself. But when I finally do solve the problem it's because I'm like a surgeon removing his 500th appendix; I've been there before.

Unity is the anchor of good writing. So, first, get your unities straight. Unity not only keeps the reader from straggling off in all directions; it satisfies the readers' subconscious need for order and reassures them that all is well at the helm. Therefore choose from among the many variables and stick to your choice.

One choice is unity of pronoun. Are you going to write in the first person, as a participant, or in the third person, as an observer? Or even in the second person, that darling of sportswriters hung up on Hemingway? ("You knew this had to be the most spine-tingling clash of giants you'd ever seen from a pressbox seat, and you weren't just some green kid who was still wet behind the ears.")

Unity of tense is another choice. Most people write mainly in the past tense ("I went up to Boston the other day"), but some people write agreeably in the present ("I'm sitting in the dining car of the Yankee Limited and we're pulling into Boston"). What is not agreeable is to switch back and forth. I'm not saying you can't use more than one tense; the whole purpose of tenses is to enable a writer to deal with time in its various gradations, from the past to the hypothetical future ("When I telephoned my mother from the Boston station, I realized that if I had written to tell her I would be coming she would have waited for me"). But you must choose the tense in which you are *principally* going to address the reader, no matter how many glances you may take backward or forward along the way.

Another choice is unity of mood. You might want to talk to the reader in the casual voice that *The New Yorker* has strenuously refined. Or you might want to approach the reader with a certain formality to describe a serious event or to present a set of important facts. Both tones are acceptable. In fact, *any* tone is acceptable. But don't mix two or three.

Such fatal mixtures are common in writers who haven't learned control. Travel writing is a conspicuous example. "My wife, Ann, and I had always wanted to visit Hong Kong," the writer begins, his blood astir with reminiscence, "and one day last spring we found ourselves looking at an airline poster and I said, 'Let's go!' The kids were grown up," he continues, and he proceeds to describe in genial detail how he and his wife stopped off in Hawaii and had such a comical time changing their money at the Hong Kong airport and finding their hotel. Fine. He is a real person taking us along on a real trip, and we can identify with him and Ann.

Suddenly he turns into a travel brochure. "Hong Kong affords many fascinating experiences to the curious sightseer," he writes. "One can ride the picturesque ferry from Kowloon and gawk at the myriad sampans as they scuttle across the teeming harbor, or take a day's trip to browse in the alleys of fabled Macao with its colorful history as a den of smuggling and intrigue. You will want to take the quaint funicular that climbs . . ." Then we get back to him and Ann and their efforts to eat at Chinese restaurants, and again all is well. Everyone is interested in food, and we are being told about a personal adventure.

Then suddenly the writer is a guidebook: "To enter Hong Kong it is necessary to have a valid passport, but no visa is required. You should definitely be immunized against hepatitis and you would also be well advised to consult your physician with regard to a possible inoculation for typhoid. The climate in Hong Kong is seasonable except in July and August when . . ." Our writer is gone, and so is Ann, and so—very soon—are we.

It's not that the scuttling sampans and the hepatitis shots shouldn't be included. What annoys us is that the writer never decided what kind of article he wanted to write or how he wanted to approach us. He comes at us in many guises, depending on what kind of material he is trying to purvey. Instead of controlling his material, his material is controlling him. That wouldn't happen if he took time to establish certain unities.

Therefore ask yourself some basic questions before you start. For example: "In what capacity am I going to address the reader?" (Reporter? Provider of information? Average man or woman?) "What pronoun and tense am I going to use?" "What style?" (Impersonal reportorial? Personal but formal? Personal and casual?) "What attitude am I going to take toward the material?" (Involved? Detached? Judgmental? Ironic? Amused?) "How much do I want to cover?" "What one point do I want to make?"

The last two questions are especially important. Most nonfiction writers have a definitiveness complex. They feel that they are under some obligation—to the subject, to their honor, to the gods of writing—to make their article the last word. It's a commendable impulse, but there is no last word. What you think is definitive today will turn undefinitive by tonight, and writers who doggedly pursue every last fact will find themselves pursuing the rainbow and never settling down to write. Nobody can write a book or an article "about" something. Tolstoy couldn't write a book about war and peace, or Melville a book about whaling. They made certain reductive decisions about time and place and about individual characters in that time and place—one man pursuing one whale. Every writing project must be reduced before you start to write.

Therefore think small. Decide what corner of your subject you're going to bite off, and be content to cover it well and stop. Often you'll find that along the way you've managed to say almost everything you wanted to say about the entire subject. This is also a matter of energy and morale. An unwieldy writing task is a drain on your enthusiasm. Enthusiasm is the force that keeps you going and keeps the reader in your grip.

When your zest begins to ebb, the reader is the first person to know it.

As for what point you want to make, every successful piece of nonfiction should leave the reader with one provocative thought that he or she didn't have before. Not two thoughts, or five—just one. So decide what single point you want to leave in the reader's mind. It will not only give you a better idea of what route you should follow and what destination you hope to reach; it will affect your decision about tone and attitude. Some points are best made by earnestness, some by dry understatement, some by humor.

Once you have your unities decided, there's no material you can't work into your frame. If the tourist in Hong Kong had chosen to write solely in the conversational vein about what he and Ann did, he would have found a natural way to weave into his narrative whatever he wanted to tell us about the Kowloon ferry and the local weather. His personality and purpose would have been intact, and his article would have held together.

Now it often happens that you'll make these prior decisions and then discover that they weren't the right ones. The material begins to lead you in an unexpected direction, where you are more comfortable writing in a different tone. That's normal— the act of writing generates some cluster of thoughts or memories that you didn't anticipate. Don't fight such a current if it feels right. Trust your material if it's taking you into terrain you didn't intend to enter but where the vibrations are good. Adjust your style accordingly and proceed to whatever destination you reach. Don't ever become the prisoner of a preconceived plan. Writing is no respecter of blueprints.

If this happens, the second part of your article will be badly out of joint with the first. But at least you know which part is truest to your instincts. Then it's just a matter of making repairs. Go back to the beginning and rewrite it so that your mood and your style are consistent from start to finish.

There's nothing in such a method to be ashamed of. Scissors and paste—or their equivalent on a word processor—are honorable writers' tools. Just remember that all the unities must be fitted into the edifice you finally put together, however backwardly they may be assembled, or it will soon come tumbling down.

9

∼∞∞∼

The Lead and the Ending

The most important sentence in any article is the first one. If it doesn't induce the reader to proceed to the second sentence, your article is dead. And if the second sentence doesn't induce him to continue to the third sentence, it's equally dead. Of such a progression of sentences, each tugging the reader forward until he is hooked, a writer constructs that fateful unit, the "lead."

How long should the lead be? One or two paragraphs? Four or five? There's no pat answer. Some leads hook the reader with just a few well-baited sentences; others amble on for several pages, exerting a slow but steady pull. Every article poses a different problem, and the only valid test is: does it work? Your lead may not be the best of all possible leads, but if it does the job it's supposed to do, be thankful and proceed.

Sometimes the length may depend on the audience you're

writing for. Readers of a literary review expect its writers to start somewhat discursively, and they will stick with those writers for the pleasure of wondering where they will emerge as they move in leisurely circles toward the eventual point. But I urge you not to count on the reader to stick around. Readers want to know— very soon—what's in it for them.

Therefore your lead must capture the reader immediately and force him to keep reading. It must cajole him with fresh- ness, or novelty, or paradox, or humor, or surprise, or with an unusual idea, or an interesting fact, or a question. Anything will do, as long as it nudges his curiosity and tugs at his sleeve.

Next the lead must do some real work. It must provide hard details that tell the reader why the piece was written and why he ought to read it. But don't dwell on the reason. Coax the reader a little more; keep him inquisitive.

Continue to build. Every paragraph should amplify the one that preceded it. Give more thought to adding solid detail and less to entertaining the reader. But take special care with the last sentence of each paragraph—it's the crucial springboard to the next paragraph. Try to give that sentence an extra twist of humor or surprise, like the periodic "snapper" in the routine of a stand- up comic. Make the reader smile and you've got him for at least one more paragraph.

Let's look at a few leads that vary in pace but are alike in maintaining pressure. I'll start with two columns of my own that first appeared in *Life* and *Look*—magazines which, judging by the comments of readers, found their consumers mainly in bar- bershops, hairdressing salons, airplanes and doctors' offices ("I was getting a haircut the other day and I saw your article"). I mention this as a reminder that far more periodical reading is done under the dryer than under the reading lamp, so there isn't much time for the writer to fool around.

The first is the lead of a piece called "Block That Chicken- furter":

I've often wondered what goes into a hot dog. Now I know and I wish I didn't.

Two very short sentences. But it would be hard not to continue to the second paragraph:

My trouble began when the Department of Agriculture published the hot dog's ingredients—everything that may legally qualify—because it was asked by the poultry industry to relax the conditions under which the ingredients might also include chicken. In other words, can a chickenfurter find happiness in the land of the frank?

One sentence that explains the incident that the column is based on. Then a snapper to restore the easygoing tone.

Judging by the 1,066 mainly hostile answers that the Department got when it sent out a questionnaire on this point, the very thought is unthinkable. The public mood was most felicitously caught by the woman who replied: "I don't eat feather meat of no kind."

Another fact and another smile. Whenever you're lucky enough to get a quotation as funny as that one, find a way to use it. The article then specifies what the Department of Agriculture says may go into a hot dog—a list that includes "the edible part of the muscle of cattle, sheep, swine or goats, in the diaphragm, in the heart or in the esophagus. . . [but not including] the muscle found in the lips, snout or ears."

From there it progresses—not without an involuntary reflex around the esophagus—into an account of the controversy between the poultry interests and the frankfurter interests, which in turn leads to the point that Americans will eat anything that even remotely resembles a hot dog. Implicit at the end is the larger point that Americans don't know, or care, what goes into the food they eat. The style of the article has remained casual and touched with humor. But its content turns out to be more serious than readers expected when they were drawn into it by a whimsical lead.

A slower lead, luring the reader more with curiosity than with humor, introduced a piece called "Thank God for Nuts":

> By any reasonable standard, nobody would want to look twice—or even once—at the piece of slippery elm bark from Clear Lake, Wisc., birthplace of pitcher Burleigh Grimes, that is on display at the National Baseball Museum and Hall of Fame in Cooperstown, N.Y. As the label explains, it is the kind of bark Grimes chewed during games "to increase saliva for throwing the spitball. When wet, the ball sailed to the plate in deceptive fashion." This would seem to be one of the least interesting facts available in America today.
>
> But baseball fans can't be judged by any reasonable standard. We are obsessed by the minutiae of the game and nagged for the rest of our lives by the memory of players we once saw play. No item is therefore too trivial that puts us back in touch with them. I am just old enough to remember Burleigh Grimes and his well-moistened pitches sailing deceptively to the plate, and when I found his bark I studied it as intently as if I had come upon the Rosetta Stone. "So *that's* how he did it," I thought, peering at the odd botanical relic. "Slippery elm! I'll be damned."
>
> This was only one of several hundred encounters I had with my own boyhood as I prowled through the Museum. Probably no other museum is so personal a pilgrimage to our past. . . .

The reader is now safely hooked, and the hardest part of the writer's job is over.

One reason for citing this lead is to note that salvation often lies not in the writer's style but in some odd fact he or she was able to discover. I went up to Cooperstown and spent a whole afternoon in the museum, taking notes. Jostled everywhere by nostalgia, I gazed with reverence at Lou Gehrig's locker and Bobby Thomson's game-winning bat. I sat in a grandstand seat brought from the Polo Grounds, dug my unspiked soles into the home plate from Ebbets Field, and dutifully copied all the labels and captions that might be useful.

"These are the shoes that touched home plate as Ted finished his journey around the bases," said a label identifying the shoes worn by Ted Williams when he famously hit a home run on his last time at bat. The shoes were in much better shape than the pair—rotted open at the sides—that belonged to Walter Johnson. But the caption provided exactly the kind of justifying fact a baseball nut would want. "My feet must be comfortable when I'm out there a-pitching," the great Walter said.

The museum closed at five and I returned to my motel secure in my memories and my research. But instinct told me to go back the next morning for one more tour, and it was only then that I noticed Burleigh Grimes's slippery elm bark, which struck me as an ideal lead. It still does.

One moral of this story is that you should always collect more material than you will use. Every article is strong in proportion to the surplus of details from which you can choose the few that will serve you best—if you don't go on gathering facts forever. At some point you must stop researching and start writing.

Another moral is to look for your material everywhere, not just by reading the obvious sources and interviewing the obvious people. Look at signs and at billboards and at all the junk written along the American roadside. Read the labels on our packages and the instructions on our toys, the claims on our medicines and the graffiti on our walls. Read the fillers, so rich in self-esteem, that come spilling out of your monthly statement from the electric company and the telephone company and the bank. Read menus and catalogues and second-class mail. Nose about in obscure crannies of the newspaper, like the Sunday real estate section—you can tell the temper of a society by what patio accessories it wants. Our daily landscape is thick with absurd messages and portents. Notice them. They not only have social significance; they are often just quirky enough to make a lead that's different from everybody else's.

Speaking of everybody else's lead, there are many categories I'd be glad never to see again. One is the future archaeologist: "When some future archaeologist stumbles on the remains of our civilization, what will he make of the jukebox?" I'm tired of him already and he's not even here. I'm also tired of the visitor from Mars: "If a creature from Mars landed on our planet he would be amazed to see hordes of scantily clad earthlings lying on the sand barbecuing their skins." I'm tired of the cute event that just happened to happen "one day not long ago" or on a conveniently recent Saturday afternoon: "One day not long ago a small button-nosed boy was walking with his dog, Terry, in a field outside Paramus, N.J., when he saw something that looked strangely like a balloon rising out of the ground." And I'm very tired of the have-in-common lead: "What did Joseph Stalin, Douglas MacArthur, Ludwig Wittgenstein, Sherwood Anderson, Jorge Luis Borges and Akira Kurosawa have in common? They all loved Westerns." Let's retire the future archaeologist and the man from Mars and the button-nosed boy. Try to give your lead a freshness of perception or detail.

Consider this lead, by Joan Didion, on a piece called "7000 Romaine, Los Angeles 38":

Seven Thousand Romaine Street is in that part of Los Angeles familiar to admirers of Raymond Chandler and Dashiell Hammett: the underside of Hollywood, south of Sunset Boulevard, a middle-class slum of "model studios" and warehouses and two-family bungalows. Because Paramount and Columbia and Desilu and the Samuel Goldwyn studios are nearby, many of the people who live around here have some tenuous connection with the motion-picture industry. They once processed fan photographs, say, or knew Jean Harlow's manicurist. 7000 Romaine looks itself like a faded movie exterior, a pastel building with chipped *art moderne* detailing, the windows now either boarded or paned with chicken-wire glass and, at the entrance, among the dusty oleander, a rubber mat that reads WELCOME.

Actually no one is welcome, for 7000 Romaine belongs to Howard Hughes, and the door is locked. That the Hughes "communications center" should lie here in the dull sunlight of Hammett-Chandler country is one of those circumstances that satisfy one's suspicion that life is indeed a scenario, for the Hughes empire has been in our time the only industrial complex in the world—involving, over the years, machinery manufacture, foreign oil-tool subsidiaries, a brewery, two airlines, immense real-estate holdings, a major motion-picture studio, and an electronics and missile operation—run by a man whose *modus operandi* most closely resembles that of a character in *The Big Sleep*.

As it happens, I live not far from 7000 Romaine, and I make a point of driving past it every now and then, I suppose in the same spirit that Arthurian scholars visit the Cornish coast. I am interested in the folklore of Howard Hughes. . . .

What is pulling us into this article—toward, we hope, some glimpse of how Hughes operates, some hint of the riddle of the Sphinx—is the steady accumulation of facts that have pathos and faded glamour. Knowing Jean Harlow's manicurist is such a minimal link to glory, the unwelcoming welcome mat such a queer relic of a golden age when Hollywood's windows weren't paned with chicken-wire glass and the roost was ruled by giants like Mayer and DeMille and Zanuck, who could actually be seen exercising their mighty power. We want to know more; we read on.

Another approach is to just tell a story. It's such a simple solution, so obvious and unsophisticated, that we often forget that it's available to us. But narrative is the oldest and most compelling method of holding someone's attention; everybody wants to be told a story. Always look for ways to convey your information in narrative form. What follows is the lead of Edmund Wilson's account of the discovery of the Dead Sea Scrolls, one of the most astonishing relics of antiquity to turn up in modern times. Wilson doesn't spend any time setting the stage. This is not the "breakfast-to-bed" format used by inexperienced writers, in which a fishing trip begins with the ringing of an alarm clock before daylight. Wilson starts right in—whap!—and we are caught:

> At some point rather early in the spring of 1947, a Bedouin boy called Muhammed the Wolf was minding some goats near a cliff on the western shore of the Dead Sea. Climbing up after one that had strayed, he noticed a cave that he had not seen before, and he idly threw a stone into it. There was an unfamiliar sound of breakage. The boy was frightened and ran away. But he later came back with another boy, and together they explored the cave. Inside were several tall clay jars, among fragments of other jars. When they took off the bowl-like lids, a very bad smell arose, which came from dark oblong lumps that were found inside all the jars. When they got these lumps out of the cave, they saw that they were wrapped up in lengths of linen and coated with a black layer of what seemed to be pitch or wax. They unrolled them and found long manuscripts, inscribed in parallel columns on thin sheets that had been sewn together. Though these manuscripts had faded and crumbled in places, they were in

general remarkably clear. The character, they saw, was not Arabic. They wondered at the scrolls and kept them, carrying them along when they moved.

These Bedouin boys belonged to a party of contrabanders, who had been smuggling their goats and other goods out of Transjordan into Palestine. They had detoured so far to the south in order to circumvent the Jordan bridge, which the customs officers guarded with guns, and had floated their commodities across the stream. They were now on their way to Bethlehem to sell their stuff in the black market. . . .

Yet there can be no firm rules for how to write a lead. Within the broad rule of not letting the reader get away, all writers must approach their subject in a manner that most naturally suits what they are writing about and who they are. Sometimes you can tell your whole story in the first sentence. Here's the opening sentence of seven memorable nonfiction books:

> In the beginning God created heaven and earth.
> —THE BIBLE

> In the summer of the Roman year 699, now described as the year 55 before the birth of Christ, the Proconsul of Gaul, Gaius Julius Caesar, turned his gaze upon Britain.
> —WINSTON S. CHURCHILL, A HISTORY OF THE ENGLISH-
> SPEAKING PEOPLES

> Put this puzzle together and you will find milk, cheese and eggs, meat, fish, beans and cereals, greens, fruits and root vegetables—foods that contain our essential daily needs.
> —IRMA S. ROMBAUER, JOY OF COOKING

> To the Manus native the world is a great platter, curving upwards on all sides, from his flat lagoon village where the

pile-houses stand like long-legged birds, placid and unstirred
by the changing tides.
     —MARGARET MEAD, GROWING UP IN NEW GUINEA

The problem lay buried, unspoken, for many years in the
minds of American women.
     —BETTY FRIEDAN, THE FEMININE MYSTIQUE

Within five minutes, or ten minutes, no more than that,
three of the others had called her on the telephone to ask her
if she had heard that something had happened out there.
     —TOM WOLFE, THE RIGHT STUFF

You know more than you think you do.
     —BENJAMIN SPOCK, BABY AND CHILD CARE

Those are some suggestions on how to get started. Now I
want to tell you how to stop. Knowing when to end an article is
far more important than most writers realize. You should give as
much thought to choosing your last sentence as you did to your
first. Well, almost as much.

That may seem hard to believe. If your readers have stuck
with you from the beginning, trailing you around blind corners
and over bumpy terrain, surely they won't leave when the end is
in sight. Surely they will, because the end that's in sight turns
out to be a mirage. Like the minister's sermon that builds to a
series of perfect conclusions that never conclude, an article that
doesn't stop where it should stop becomes a drag and therefore
a failure.

Most of us are still prisoners of the lesson pounded into us
by the composition teachers of our youth: that every story must
have a beginning, a middle and an end. We can still visualize the
outline, with its Roman numerals (I, II and III), which staked
out the road we would faithfully trudge, and its subnumerals

(IIa and IIb) denoting lesser paths down which we would briefly poke. But we always promised to get back to III and summarize our journey.

That's all right for elementary and high school students uncertain of their ground. It forces them to see that every piece of writing should have a logical design. It's a lesson worth knowing at any age—even professional writers are adrift more often than they would like to admit. But if you're going to write good nonfiction you must wriggle out of III's dread grip.

You'll know you have arrived at III when you see emerging on your screen a sentence that begins, "In sum, it can be noted that . . ." Or a question that asks, "What insights, then, have we been able to glean from. . . ?" These are signals that you are about to repeat in compressed form what you have already said in detail. The reader's interest begins to falter; the tension you have built begins to sag. Yet you will be true to Miss Potter, your teacher, who made you swear fealty to the holy outline. You remind the reader of what can, in sum, be noted. You go gleaning one more time in insights you have already adduced.

But your readers hear the laborious sound of cranking. They notice what you are doing and how bored you are by it. They feel the stirrings of resentment. Why didn't you give more thought to how you were going to wind this thing up? Or are you summarizing because you think they're too dumb to get the point? Still, you keep cranking. But the readers have another option. They quit.

That's the negative reason for not forgetting the importance of the last sentence. Failure to know where that sentence should occur can wreck an article that until its final stage has been tightly constructed. The positive reason for ending well is that a good last sentence—or last paragraph—is a joy in itself. It gives the reader a lift, and it lingers when the article is over.

The perfect ending should take your readers slightly by surprise and yet seem exactly right. They didn't expect the article to end so soon, or so abruptly, or to say what it said. But they know it when they see it. Like a good lead, it works. It's like the curtain line in a theatrical comedy. We are in the middle of a scene (we think), when suddenly one of the actors says something funny, or outrageous, or epigrammatic, and the lights go out. We are startled to find the scene over, and then delighted by the aptness of how it ended. What delights us is the playwright's perfect control.

For the nonfiction writer, the simplest way of putting this into a rule is: when you're ready to stop, stop. If you have presented all the facts and made the point you want to make, look for the nearest exit.

Often it takes just a few sentences to wrap things up. Ideally they should encapsulate the idea of the piece and conclude with a sentence that jolts us with its fitness or unexpectedness. Here's how H. L. Mencken ends his appraisal of President Calvin Coolidge, whose appeal to the "customers" was that his "government governed hardly at all; thus the ideal of Jefferson was realized at last, and the Jeffersonians were delighted":

> We suffer most, not when the White House is a peaceful dormitory, but when it [has] a tin-pot Paul bawling from the roof. Counting out Harding as a cipher only, Dr. Coolidge was preceded by one World Saver and followed by two more. What enlightened American, having to choose between any of them and another Coolidge, would hesitate for an instant? There were no thrills while he reigned, but neither were there any headaches. He had no ideas, and he was not a nuisance.

The five short sentences send the reader on his way quickly and with an arresting thought to take along. The notion of Coolidge having no ideas and not being a nuisance can't help leaving a residue of enjoyment. It works.

Something I often do in my own work is to bring the story full circle—to strike at the end an echo of a note that was sounded at the beginning. It gratifies my sense of symmetry, and it also pleases the reader, completing with its resonance the journey we set out on together.

But what usually works best is a quotation. Go back through your notes to find some remark that has a sense of finality, or that's funny, or that adds an unexpected closing detail. Sometimes it will jump out at you during the interview—I've often thought, "That's my ending!"—or during the process of writing. In the mid–1960s, when Woody Allen was just becoming established as America's resident neurotic, doing nightclub monologues, I wrote the first long magazine piece that took note of his arrival. It ended like this:

> "If people come away relating to me as a person," Allen says, "rather than just enjoying my jokes; if they come away wanting to hear me again, no matter what I might talk about, then I'm succeeding." Judging by the returns, he is. Woody Allen is Mr. Related-To, and he seems a good bet to hold the franchise for many years.
>
> Yet he does have a problem all his own, unshared by, unrelated to, the rest of America. "I'm obsessed," he says, "by the fact that my mother genuinely resembles Groucho Marx."

There's a remark from so far out in left field that nobody could see it coming. The surprise it carries is tremendous. How could it not be a perfect ending? Surprise is one of the most refreshing elements in nonfiction writing. If something surprises you it will also surprise—and delight—the people you are writing for, especially as you conclude your story and send them on their way.

1 0

Bits & Pieces

This is a chapter of scraps and morsels—small admonitions on many points that I have collected under one, as they say, umbrella.

VERBS.

Use active verbs unless there is no comfortable way to get around using a passive verb. The difference between an active-verb style and a passive-verb style—in clarity and vigor—is the difference between life and death for a writer.

"Joe saw him" is strong. "He was seen by Joe" is weak. The first is short and precise; it leaves no doubt about who did what. The second is necessarily longer and it has an insipid quality: something was done by somebody to someone else. It's also ambiguous. How often was he seen by Joe? Once? Every day? Once a week? A style that consists of passive constructions will sap the reader's energy. Nobody ever quite knows what is being perpetrated by whom and on whom.

I use "perpetrated" because it's the kind of word that passive-voice writers are fond of. They prefer long words of Latin origin to short Anglo-Saxon words—which compounds their trouble and makes their sentences still more glutinous. Short is generally better than long. Of the 701 words in Lincoln's Second Inaugural Address, a marvel of economy in itself, 505 are words of one syllable and 122 are words of two syllables.

Verbs are the most important of all your tools. They push the sentence forward and give it momentum. Active verbs push hard; passive verbs tug fitfully. Active verbs also enable us to visualize an activity because they require a pronoun ("he"), or a noun ("the boy"), or a person ("Mrs. Scott") to put them in motion. Many verbs also carry in their imagery or in their sound a suggestion of what they mean: glitter, dazzle, twirl, beguile, scatter, swagger, poke, pamper, vex. Probably no other language has such a vast supply of verbs so bright with color. Don't choose one that is dull or merely serviceable. Make active verbs activate your sentences, and try to avoid the kind that need an appended preposition to complete their work. Don't set up a business that you can start or launch. Don't say that the president of the company stepped down. Did he resign? Did he retire? Did he get fired? Be precise. Use precise verbs.

If you want to see how active verbs give vitality to the written word, don't just go back to Hemingway or Thurber or Thoreau. I commend the King James Bible and William Shakespeare.

ADVERBS.

Most adverbs are unnecessary. You will clutter your sentence and annoy the reader if you choose a verb that has a specific meaning and then add an adverb that carries the same meaning. Don't tell us that the radio blared loudly; "blare" connotes loudness. Don't write that someone clenched his teeth tightly; there's no other way to clench teeth. Again and again in careless writing, strong verbs are weakened by redundant adverbs. So are adjectives and other parts of speech: "effortlessly easy," "slightly spartan," "totally flabbergasted." The beauty of "flab-bergasted" is that it implies an astonishment that is total; I can't picture someone being partly flabbergasted. If an action is so easy as to be effortless, use "effortless." And what is "slightly spartan"? Perhaps a monk's cell with wall-to-wall carpeting. Don't use adverbs unless they do necessary work. Spare us the news that the winning athlete grinned widely.

And while we're at it, let's retire "decidedly" and all its slip-pery cousins. Every day I see in the paper that some situations are decidedly better and others are decidedly worse, but I never know how decided the improvement is, or who did the deciding, just as I never know how eminent a result is that's eminently fair, or whether to believe a fact that's arguably true. "He's arguably the best pitcher on the Mets," the preening sportswriter writes, aspiring to Parnassus, which Red Smith reached by never using words like "arguably." Is the pitcher—it can be proved by argument—the best pitcher on the team? If so, please omit "arguably." Or is he *perhaps*—the opinion is open to argument—the best pitcher? Admittedly I don't know. It's virtually a toss-up.

ADJECTIVES.

Most adjectives are also unnecessary. Like adverbs, they are sprinkled into sentences by writers who don't stop to think that the concept is already in the noun. This kind of prose is littered with precipitous cliffs and lacy spiderwebs, or with adjectives denoting the color of an object whose color is well known: yel-low daffodils and brownish dirt. If you want to make a value judgment about daffodils, choose an adjective like "garish." If you're in a part of the country where the dirt is red, feel free to mention the red dirt. Those adjectives would do a job that the noun alone wouldn't be doing.

Most writers sow adjectives almost unconsciously into the soil of their prose to make it more lush and pretty, and the sentences become longer and longer as they fill up with stately elms and frisky kittens and hard-bitten detectives and sleepy lagoons. This is adjective-by-habit—a habit you should get rid of. Not every oak has to be gnarled. The adjective that exists solely as decoration is a self-indulgence for the writer and a burden for the reader.

Again, the rule is simple: make your adjectives do work that needs to be done. "He looked at the gray sky and the black clouds and decided to sail back to the harbor." The darkness of the sky and the clouds is the reason for the decision. If it's important to tell the reader that a house was drab or a girl was beautiful, by all means use "drab" and "beautiful." They will have their proper power because you have learned to use adjectives sparsely.

LITTLE QUALIFIERS.

Prune out the small words that qualify how you feel and how you think and what you saw: "a bit," "a little," "sort of," "kind of," "rather," "quite," "very," "too," "pretty much," "in a sense" and dozens more. They dilute your style and your persuasiveness.

Don't say you were a bit confused and sort of tired and a little depressed and somewhat annoyed. Be confused. Be tired. Be depressed. Be annoyed. Don't hedge your prose with little timidities. Good writing is lean and confident.

Don't say you weren't too happy because the hotel was pretty expensive. Say you weren't happy because the hotel was expensive. Don't tell us you were quite fortunate. How fortunate is that? Don't describe an event as rather spectacular or very awesome. Words like "spectacular" and "awesome" don't submit to measurement. "Very" is a useful word to achieve emphasis, but far more often it's clutter. There's no need to call someone very methodical. Either he is methodical or he isn't.

The larger point is one of authority. Every little qualifier whittles away some fraction of the reader's trust. Readers want a

writer who believes in himself and in what he is saying. Don't
diminish that belief. Don't be kind of bold. Be bold.

PUNCTUATION.

These are brief thoughts on punctuation, in no way intended
as a primer. If you don't know how to punctuate—and many college students still don't—get a grammar book.

The Period. There's not much to be said about the period
except that most writers don't reach it soon enough. If you find
yourself hopelessly mired in a long sentence, it's probably
because you're trying to make the sentence do more than it can
reasonably do—perhaps express two dissimilar thoughts. The
quickest way out is to break the long sentence into two short
sentences, or even three. There is no minimum length for a sentence that's acceptable in the eyes of God. Among good writers
it is the short sentence that predominates, and don't tell me
about Norman Mailer—he's a genius. If you want to write long
sentences, be a genius. Or at least make sure that the sentence
is under control from beginning to end, in syntax and punctuation, so that the reader knows where he is at every step of the
winding trail.

The Exclamation Point. Don't use it unless you must to
achieve a certain effect. It has a gushy aura, the breathless excitement of a debutante commenting on an event that was exciting
only to her: "Daddy says I must have had too much champagne!"
"But honestly, I could have danced all night!" We have all suffered
more than our share of these sentences in which an exclamation
point knocks us over the head with how cute or wonderful something was. Instead, construct your sentence so that the order of
the words will put the emphasis where you want it. Also resist
using an exclamation point to notify the reader that you are making a joke or being ironic. "It never occurred to me that the water

pistol might be loaded!" Readers are annoyed by your reminder that this was a comical moment. They are also robbed of the pleasure of finding it funny on their own. Humor is best achieved by understatement, and there's nothing subtle about an exclamation point.

The Semicolon. There is a 19th-century mustiness that hangs over the semicolon. We associate it with the carefully balanced sentences, the judicious weighing of "on the one hand" and "on the other hand," of Conrad and Thackeray and Hardy. Therefore it should be used sparingly by modern writers of nonfiction. Yet I notice that it turns up quite often in the passages I've quoted in this book and that I use it fairly often myself—usually to add a related thought to the first half of a sentence. Still, the semicolon brings the reader, if not to a halt, at least to a pause. So use it with discretion, remembering that it will slow to a Victorian pace the late–20th-century momentum you're striving for, and rely instead on the period and the dash.

The Dash. Somehow this invaluable tool is widely regarded as not quite proper—a bumpkin at the genteel dinner table of good English. But it has full membership and will get you out of many tight corners. The dash is used in two ways. One is to amplify or justify in the second part of the sentence a thought you stated in the first part. "We decided to keep going—it was only 100 miles more and we could get there in time for dinner." By its very shape the dash pushes the sentence ahead and explains why they decided to keep going. The other use involves two dashes, which set apart a parenthetical thought within a longer sentence. "She told me to get in the car—she had been after me all summer to have a haircut—and we drove silently into town." An explanatory detail that might otherwise have required a separate sentence is dispatched along the way.

The Colon. The colon has begun to look even more antique than the semicolon, and many of its functions have been taken over by the dash. But it still serves well its pure role of bringing your sentence to a brief halt before you plunge into, say, an itemized list. "The brochure said the ship would stop at the following ports: Oran, Algiers, Naples, Brindisi, Piraeus, Istanbul and Beirut." You can't beat the colon for work like that.

MOOD CHANGERS.

Learn to alert the reader as soon as possible to any change in mood from the previous sentence. At least a dozen words will do this job for you: "but," "yet," "however," "nevertheless," "still," "instead," "thus," "therefore," "meanwhile," "now," "later," "today," "subsequently" and several more. I can't overstate how much easier it is for readers to process a sentence if you start with "but" when you're shifting direction. Or, conversely, how much harder it is if they must wait until the end to realize that you have shifted.

Many of us were taught that no sentence should begin with "but." If that's what you learned, unlearn it—there's no stronger word at the start. It announces total contrast with what has gone before, and the reader is thereby primed for the change. If you need relief from too many sentences beginning with "but," switch to "however." It is, however, a weaker word and needs careful placement. Don't start a sentence with "however"—it hangs there like a wet dishrag. And don't end with "however"—by that time it has lost its howeverness. Put it as early as you reasonably can, as I did three sentences ago. Its abruptness then becomes a virtue.

"Yet" does almost the same job as "but," though its meaning is closer to "nevertheless." Either of those words at the beginning of a sentence—"Yet he decided to go" or "Nevertheless he decided to go"—can replace a whole long phrase that summarizes what the reader has just been told: *"Despite the fact that all these dangers had been pointed out to him,* he decided to go." Look for all the places where one of these short words will instantly convey the same meaning as a long and dismal clause. "Instead I took the train." "Still I had to admire him." "Thus I learned how to smoke." "It was therefore easy to meet him." "Meanwhile I had talked to John." What a vast amount of huffing and puffing these pivotal words save! (The exclamation point is to show that I really mean it.)

As for "meanwhile," "now," "today" and "later," what they also save is confusion, for careless writers often change their time frame without remembering to tip the reader off. "Now I know better." "Today you can't find such an item." "Later I found out why." Always make sure your readers are oriented. Always ask yourself where you left them in the previous sentence.

CONTRACTIONS.

Your style will be warmer and truer to your personality if you use contractions like "I'll" and "won't" and "can't" when they fit comfortably into what you're writing. "I'll be glad to see them if they don't get mad" is less stiff than "I will be glad to see them if they do not get mad." (Read that aloud and hear how stilted it sounds.) There's no rule against such informality—trust your ear and your instincts. I only suggest avoiding one form—"I'd," "he'd," "we'd," etc.—because "I'd" can mean both "I had" and "I would," and readers can get well into a sentence before learning which meaning it is. Often it's not the one they thought it was. Also, don't invent contractions, like "could've." They cheapen your style. Stick with the ones you can find in the dictionary.

THAT AND WHICH.

Anyone who tries to explain "that" and "which" in less than an hour is asking for trouble. Fowler, in his *Modern English Usage,* takes 25 columns of type. I'm going for two minutes, perhaps the world record. Here (I hope) is much of what you need to bear in mind:

Always use "that" unless it makes your meaning ambiguous. Notice that in carefully edited magazines, such as *The New Yorker*, "that" is by far the predominant usage. I mention this because it is still widely believed—a residue from school and college—that "which" is more correct, more acceptable, more literary. It's not. In most situations, "that" is what you would naturally say and therefore what you should write.

If your sentence needs a comma to achieve its precise meaning, it probably needs "which." "Which" serves a particular identifying function, different from "that." (A) "Take the shoes that are in the closet." This means: take the shoes that are in the closet, not the ones under the bed. (B) "Take the shoes, which are in the closet." Only one pair of shoes is under discussion; the "which" usage tells you where they are. Note that the comma is necessary in B, but not in A.

A high proportion of "which" usages narrowly describe, or identify, or locate, or explain, or otherwise qualify the phrase that preceded the comma:

> The house, which has a red roof,
> The store, which is called Bob's Hardware,
> The Rhine, which is in Germany,
> The monsoon, which is a seasonal wind,
> The moon, which I saw from the porch,

That's all I'm going to say that I think you initially need to know to write good nonfiction, which is a form that requires exact marshaling of information.

CONCEPT NOUNS.

Nouns that express a concept are commonly used in bad writing instead of verbs that tell what somebody did. Here are three typical dead sentences:

The common reaction is incredulous laughter.
Bemused cynicism isn't the only response to the old system.
The current campus hostility is a symptom of the change.

What is so eerie about these sentences is that they have no people in them. They also have no working verbs—only "is" or "isn't." The reader can't visualize anybody performing some activity; all the meaning lies in impersonal nouns that embody a vague concept: "reaction," "cynicism," "response," "hostility." Turn these cold sentences around. Get people doing things:

Most people just laugh with disbelief.
Some people respond to the old system by turning cynical; others say. . .
It's easy to notice the change—you can see how angry all the students are.

My revised sentences aren't jumping with vigor, partly because the material I'm trying to knead into shape is shapeless dough. But at least they have real people and real verbs. Don't get caught holding a bag full of abstract nouns. You'll sink to the bottom of the lake and never be seen again.

CREEPING NOUNISM.

This is a new American disease that strings two or three nouns together where one noun—or, better yet, one verb—will do. Nobody goes broke now; we have money problem areas. It no longer rains; we have precipitation activity or a thunderstorm probability situation. Please, let it rain.

Today as many as four or five concept nouns will attach themselves to each other, like a molecule chain. Here's a brilliant specimen I recently found: "Communication facilitation skills development intervention." Not a person in sight, or a working verb. I think it's a program to help students write better.

OVERSTATEMENT.

"The living room looked as if an atomic bomb had gone off there," writes the novice writer, describing what he saw on Sunday morning after a party that got out of hand. Well, we all know he's exaggerating to make a droll point, but we also know that an atomic bomb *didn't* go off there, or any other bomb except maybe a water bomb. "I felt as if ten 747 jets were flying through my brain," he writes, "and I seriously considered jumping out the window and killing myself." These verbal high jinks can get just so high—and this writer is already well over the limit—before the reader feels an overpowering drowsiness. It's like being trapped with a man who can't stop reciting limericks. Don't overstate. You didn't really consider jumping out the window. Life has more than enough truly horrible funny situations. Let the humor sneak up so we hardly hear it coming.

CREDIBILITY.

Credibility is just as fragile for a writer as for a President. Don't inflate an incident to make it more outlandish than it actually was. If the reader catches you in just one bogus statement that you are trying to pass off as true, everything you write thereafter will be suspect. It's too great a risk, and not worth taking.

DICTATION.

Much of the "writing" done in America is done by dictation. Administrators, executives, managers, educators and other officials think in terms of using their time efficiently. They think the quickest way of getting something "written" is to dictate it to a secretary and never look at it. This is false economy—they save a few hours and blow their whole personality. Dictated sentences tend to be pompous, sloppy and redundant. Executives who are so busy that they can't avoid dictating should at least find time to edit what they have dictated, crossing words out and putting words in, making sure that what they finally write is a true reflection of who they are, especially if it's a document that will go to customers who will judge their personality and their company on the basis of their style.

WRITING IS NOT A CONTEST.

Every writer is starting from a different point and is bound for a different destination. Yet many writers are paralyzed by the thought that they are competing with everybody else who is trying to write and presumably doing it better. This can often happen in a writing class. Inexperienced students are chilled to find themselves in the same class with students whose byline has appeared in the college newspaper. But writing for the college paper is no great credential; I've often found that the hares who write for the paper are overtaken by the tortoises who move studiously toward the goal of mastering the craft. The same fear hobbles freelance writers, who see the work of other writers appearing in magazines while their own keeps returning in the mail. Forget the competition and go at your own pace. Your only contest is with yourself.

THE SUBCONSCIOUS MIND.

Your subconscious mind does more writing than you think. Often you'll spend a whole day trying to fight your way out of some verbal thicket in which you seem to be tangled beyond salvation. Frequently a solution will occur to you the next morning when you plunge back in. While you slept, your writer's mind didn't. A writer is always working. Stay alert to the currents around you. Much of what you see and hear will come back, having percolated for days or months or even years through your subconscious mind, just when your conscious mind, laboring to write, needs it.

THE QUICKEST FIX.

Surprisingly often a difficult problem in a sentence can be solved by simply getting rid of it. Unfortunately, this solution is usually the last one that occurs to writers in a jam. First they will put the troublesome phrase through all kinds of exertions—moving it to some other part of the sentence, trying to rephrase it, adding new words to clarify the thought or to oil whatever is stuck. These efforts only make the situation worse, and the writer is left to conclude that there *is* no solution to the problem—not a comforting thought. When you find yourself at such an impasse, look at the troublesome element and ask, "Do I need it at all?" Probably you don't. It was trying to do an unnecessary job all along—that's why it was giving you so much grief. Remove it and watch the afflicted sentence spring to life and breathe normally. It's the quickest cure and very often the best.

PARAGRAPHS.

Keep your paragraphs short. Writing is visual—it catches the eye before it has a chance to catch the brain. Short paragraphs put air around what you write and make it look inviting, whereas a long chunk of type can discourage a reader from even starting to read.

Newspaper paragraphs should be only two or three sentences long; newspaper type is set in a narrow width, and the inches quickly add up. You may think such frequent paragraphing will damage the development of your point. Obviously *The New Yorker* is obsessed by this fear—a reader can go for miles without relief. Don't worry; the gains far outweigh the hazards.

But don't go berserk. A succession of tiny paragraphs is as annoying as a paragraph that's too long. I'm thinking of all those midget paragraphs—verbless wonders—written by modern journalists trying to make their articles quick 'n' easy. Actually they make the reader's job harder by chopping up a natural train of thought. Compare the following two arrangements of the same article—how they look at a glance and how they read:

The No. 2 lawyer at the White House left work early on Tuesday, drove to an isolated park overlooking the Potomac River and took his life.

A revolver in his hand, slumped against a Civil War–era cannon, he left behind no note, no explanation.

Only friends, family and colleagues in stunned sorrow.

And a life story that until Tuesday had read like any man's fantasy.

The No. 2 lawyer at the White House left work early on Tuesday, drove to an isolated park overlooking the Potomac River and took his life. A revolver in his hand, slumped against a Civil War–era cannon, he left behind no note, no explanation—only friends, family and colleagues in stunned sorrow. He also left behind a life story that until Tuesday had read like any man's fantasy.

The Associated Press version *(left)*, with its breezy paragraphing and verbless third and fourth sentences, is disruptive and condescending. "Yoo-hoo! Look how simple I'm making this for you!" the reporter is calling to us. My version *(right)* gives the reporter the dignity of writing good English and building three sentences into a logical unit.

Paragraphing is a subtle but important element in writing nonfiction articles and books, a road map constantly telling your reader how you have organized your ideas. Study good nonfiction writers to see how they do it. You'll find that almost all of them think in paragraph units, not in sentence units. Each paragraph has its own integrity of content and structure.

SEXISM.

One of the most vexing new questions for writers is what to do about sexist language, especially the "he-she" pronoun. The feminist movement helpfully revealed how much sexism lurks in our language, not only in the offensive "he" but in the hundreds of words that carry an invidious meaning or some overtone of judgment. They are words that patronize ("gal"), or that imply second-class status ("poetess"), or a second-class role ("house-wife"), or a certain kind of empty-headedness ("the girls"), or that demean the ability of a woman to do a certain kind of job ("lady lawyer"), or that are deliberately prurient ("divorcée," "coed," "blonde") and are seldom applied to men. Men get mugged; a woman who gets mugged is a shapely stewardess or a pert brunette.

More damaging—and more subtle—are all the usages that treat women as possessions of the family male, not as people with their own identity who played an equal part in the family saga: "Early settlers pushed west with their wives and children." Turn those settlers into pioneer families, or pioneer couples who went west with their sons and daughters, or men and women who settled the West. Today there are very few roles that aren't open to both sexes. Don't use constructions that suggest that only men can be settlers or farmers or cops or firefighters.

A thornier problem is raised by the feminists' annoyance with words that contain "man," such as "chairman" and "spokesman." Their point is that women can chair a committee as well as a man and are equally good at spoking. Hence the flurry of new words like "chairperson" and "spokeswoman." Those makeshift words from the 1960s raised our consciousness about sex discrimination, both in words and in attitudes. But in the end they are makeshift words, sometimes hurting the cause more than helping it. One solution is to find another term: "chair" for "chairman," "company representative" for "spokesman." You can also convert the noun into a verb: "Speaking for the company, Ms. Jones said . . ." Where a certain occupation has both a masculine and a feminine form, look for a generic substitute. Actors and actresses can become performers.

This still leaves the bothersome pronoun. "He" and "him" and "his" are words that rankle. "Every employee should decide what he thinks is best for him and his dependents." What are we to do about these countless sentences? One solution is to turn them into the plural: "All employees should decide what they think is best for them and their dependents." But this is good only in small doses. A style that converts every "he" into a "they" will quickly turn to mush.

Another common solution is to use "or": "Every employee should decide what he or she thinks is best for him or her." But again, it should be used sparingly. Often a writer will find several situations in an article where he or she can use "he or she," or "him or her," if it seems natural. By "natural" I mean that the writer is serving notice that he (or she) has the problem in mind and is trying his (or her) best within reasonable limits. But let's face it: the English language is stuck with the generic masculine ("Man shall not live by bread alone"). To turn every "he" into a "he or she," and every "his" into a "his or her," would clog the language.

In early editions of *On Writing Well* I used "he" and "him" to refer to "the reader," "the writer," "the critic," "the humorist," etc. I felt that the book would be harder to read if I used "he or she" with every such mention. (I reject "he/she" altogether; the slant has no place in good English.) Over the years, however, many women wrote to nudge me about this. They said that as writers and readers themselves they resent always having to visualize a man doing the writing and reading, and they're right; I stand nudged. Most of the nudgers urged me to adopt the plural: to use "readers" and "writers," followed thereafter by "they." I don't like plurals; they weaken writing because they are less specific than the singular, less easy to visualize. I'd like every writer to visualize *one* reader struggling to read what he or she has written. Nevertheless I found three or four hundred places where I could eliminate "he," "him," "his," "himself" or "man," mainly by switching to the plural, with no harm done; the sky didn't fall in. Where the male pronoun remains in this edition I felt it was the only solution that wasn't cumbersome.

The best solutions simply eliminate "he" and its connotations of male ownership by using other pronouns or by altering some other component of the sentence. "We" is a handy replacement for "he." "Our" and "the" can often replace "his." (A) "First *he* notices what's happening to *his* kids and he blames it on *his* neighborhood." (B) "First *we* notice what's happening to *our* kids and we blame it on *the* neighborhood." General nouns can replace specific nouns. (A) "Doctors often neglect their wives and children." (B) "Doctors often neglect their families." Countless sins can be erased by such small changes.

One other pronoun that helped me in my repairs was "you." Instead of talking about what "the writer" does and the trouble *he* gets into, I found more places where I could address the writer directly ("You'll often find. . . "). It doesn't work for every kind of writing, but it's a godsend to anyone writing an instructional book or a self-help book. The voice of a Dr. Spock talking to the mother of a child with a fever, or the voice of a Julia Child talking to the cook stalled in mid-recipe, is one of the most reassuring sounds a reader can hear. Always look for ways to make yourself available to the people you're trying to reach.

REWRITING.

Rewriting is the essence of writing well: it's where the game is won or lost. That idea is hard to accept. We all have an emotional equity in our first draft; we can't believe that it wasn't born perfect. But the odds are close to 100 percent that it wasn't. Most writers don't initially say what they want to say, or say it as well as they could. The newly hatched sentence almost always has something wrong with it. It's not clear. It's not logical. It's verbose. It's klunky. It's pretentious. It's boring. It's full of clutter. It's full of clichés. It lacks rhythm. It can be read in sev-

eral different ways. It doesn't lead out of the previous sentence.
It doesn't. . . . The point is that clear writing is the result of a lot
of tinkering.

Many people assume that professional writers don't need to
rewrite; the words just fall into place. On the contrary, careful
writers can't stop fiddling. I've never thought of rewriting as an
unfair burden; I'm grateful for every chance to keep improving
my work. Writing is like a good watch—it should run smoothly
and have no extra parts. Students, I realize, don't share my love
of rewriting. They think of it as punishment: extra homework or
extra infield practice. Please—if you're such a student—think of
it as a gift. You won't write well until you understand that writing is an evolving *process*, not a *product*. Nobody expects you to
get it right the first time, or even the second time.

What do I mean by "rewriting"? I don't mean writing one
draft and then writing a different second version, and then a
third. Most rewriting consists of reshaping and tightening and
refining the raw material you wrote on your first try. Much of it
consists of making sure you've given the reader a narrative flow
he can follow with no trouble from beginning to end. Keep
putting yourself in the reader's place. Is there something he
should have been told early in the sentence that you put near
the end? Does he know when he starts sentence B that you've
made a shift—of subject, tense, tone, emphasis—from sentence A?

Let's look at a typical paragraph and imagine that it's the
writer's first draft. There's nothing really wrong with it; it's clear
and it's grammatical. But it's full of ragged edges: failures of the
writer to keep the reader notified of changes in time, place and
mood, or to vary and animate the style. What I've done is to add,
in bracketed italics after each sentence, some of the thoughts
that might occur to an editor taking a first look at this draft.
After that you'll find my revised paragraph, which incorporates
those corrective thoughts.

There used to be a time when neighbors took care of one another, he remembered. [*Put "he remembered" first to establish reflective tone.*] It no longer seemed to happen that way, however. [*The contrast supplied by "however" must come first. Start with "But." Also establish America locale.*] He wondered if it was because everyone in the modern world was so busy. [*All these sentences are the same length and have the same soporific rhythm; turn this one into a question?*] It occurred to him that people today have so many things to do that they don't have time for old-fashioned friendship. [*Sentence essentially repeats previous sentence; kill it or warm it up with specific detail.*] Things didn't work that way in America in previous eras. [*Reader is still in the present; reverse the sentence to tell him he's now in the past. "America" no longer needed if inserted earlier.*] And he knew that the situation was very different in other countries, as he recalled from the years when he lived in villages in Spain and Italy. [*Reader is still in America. Use a negative transition word to get him to Europe. Sentence is also too flabby. Break it into two sentences?*] It almost seemed to him that as people got richer and built their houses farther apart they isolated themselves from the essentials of life. [*Irony deferred too long. Plant irony early. Sharpen the paradox about richness.*] And there was another thought that troubled him. [*This is the real point of the paragraph; signal the reader that it's important. Avoid weak "there was" construction.*] His friends had deserted him when he needed them most during his recent illness. [*Reshape to end with "most"; the last word is the one that stays in the reader's ear and gives the sentence its punch. Hold sickness for next sentence; it's a separate thought.*] It was almost as if they found him guilty of doing something shameful. [*Introduce sickness here as the reason for the shame. Omit "guilty"; it's implicit.*] He recalled reading somewhere about societies in primitive parts of the world in which sick people were shunned, though he had never heard of any such ritual in America. [*Sentence starts slowly and stays sluggish and dull. Break it into shorter units. Snap off the ironic point.*]

He remembered that neighbors used to take care of one another. But that no longer seemed to happen in America. Was it because everyone was so busy? Were people really so preoccupied with their television sets and their cars and their fitness programs that they had no time for friendship? In previous eras that was never true. Nor was it how families lived in other parts of the world. Even in the poorest villages of Spain and Italy, he recalled, people would drop in with a loaf of bread. An ironic idea struck him: as people got richer they cut themselves off from the richness of life. But what really troubled him was an even more shocking fact. The time when his friends deserted him was the time when he needed them most. By getting sick he almost seemed to have done something shameful. He knew that other societies had a custom of "shunning" people who were very ill. But that ritual only existed in primitive cultures. Or did it?

My revisions aren't the best ones that could be made, or the only ones. They're mainly matters of carpentry: altering the sequence, tightening the flow, sharpening the point. Much could still be done in such areas as cadence, detail and freshness of language. Beyond these repairs, which only apply to individual sentences; the total construction is equally important. Read your article aloud from beginning to end, always remembering where you left the reader in the previous sentence. You might find you had written two sentences like this:

The tragic hero of the play is Othello. Small and malevolent, Iago feeds his jealous suspicions.

In itself there's nothing wrong with the Iago sentence. But as a sequel to the previous sentence it's very wrong. The name lingering in the reader's ear is Othello; the reader naturally assumes that Othello is small and malevolent.

When you read your writing aloud with these connecting links in mind you'll hear a dismaying number of places where you lost the reader, or confused the reader, or failed to tell him the one fact he needed to know, or told him the same thing twice: the inevitable loose ends of every early draft. What you must do is make an arrangement—one that holds together from start to finish and that moves with economy and warmth.

Learn to enjoy this tidying process. I don't like to write (I like to have written). But I love to rewrite. I especially like to cut: to press the DELETE key and see an unnecessary word or phrase or sentence vanish into the electricity. I like to replace a humdrum word with one that has more precision or color. I like to strengthen the transition between one sentence and another. I like to rephrase a drab sentence to give it a more pleasing rhythm or a more graceful musical line. With every small refinement I feel that I'm coming nearer to where I would like to arrive, and when I finally get there I know it was the rewriting, not the writing, that won the game.

WORD PROCESSING.

The word processor is God's gift, or technology's gift, to rewriting and reorganizing. It puts your words right in front of your eyes for your instant consideration—and reconsideration; you can play with your sentences until you get them right. The paragraphs and pages will keep rearranging themselves, no matter how much you cut and change, and then your printer will type everything neatly while you go and have a beer. Sweeter music could hardly be sung to writers than the sound of their article being retyped with all its improvements—but not by them.

It's no longer necessary for this book to explain, as earlier editions did, how to operate the wonderful new machine that had come into our lives and how to put its wonders to use in writing, rewriting, and organizing. That's now common knowledge. I'll just remind you (if you're still not a believer) that the savings in time and drudgery are enormous. With a word processor I sit down to write more willingly than I did when I used a typewriter, especially if I'm facing a complex task of organization, and I finish the task sooner and with far less fatigue. These are crucial gains for a writer: time, output, energy, enjoyment and control.

TRUST YOUR MATERIAL.

The longer I work at the craft of writing, the more I realize that there's nothing more interesting than the truth. What people do—and what people say—continues to take me by surprise with its wonderfulness, or its quirkiness, or its drama, or its humor, or its pain. Who could invent all the astonishing things that really happen? I increasingly find myself saying to writers and students, "Trust your material." It's hard advice to follow.

Recently I spent some time as a writing coach at a newspaper in a small American city. I noticed that many reporters had fallen into the habit of trying to make the news more palatable by writing in a feature style. Their leads consisted of a series of snippets that went something like this:

> Whoosh!
> It was incredible.
> Ed Barnes wondered if he was seeing things.
> Or maybe it was just spring fever. Funny how April can do that to a guy.
> It wasn't as if he hadn't checked his car before leaving the house.
> But then again, he didn't remember to tell Linda.

Which was odd, because he always remembered to tell Linda. Ever since they started going together back in junior high.

Was that really 20 years ago?

And now there was also little Scooter to worry about.

Come to think of it, the dog was acting kind of suspicious.

The articles often began on page 1, and I would read as far as "Continued on page 9" and still have no idea of what they were about. Then I would dutifully turn to page 9 and find myself in an interesting story, full of specific details. I'd say to the reporter, "That was a good story when I finally got over here to page 9. Why didn't you put that stuff in the lead?" The reporter would say, "Well, in the lead I was writing color." The assumption is that fact and color are two separate ingredients. They're not; color is organic to the fact. Your job is to present the colorful fact.

In 1988 I wrote a baseball book called *Spring Training*. It combined my lifelong vocation with my lifelong addiction—which is one of the best things that can happen to a writer. People of every age will write better and with more enjoyment if they write about what they care about. I chose spring training as my small corner of the large subject of baseball because it's a time of renewal, both for the players and for the fans. The game is given back to us in its original purity: it's played outside, in the sun, on grass, without organ music, by young men who are almost near enough to touch and whose salaries and grievances are mercifully put aside for six weeks. Above all, it's a time of teaching and learning. I chose the Pittsburgh Pirates as the team I would cover because they trained in an old-time ballpark in Bradenton, Florida, and were a young club just starting to rebuild, with a manager, Jim Leyland, who was committed to teaching.

I knew that I didn't want to romanticize the game. I don't like baseball movies that go into slow motion when the batter hits a home run, to notify me that it's a pregnant moment. I *know* that about home runs, especially if they're hit with two out in the bottom of the ninth to win the game. I resolved not to let my writing go into slow motion—not to nudge the reader with significance—or to claim baseball as a metaphor for life, death, middle age, lost youth or a more innocent America. My premise was that baseball is a job—honorable work—and I wanted to know how that job gets taught and learned.

So I went to Jim Leyland and his coaches and I said, "You're a teacher. I'm a teacher. Tell me: How do you teach hitting? How do you teach pitching? How do you teach fielding? How do you teach baserunning? How do you keep these young men *up* for such a brutally long schedule?" All of them responded generously and told me in detail how they do what they do. So did the players and all the other men and women who had information I wanted: umpires, scouts, ticket sellers, local boosters.

One day I climbed up into the stands behind home plate to look for a scout. Spring training is baseball's ultimate talent show, and the camps are infested with laconic men who have spent a lifetime appraising talent. I spotted an empty seat next to a weathered man in his sixties who was using a stopwatch and taking notes. When the inning was over I asked him what he was timing. He said he was Nick Kamzic, Northern Scouting Coordinator of the California Angels, and he was timing runners on the base paths. I asked him what kind of information he was looking for.

> "Well, it takes a right-handed batter 4.3 seconds to reach first base," he said, "and a left-handed batter 4.1 or 4.2 seconds. Naturally that varies a little—you've got to take the human element into consideration."
>
> "What do those numbers tell you?" I asked.
>
> "Well, of course the average double play takes 4.3 seconds," he said. He said it as if it was common knowledge. I had never given any thought to the elapsed time of a double play.

"So that means. . ."

"If you see a player who gets to first base in less than 4.3 seconds you're interested in him."

As a fact that's self-sufficient. There's no need to add a sentence pointing out that 4.3 seconds is remarkably little time to execute a play that involves one batted ball, two thrown balls and three infielders. Given 4.3 seconds, readers can do their own marveling. They will also enjoy being allowed to think for themselves. The reader plays a major role in the act of writing and must be given room to play it. Don't annoy your readers by over-explaining—by telling them something they already know or can surmise. Try not to use words like "surprisingly," "predictably" and "of course," which put a value on a fact before the reader encounters the fact. Trust your material.

GO WITH YOUR INTERESTS.

There's no subject you don't have permission to write about. Students often avoid subjects close to their heart—skateboarding, cheerleading, rock music, cars—because they assume that their teachers will regard those topics as "stupid." No area of life is stupid to someone who takes it seriously. If you follow your affections you will write well and will engage your readers.

I've read elegant books on fishing and poker, billiards and rodeos, mountain climbing and giant sea turtles and many other subjects I didn't think I was interested in. Write about your hobbies: cooking, gardening, photography, knitting, antiques, jogging, sailing, scuba diving, tropical birds, tropical fish. Write about your work: teaching, nursing, running a business, running a store. Write about a field you enjoyed in college and always meant to get back to: history, biography, art, archeology. No subject is too specialized or too quirky if you make an honest connection with it when you write about it.

PART III

———— ∞∞∞ ————

Forms

11

Nonfiction as Literature

One weekend a few years ago I went to Buffalo to talk at a writers' conference that had been organized by a group of women writers in that city. The women were serious about their craft, and the books and articles they had written were solid and useful. They asked me if I would take part in a radio talk show earlier in the week to publicize the conference—they would be with the host in the studio and I would be on a telephone hookup from my apartment in New York.

The appointed evening arrived, and my phone rang, and the host came on and greeted me with the strenuous joviality of his trade. He said he had three lovely ladies in the studio with him and he was eager to find out what we all thought of the present state of literature and what advice we had for all his listeners who were members of the literati and had literary ambitions themselves. This hearty introduction dropped like a stone in our midst, and none of the three lovely ladies said anything, which I thought was the proper response.

The silence lengthened, and finally I said, "I think we should banish all further mention of the words 'literature' and 'literary' and 'literati.'" I knew that the host had been briefed about what kind of writers we were and what we wanted to discuss. But he had no other frame of reference. "Tell me," he said, "what insights do you all have about the literary experience in America today?" Silence also greeted this question. Finally I said, "We're here to talk about the craft of writing."

He didn't know what to make of that, and he began to invoke the names of authors like Ernest Hemingway and Saul Bellow and William Styron, whom we surely regarded as literary giants. We said that those writers didn't happen to be our models, and we mentioned people like Lewis Thomas and Joan Didion and Gary Wills. He had never heard of them. One of the women mentioned Tom Wolfe's *The Right Stuff*, and he hadn't heard of that. We explained that these were writers we admired for their ability to harness the issues and concerns of the day.

"But don't you want to write anything literary?" our host said. The three women said they felt they were already doing satisfying work. That brought the program to another halt, and the host began to accept phone calls from his listeners, all of whom were interested in the craft of writing and wanted to know how we went about it. "And yet, in the stillness of the night," the host said to several callers, "don't you ever dream of writing the great American novel?" They didn't. They had no such dreams—in the stillness of the night or at any other time. It was one of the all-time lousy radio talk shows.

The story sums up a situation that any practitioner of nonfiction will recognize. Those of us who are trying to write well about the world we live in, or to teach students to write well about the world *they* live in, are caught in a time warp, where literature by definition still consists of forms that were certified as "literary" in the 19th century: novels and short stories and poems. But in fact the great preponderance of what writers now write and sell, what book and magazine publishers publish and what readers demand is nonfiction.

The shift can be documented by all kinds of examples. One is the history of the Book-of-the-Month Club. When the club was founded in 1926 by Harry Scherman, Americans had little access to good new literature and were mainly reading junk like *Ben-Hur.* Scherman's idea was that any town that had a post office had the equivalent of a bookstore, and he began sending the best new books to his newly recruited readers all over the country.

Much of what he sent was fiction. The list of main selections chosen by the club from 1926 through 1941 is heavily laced with novelists: Ellen Glasgow, Sinclair Lewis, Virginia Woolf, John Galsworthy, Elinor Wylie, Ignazio Silone, Rosamond Lehmann, Edith Wharton, Somerset Maugham, Willa Cather, Booth Tarkington, Isak Dinesen, James Gould Cozzens, Thornton Wilder, Sigrid Undset, Ernest Hemingway, William Saroyan, John P. Marquand, John Steinbeck and many others. That was the high tide of "literature" in America. Members of the Book-of-the-Month Club hardly heard the approach of World War II. Not until 1940 was it brought home to them in a book, *Mrs. Miniver,* a stiff-upper-lip novel about the early days of the Battle of Britain.

All of this changed with Pearl Harbor. World War II sent seven million Americans overseas and opened their eyes to reality: to new places and issues and events. After the war that trend was reinforced by the advent of television. People who saw reality every evening in their living room lost patience with the slower rhythms and glancing allusions of the novelist. Overnight, America became a fact-minded nation. Since 1946 the Book-of-the-Month Club's members have predominantly demanded—and therefore received—nonfiction.

Magazines were swept along on the same tide. The *Saturday Evening Post*, which had long spoon-fed its readers a heavy diet of short stories by writers who all seemed to have three names— Clarence Budington Kelland, Octavus Roy Cohen—reversed the ratio in the early 1960s. Ninety percent of the magazine was now allotted to nonfiction articles, with just one short story by a three-named author to keep the faithful from feeling abandoned. It was the beginning of a golden era of nonfiction, especially in *Life*, which ran finely crafted articles every week; in *The New Yorker*, which elevated the form by originating such landmarks of modern American writing as Rachel Carson's *Silent Spring* and Truman Capote's *In Cold Blood;* and in *Harper's*, which commissioned such remarkable pieces as Norman Mailer's *Armies of the Night*. Nonfiction became the new American literature.

Today there's no area of life—present or past—that isn't being made accessible to ordinary readers by men and women writing with high seriousness and grace. Add to this literature of fact all the disciplines that were once regarded as academic, like anthropology and economics and social history, that have become the domain of nonfiction writers and of broadly curious readers. Add all the books combining history and biography that have distinguished American letters in recent years: David McCullough's *Truman* and *The Path Between the Seas*, Robert A. Caro's *The Power Broker* and *The Years of Lyndon Johnson*, Taylor Branch's *Parting the Waters: America in the King Years, 1954–63*, Richard Rhodes's *The Making of the Atomic Bomb*, Thomas L. Friedman's *From Beirut to Jerusalem*, J. Anthony Lukas's *Common Ground*, Ronald Steel's *Walter Lippmann and the American Century*, David Remnick's *Lenin's Tomb.* My roster of the new literature of nonfiction, in short, would include all the writers who come bearing information and who present it with vigor, clarity and humanity.

I'm not saying that fiction is dead. Obviously the novelist can take us into hidden places where no other writer can go: into the deep emotions and the interior life. What I'm saying is that I have no patience with the snobbery that says nonfiction is only journalism by another name and that journalism by any name is a dirty word. While we're redefining literature, let's also redefine journalism. Journalism is writing that first appears in any periodic journal, whatever its constituency: *American Heritage, Natural History, The New York Review of Books, Scientific American, Granta, Harvard Magazine, Audubon, Lingua Franca.* Lewis Thomas's first two books, *Lives of a Cell* and *The Medusa and the Snail,* were first written as essays for the *New England Journal of Medicine.* Historically, in America, good journalism becomes good literature. H. L. Mencken, Ring Lardner, Joseph Mitchell, Edmund Wilson and dozens of other major American writers were working journalists before they were canonized in the church of literature. They just did what they did best and never worried about how it was defined.

Ultimately every writer must follow the path that feels most comfortable. For most people learning to write, that path is nonfiction. It enables them to write about what they know or can observe or can find out. This is especially true of young people and students. They will write far more willingly about subjects that touch their own lives or that they have an aptitude for. Motivation is at the heart of writing. If nonfiction is where you do your best writing, or your best teaching of writing, don't be buffaloed into the idea that it's an inferior species. The only important distinction is between good writing and bad writing. Good writing is good writing, whatever form it takes and whatever we call it.

12

Writing About People

The Interview

Get people talking. Learn to ask questions that will elicit answers about what is most interesting or vivid in their lives. Nothing so animates writing as someone telling what he thinks or what he does—in his own words.

His own words will always be better than your words, even if you are the most elegant stylist in the land. They carry the inflection of his speaking voice and the idiosyncrasies of how he puts a sentence together. They contain the regionalisms of his conversation and the lingo of his trade. They convey his enthusiasms. This is a person talking to the reader directly, not through the filter of a writer. As soon as a writer steps in, everyone else's experience becomes secondhand.

Therefore learn how to conduct an interview. Whatever form of nonfiction you write, it will come alive in proportion to the number of "quotes" you can weave into it as you go along. Often you'll find yourself embarking on an article so apparently lifeless—the history of an institution, or some local issue such as storm sewers—that you will quail at the prospect of keeping your readers, or even yourself, awake.

Take heart. You'll find the solution if you look for the human element. Somewhere in every drab institution are men and women who have a fierce attachment to what they are doing and are rich repositories of lore. Somewhere behind every storm sewer is a politician whose future hangs on getting it installed and a widow who has always lived on the block and is outraged that some damn-fool legislator thinks it will wash away. Find these people to tell your story and it won't be drab.

I've proved this to myself often. Many years ago I was invited to write a small book for the New York Public Library to celebrate the 50th anniversary of its main building on Fifth Avenue. On the surface it seemed to be just the story of a marble building and millions of musty volumes. But behind the facade I found that the library had 19 research divisions, each with a curator supervising a hoard of treasures and oddities, from Washington's handwritten Farewell Address to 750,000 movie stills. I decided to interview all those curators to learn what was in their collections, what they were adding to keep up with new areas of knowledge, and how their rooms were being used.

I found that the Science & Technology division had a collection of patents second only to that of the United States Patent Office and was therefore almost a second home to the city's patent lawyers. But it also had a daily stream of men and women who thought they were on the verge of discovering perpetual motion. "Everybody's got something to invent," the curator explained, "but they won't tell us what they're looking for—maybe because they think we'll patent it ourselves." The whole building turned out to be just such a mixture of scholars and searchers and crackpots, and my story, though ostensibly the chronicle of an institution, was really a story about people.

I used the same approach in a long article about Sotheby's, the London auction firm. Sotheby's was also divided into various domains, such as silver and porcelain and art, each with an expert in charge, and, like the Library, it subsisted on the whims of a capricious public. The experts were like department heads in a small college, and all of them had anecdotes that were unique both in substance and in the manner of telling:

> "We just sit here like Micawber waiting for things to come in," said R. S. Timewell, head of the furniture department. "Recently an old lady near Cambridge wrote that she wanted to raise two thousand pounds and asked if I would go through her house and see if her furniture would fetch that much. I did, and there was absolutely nothing of value. As I was about to leave I said, 'Have I seen *every*thing?' She said I had, except for a maid's room that she hadn't bothered to show me. The room had a very fine 18th-century chest that the old lady was using to store blankets in. 'Your worries are over,' I told her, 'if you sell that chest.' She said, 'But that's quite impossible—where will I store my blankets?'"

My worries were over, too. By listening to the quizzical scholars who ran the business and to the men and women who flocked there every morning bearing unloved objects found in British attics ("I'm afraid it *isn't* Queen Anne, madam—much nearer Queen Victoria, unfortunately"), I got as much human detail as a writer could want.

Again, when I was asked in 1966 to write a history of the Book-of-the-Month Club to mark its 40th birthday, I thought I might encounter nothing but inert matter. But I found a peppery human element on both sides of the fence, for the books had always been selected by a panel of strong-minded judges and sent to equally stubborn subscribers, who never hesitated to wrap up a book they didn't like and send it right back. I was given more than a thousand pages of transcribed interviews with the five original judges (Heywood Broun, Henry Seidel Canby, Dorothy Canfield, Christopher Morley and William Allen White), to which I added my own interviews with the club's founder, Harry Scherman, and with the judges who were then active. The result was four decades' worth of personal memories on how America's reading tastes had changed, and even the books took on a life of their own and became characters in my story:

> "Probably it's difficult for anyone who remembers the prodigious success of *Gone With the Wind*," Dorothy Can-field said, "to think how it would have seemed to people who encountered it simply as a very, very long and detailed book about the Civil War and its aftermath. We had never heard of the author and didn't have anybody else's opinion on it. It was chosen with a little difficulty, because some of the characteri-zation was not very authentic or convincing. But as a narrative it had the quality which the French call *attention:* it made you want to turn over the page to see what happens next. I remember that someone commented, 'Well, people may not like it very much, but nobody can deny that it gives a lot of reading for your money.' Its tremendous success was, I must say, about as surprising to us as to anybody else."

Those three examples are typical of the kind of information that is locked inside people's heads, which a good nonfiction writer must unlock. The best way to practice is to go out and interview people. The interview itself is one of the most popular nonfiction forms, so you should master it early.

How should you start? First, decide what person you want to interview. If you are a college student, don't interview your roommate. With all due respect for what terrific roommates you've got, they probably don't have much to say that the rest of us want to hear. To learn the craft of nonfiction you must push yourself out into the real world—your town or your city or your county—and pretend that you're writing for a real publication. If it helps, decide which publication you are hypothetically writing for. Choose as your subject someone whose job is so important, or so interesting, or so unusual that the average reader would want to read about that person.

That doesn't mean he or she has to be president of the bank. It can be the owner of the local pizza parlor or supermarket or hairdressing academy. It can be the fisherman who puts out to sea every morning, or the Little League manager, or the nurse. It can be the butcher, the baker or—better yet, if you can find him—the candlestick maker. Look for the women in your community who are unraveling the old myths about what the two sexes were foreordained to do. Choose, in short, someone who touches some corner of the reader's life.

Interviewing is one of those skills you can only get better at. You will never again feel so ill at ease as when you try it for the first time, and probably you'll never feel entirely comfortable prodding another person for answers he or she may be too shy or too inarticulate to reveal. But much of the skill is mechanical. The rest is instinct—knowing how to make the other person relax, when to push, when to listen, when to stop. This can all be learned with experience.

The basic tools for an interview are paper and some well-sharpened pencils. Is that insultingly obvious advice? You'd be surprised how many writers venture forth to stalk their quarry with no pencil, or with one that breaks, or with a pen that doesn't work, and with nothing to write on. "Be prepared" is as apt a motto for the nonfiction writer on his rounds as it is for the Boy Scout.

But keep your notebook out of sight until you need it.

There's nothing less likely to relax a person than the arrival of a stranger with a stenographer's pad. Both of you need time to get to know each other. Take a while just to chat, gauging what sort of person you're dealing with, getting him or her to trust you.

Never go into an interview without doing whatever homework you can. If you are interviewing a town official, know his or her voting record. If it's an actress, know what plays or movies she has been in. You will be resented if you inquire about facts you could have learned in advance.

Make a list of likely questions—it will save you the vast embarrassment of going dry in mid-interview. Perhaps you won't need the list; better questions will occur to you, or the people being interviewed will veer off at an angle you couldn't have foreseen. Here you can only go by intuition. If they stray hopelessly off the subject, drag them back. If you like the new direction, follow along and forget the questions you intended to ask.

Many beginning interviewers are inhibited by the fear that they are imposing on other people and have no right to invade their privacy. This fear is almost wholly unfounded. The so-called man in the street is delighted that somebody wants to interview him. Most men and women lead lives, if not of quiet desperation, at least of desperate quietness, and they jump at a chance to talk about their work to an outsider who seems eager to listen.

This doesn't necessarily mean it will go well. Often you will be talking to people who have never been interviewed before, and they will warm to the process awkwardly, self-consciously, perhaps not giving you anything you can use. Come back another day; it will go better. You will both even begin to enjoy it—proof that you aren't forcing your victims to do something they really don't want to do.

Speaking of tools, is it all right (you ask) to use a tape recorder? Why not just take one along, start it going, and forget all that business of pencil and paper?

Obviously the tape recorder is a superb machine for capturing what people have to say—especially people who, for reasons of their culture or temperament, would never get around to writing it down. In such areas as social history and anthropology it's invaluable. I admire the books of Studs Terkel, such as *Hard Times: An Oral History of the Great Depression,* which he "wrote" by recording interviews with ordinary people and patching the results into coherent shape. I also like the question-and-answer interviews, obtained by tape recorder, that are published in certain magazines. They have the sound of spontaneity, the refreshing absence of a writer hovering over the product and burnishing it to a high gloss.

Strictly, however, this isn't writing. It's a process of asking questions and then pruning and splicing and editing the transcribed answers, and it takes a tremendous amount of time and labor. Educated people who you think have been talking into your tape recorder with linear precision turn out to have been stumbling so aimlessly over the sands of language that they haven't completed a single decent sentence. The ear makes repeated allowances for missing grammar, syntax and transitions that the eye wouldn't tolerate in print. The seemingly simple use of a tape recorder isn't simple; infinite stitchery is required.

But my main reasons for warning you off it are practical. One hazard is that you don't usually have a tape recorder with you; you are more likely to have a pencil. Another is that tape recorders malfunction. Few moments in journalism are as glum as the return of a reporter with "a really great story," followed by his pushing of the PLAY button and silence. But above all, a writer should be able to see his materials. If your interview is on tape you become a listener, forever fussing with the machine, running it backward to find the brilliant remark you can never quite find, running it forward, stopping, starting, driving yourself crazy. Be a writer. Write things down.

I do my interviewing by hand, with a sharp No. 1 pencil. I

like the transaction with another person. I like the fact that that person can see me *working*—doing a job, not just sitting there letting a machine do it for me. Only once did I use a tape recorder extensively: for my book, *Willie and Dwike,* about the jazz musicians Willie Ruff and Dwike Mitchell. Although I knew both men well, I felt that a white writer who presumes to write about the black experience has an obligation to get the tonalities right. It's not that Ruff and Mitchell speak a different kind of English; they speak good and often eloquent English. But as Southern blacks they use certain words and idioms that are distinctive to their heritage, adding richness and humor to what they say. I didn't want to miss any of those usages. My tape recorder caught them all, and readers of the book can hear that I got the two men right. Consider using a tape recorder in situations where you might violate the cultural integrity of the people you're interviewing.

Taking notes, however, has one big problem: the person you're interviewing often starts talking faster than you can write. You are still scribbling Sentence A when he zooms into Sentence B. You drop Sentence A and pursue him into Sentence B, meanwhile trying to hold the rest of Sentence A in your inner ear and hoping Sentence C will be a dud that you can skip altogether, using the time to catch up. Unfortunately, you now have your subject going at high speed. He is finally saying all the things you have been trying to cajole out of him for an hour, and saying them with what seems to be Churchillian eloquence. Your inner ear is clogging up with sentences you want to grab before they slip away.

Tell him to stop. Just say, "Hold it a minute, please," and write until you catch up. What you are trying to do with your feverish scribbling is to quote him correctly, and nobody wants to be misquoted.

With practice you will write faster and develop some form of shorthand. You'll find yourself devising abbreviations for often-

extent that you get the main points made without waste. Therefore if you find on page 5 of your notes a comment that perfectly amplifies a point on page 2—a point made earlier in the
interview—you will do everyone a favor if you link the two
thoughts, letting the second sentence follow and illustrate the
first. This may violate the truth of how the interview actually
progressed, but you will be true to the intent of what was said.
Play with the quotes by all means—selecting, rejecting, thin-
ning, transposing their order, saving a good one for the end. Just
make sure the play is fair. Don't change any words or let the cutting of a sentence distort the proper context of what remains.

Do I literally mean "don't change any words"? Yes and no. If
a speaker chooses his words carefully you should make it a point
of professional pride to quote him verbatim. Most interviewers
are sloppy about this; they think that if they achieve a rough
approximation it's good enough. It's not good enough: nobody
wants to see himself in print using words or phrases he would
never use. But if the speaker's conversation is ragged—if his
sentences trail off, if his thoughts are disorderly, if his language
is so tangled that it would embarrass him—the writer has no
choice but to clean up the English and provide the missing
links.

Sometimes you can fall into a trap by trying to be too true to
the speaker. As you write your article, you type his words exactly
as you took them down. You even allow yourself a moment of
satisfaction at being such a faithful scribe. Later, editing what
you've written, you realize that several of the quotes don't quite
make sense. When you first heard them they sounded so felici-
tous that you didn't give them a second thought. Now, on second thought, there's a hole in the language or the logic. To leave
the hole is no favor to the reader or the speaker—and no credit
to the writer. Often you only need to add one or two clarifying
words. Or you might find another quote in your notes that
makes the same point clearly. But also remember that you can

call the person you interviewed. Tell him you want to check a few of the things he said. Get him to rephrase his points until you understand them. Don't become the prisoner of your quotes—so lulled by how wonderful they sound that you don't stop to analyze them. Never let anything go out into the world that *you* don't understand.

As for how to organize the interview, the lead should obviously tell the reader why the person is worth reading about. What is his claim to our time and attention? Thereafter, try to achieve a balance between what the subject is saying in *his* words and what you are writing in *your* words. If you quote a person for three or four consecutive paragraphs it becomes monotonous. Quotes are livelier when you break them up, making periodic appearances in your role as guide. You are still the writer—don't relinquish control. But make your appearances useful; don't just insert one of those dreary sentences that shout to the reader that your sole purpose is to break up a string of quotations ("He tapped his pipe on a nearby ashtray and I noticed that his fingers were quite long." "She toyed idly with her arugula salad").

When you use a quotation, start the sentence with it. Don't lead up to it with a vapid phrase saying what the man said.

> BAD: Mr. Smith said that he liked to "go downtown once a
>   week and have lunch with some of my old friends."
> GOOD: "I usually like to go downtown once a week," Mr.
>   Smith said, "and have lunch with some of my old friends."

The second sentence has vitality, the first one is dead. Nothing is deader than to start a sentence with a "Mr. Smith said" construction—it's where many readers stop reading. If the man said it, let him say it and get the sentence off to a warm, human start.

But be careful where you break the quotation. Do it as soon as you naturally can, so that the reader knows who is talking, but not where the break will destroy the rhythm or the meaning. Notice how the following three variants all inflict some kind of damage:

> "I usually like," Mr. Smith said, "to go downtown once a week and have lunch with some of my old friends."
> "I usually like to go downtown," Mr. Smith said, "once a week and have lunch with some of my old friends."
> "I usually like to go downtown once a week and have lunch," Mr. Smith said, "with some of my old friends."

Finally, don't strain to find synonyms for "he said." Don't make your man assert, aver and expostulate just to avoid repeating "he said," and please—please!—don't write "he smiled" or "he grinned." I've never heard anybody smile. The reader's eye skips over "he said" anyway, so it's not worth a lot of fuss. If you crave variety, choose synonyms that catch the shifting nature of the conversation. "He pointed out," "he explained," "he replied," "he added"—these all carry a particular meaning. But don't use "he added" if the man is merely averring and not putting a postscript on what he just said.

All these technical skills, however, can take you just so far. Conducting a good interview is finally related to the character and personality of the writer, because the person you're interviewing will always know more about the subject than you do. Some ideas on how to overcome your anxiety in this uneven situation, learning to trust your general intelligence, are offered in Chapter 21, "Enjoyment, Fear and Confidence."

The proper and improper use of quotations has been much in the news, dragged there by two highly visible events. One was the libel and defamation trial of Janet Malcolm, whom a jury found guilty of "fabricating" certain quotes in her *New Yorker* profile of the psychiatrist Jeffrey M. Masson. The other was the revelation by Joe McGinniss that in his biography of Senator Edward M. Kennedy, *The Last Brother*, he had "written certain scenes and described certain events from what I have inferred to be his point of view," though he never interviewed Kennedy himself. Such blurring of fact and fiction is a trend that bothers careful writers of nonfiction—an assault on the craft. Yet even for a conscientious reporter this is uncertain terrain. Let me invoke the work of Joseph Mitchell to suggest some guidelines. The seamless weaving of quotes through his prose was a hallmark of Mitchell's achievement in the brilliant articles he wrote for *The New Yorker* from 1938 to 1965, many of them dealing with people who worked around the New York waterfront. Those articles were hugely influential on nonfiction writers of my generation—a primary textbook.

The six Mitchell pieces that would eventually constitute his book, *The Bottom of the Harbor*, a classic of American nonfiction, ran with maddening infrequency in *The New Yorker* during the late 1940s and early '50s, often several years apart. Sometimes I would ask friends who worked at the magazine when I might expect a new one, but they never knew or even presumed to guess. This was mosaic work, they reminded me, and the mosaicist was finicky about fitting the pieces together until he got them right. When at last a new article did appear I saw why it had taken so long; it *was* exactly right. I still remember the excitement of reading "Mr. Hunter's Grave," my favorite Mitchell piece. It's about an 87-year-old elder of the African Methodist Church, who was one of the last survivors of a 19th-century village of Negro oystermen on Staten Island called Sandy Ground. With *The Bottom of the Harbor* the past became a major character in Mitchell's work, giving it a tone both elegiac and historical. The old men who were his main subject were custodians of memory, a living link with an earlier New York.

The following paragraph, quoting George H. Hunter on the

subject of pokeweed, is typical of many very long quotes in "Mr.
Hunter's Grave" in its leisurely accretion of enjoyable detail:

"In the spring, when it first comes up, the young shoots
above the root are good to eat. They taste like asparagus. The
old women in Sandy Ground used to believe in eating pokeweed shoots, the old Southern women. They said it renewed
your blood. My mother believed it. Every spring she used to
send me out in the woods to pick pokeweed shoots. And I
believe it. So every spring, if I think about it, I go pick some and
cook them. It's not that I like them so much—in fact, they give
me gas—but they remind me of the days gone by, they remind
me of my mother. Now, away down here in the woods in this
part of Staten Island, you might think you were fifteen miles on
the other side of nowhere, but just a little ways up Arthur Kill
Road, up near Arden Avenue, there's a bend in the road where
you can sometimes see the tops of the skyscrapers in New York.
Just the tallest skyscrapers, and just the tops of them. It has to
be an extremely clear day. Even then, you might be able to see
them one moment and the next moment they're gone. Right
beside this bend in the road there's a little swamp, and the edge
of this swamp is the best place I know to pick pokeweed. I went
up there one morning this spring to pick some, but we had a
late spring, if you remember, and the pokeweed hadn't come
up. The fiddleheads were up, and golden club, and spring
beauty, and skunk cabbage, and bluets, but no pokeweed. So I
was looking here and looking there, and not noticing where I
was stepping, and I made a misstep, and the next thing I knew
I was up to my knees in mud. I floundered around in the mud
a minute, getting my bearings, and then I happened to raise my
head and look up, and suddenly I saw, away off in the distance,
miles and miles away, the tops of the skyscrapers in New York
shining in the morning sun. I wasn't expecting it, and it was
amazing. It was like a vision in the Bible."

Now, nobody thinks Mr. Hunter really said all that in one spurt; Mitchell did a heap of splicing. Yet I have no doubt that Mr. Hunter did say it at one moment or another—that all the words and turns of phrase are his. It sounds like him; Mitchell didn't write the scene from what he "inferred" to be his subject's point of view. He made a literary arrangement, pretending to have spent one afternoon being shown around the cemetery, whereas I would guess, knowing his famously patient and courteous manner and his lapidary methods, that the article took at least a year of strolling, chatting, writing and rewriting. I've seldom read a piece so rich in texture; Mitchell's "afternoon" has the unhurried quality of an actual afternoon. By the time it's over, Mr. Hunter, reflecting on the history of oyster fishing in New York harbor, on the passing of generations in Sandy Ground, on families and family names, planting and cooking, wildflowers and fruit, birds and trees, churches and funerals, change and decay, has touched on much of what living is all about.

I have no problem calling "Mr. Hunter's Grave" nonfiction. Although Mitchell altered the truth about elapsed time, he used a dramatist's prerogative to compress and focus his story, thereby giving the reader a manageable framework. If he had told the story in real time, strung across all the days and months he did spend on Staten Island, he would have achieved the numbing truth of Andy Warhol's eight-hour film of a man having an eight-hour sleep. By careful manipulation he raised the craft of nonfiction to art. But he never manipulated Mr. Hunter's truth; there has been no "inferring," no "fabricating." He has played fair.

That, finally, is my standard. I know that it's just not possible to write a competent interview without some juggling and eliding of quotes; don't believe any writer who claims he never does it. But many shades of opinion exist on both sides of mine. Purists would say that Joseph Mitchell has taken a novelist's wand to the facts. Progressives would say that Mitchell was a pioneer—that he anticipated by several decades the "new journalism" that writers like Gay Talese and Tom Wolfe were hailed for inventing in the 1960s, using fictional techniques of imagined dialogue and emotion to give narrative flair to works whose facts they had punctiliously researched. Both views are partly right.

What's wrong, I believe, is to fabricate quotes or to surmise what someone might have said. Writing is a public trust. The nonfiction writer's rare privilege is to have the whole wonderful world of real people to write about. When you get people talking, handle what they say as you would handle a valuable gift.

1 3

❧

Writing About Places

The Travel Article

Next to knowing how to write about people, you should know how to write about a place. People and places are the twin pillars on which most nonfiction is built. Every human event happens somewhere, and the reader wants to know what that somewhere was like.

In a few cases you'll need only a paragraph or two to sketch the setting of an event. But more often you'll need to evoke the mood of a whole neighborhood or town to give texture to the story you're telling. And in certain cases, such as the travel piece itself—that hardy form in which you recall how you took a boat through the isles of Greece or went backpacking in the Rockies—descriptive detail will be the main substance.

Whatever the proportion, it would seem to be relatively easy. The dismal truth is that it's very hard. It must be hard, because it's in this area that most writers—professional and amateur—produce not only their worst work but work that is just plain terrible. The terrible work has nothing to do with some terrible flaw of character. On the contrary, it results from the virtue of enthusiasm. Nobody turns so quickly into a bore as a traveler home from his travels. He enjoyed his trip so much that he wants to tell us all about it—and "all" is what we don't want to hear. We only want to hear some. What made his trip different from everybody else's? What can he tell us that we don't already know? We don't want him to describe every ride at Disneyland, or tell us that the Grand Canyon is awesome, or that Venice has canals. If one of the rides at Disneyland got stuck, if somebody fell into the awesome Grand Canyon, *that* would be worth hearing about.

It's natural for all of us when we have gone to a certain place to feel that we are the first people who ever went there or thought such sensitive thoughts about it. Fair enough: it's what keeps us going and validates our experience. Who can visit the Tower of London without musing on the wives of Henry VIII, or visit Egypt and not be moved by the size and antiquity of the pyramids? But that is ground already covered by multitudes of people. As a writer you must keep a tight rein on your subjective self—the traveler touched by new sights and sounds and smells—and keep an objective eye on the reader. The article that records everything you did on your trip will fascinate you because it was your trip. Will it fascinate the reader? It won't. The mere agglomeration of detail is no free pass to the reader's interest. The detail must be significant.

The other big trap is style. Nowhere else in nonfiction do writers use such syrupy words and groaning platitudes. Adjectives you would squirm to use in conversation—"wondrous," "dappled," "roseate," "fabled," "scudding"—are common currency. Half the sights seen in a day's sightseeing are quaint, especially windmills and covered bridges; they are certified for quaintness. Towns situated in hills (or foothills) are nestled—I hardly ever read about an unnestled town in the hills—and the countryside is dotted with byways, preferably half forgotten. In Europe you awake to the clip-clop of horse-drawn wagons along a history-haunted river; you seem to hear the scratch of a quill pen. This is a world where old meets new—old never meets old. It's a world where inanimate objects spring to life: storefronts smile, buildings boast, ruins beckon and the very chimneytops sing their immemorial song of welcome.

Travelese is also a style of soft words that under hard examination mean nothing, or that mean different things to different people: "attractive," "charming," "romantic." To write that "the city has its own attractiveness" is no help. And who will define "charm," except the owner of a charm school? Or "romantic"? These are subjective concepts in the eye of the beholder. One man's romantic sunrise is another man's hangover.

How can you overcome such fearful odds and write well about a place? My advice can be reduced to two principles— one of style, the other of substance.

First, choose your words with unusual care. If a phrase comes to you easily, look at it with deep suspicion; it's probably one of the countless clichés that have woven their way so tightly into the fabric of travel writing that you have to make a special effort *not* to use them. Also resist straining for the luminous lyrical phrase to describe the wondrous waterfall. At best it will make you sound artificial—unlike yourself—and at worst pompous. Strive for fresh words and images. Leave "myriad" and their ilk to the poets. Leave "ilk" to anyone who will take it away.

As for substance, be intensely selective. If you are describing a beach, don't write that "the shore was scattered with rocks" or that "occasionally a seagull flew over." Shores have a tendency to be scattered with rocks and to be flown over by seagulls. Eliminate every such fact that is a known attribute: don't tell us that the sea had waves and the sand was white. Find details that are significant. They may be important to your narrative; they may be unusual, or colorful, or comic, or entertaining. But make sure they do useful work.

I'll give you some examples from various writers, widely different in temperament but alike in the power of the details they choose. The first is from an article by Joan Didion called "Some Dreamers of the Golden Dream." It's about a lurid crime that occurred in the San Bernardino Valley of California, and in this early passage the writer is taking us, as if in her own car, away from urban civilization to the lonely stretch of road where Lucille Miller's Volkswagen so unaccountably caught fire:

> This is the California where it is easy to Dial-A-Devotion, but hard to buy a book. This is the country of the teased hair and the Capris and the girls for whom all life's promise comes down to a waltz-length white wedding dress and the birth of a Kimberly or a Sherry or a Debbi and a Tijuana divorce and a return to hairdresser's school. "We were just crazy kids," they say without regret, and look to the future. The future always looks good in the golden land, because no one remembers the past. Here is where the hot wind blows and the old ways do not seem relevant, where the divorce rate is double the national average and where one person in every 38 lives in a trailer. Here is the last stop for all those who come from somewhere else, for all those who drifted away from the cold and the past and the old ways. Here is where they are trying to find a new life style, trying to find it in the only places they know to look: the movies and the newspapers. The case of Lucille Marie Maxwell Miller is a tabloid monument to the new style.
>
> Imagine Banyan Street first, because Banyan is where it happened. The way to Banyan is to drive west from San

Bernardino out Foothill Boulevard, Route 66: past the Santa
Fe switching yards, the Forty Winks Motel. Past the motel
that is 19 stucco tepees: "SLEEP IN A WIGWAM—GET MORE FOR
YOUR WAMPUM." Past Fontana Drag City and Fontana Church
of the Nazarene and the Pit Stop A Go-Go; past Kaiser Steel,
through Cucamonga, out to the Kapu Kai Restaurant-Bar and
Coffee Shop, at the corner of Route 66 and Carnelian
Avenue. Up Carnelian Avenue from the Kapu Kai, which
means "Forbidden Seas," the subdivision flags whip in the
harsh wind. "HALF-ACRE RANCHES! SNACK BARS! TRAVERTINE
ENTRIES! $95 DOWN." It is the trail of an intention gone hay-
wire, the flotsam of the New California. But after a while the
signs thin out on Carnelian Avenue, and the houses are no
longer the bright pastels of the Springtime Home owners but
the faded bungalows of the people who grow a few grapes
and keep a few chickens out here, and then the hill gets
steeper and the road climbs and even the bungalows are few,
and here—desolate, roughly surfaced, lined with eucalyptus
and lemon groves—is Banyan Street.

In only two paragraphs we have a feeling not only for the
tackiness of the New California landscape, with its stucco tepees
and instant housing and borrowed Hawaiian romance, but for
the pathetic impermanence of the lives and pretensions of the
people who have alighted there. All the details—statistics and
names and signs—are doing useful work.

Concrete detail is also the anchor of John McPhee's prose.
Coming Into the Country, his book about Alaska—to choose
one example from his many craftsmanlike books—has a section
devoted to the quest for a possible new state capital. It takes
McPhee only a few sentences to give us a sense of what's wrong
with the present capital, both as a place to live and as a place for
lawmakers to make good laws:

A pedestrian today in Juneau, head down and charging, can be stopped for no gain by the wind. There are railings along the streets by which senators and representatives can haul themselves to work. Over the past couple of years, a succession of wind gauges were placed on a ridge above the town. They could measure velocities up to 200 miles per hour. They did not survive. The taku winds tore them apart after driving their indicators to the end of the scale. The weather is not always so bad; but under its influence the town took shape, and so Juneau is a tight community of adjacent buildings and narrow European streets, adhering to its mountainsides and fronting the salt water. . . .

The urge to move the capital came over Harris during those two years [in the Alaska State Senate]. Sessions began in January and ran on at least three months, and Harris developed what he called "a complete sense of isolation—stuck there. People couldn't get at you. You were in a cage. You talked to the hard lobbyists every day. Every day the same people. What was going on needed more airing."

The oddity of the city, so remote from the ordinary American experience, is instantly clear. One possibility for the legislators was to move the capital to Anchorage. There at least people wouldn't feel they were in an alien town. McPhee distills its essence in a paragraph that is brilliant both in detail and in metaphor:

Almost all Americans would recognize Anchorage, because Anchorage is that part of any city where the city has burst its seams and extruded Colonel Sanders. Anchorage is sometimes excused in the name of pioneering. Build now, civilize later. But Anchorage is not a frontier town. It is virtually unrelated to its environment. It has come in on the wind, an

American spore. A large cookie cutter brought down on El Paso could lift something like Anchorage into the air. Anchorage is the northern rim of Trenton, the center of Oxnard, the ocean-blind precincts of Daytona Beach. It is condensed, instant Albuquerque.

What McPhee has done is to capture the *idea* of Juneau and Anchorage. Your main task as a travel writer is to find the central idea of the place you're dealing with. Over the decades countless writers have tried to harness the Mississippi River, to catch the essence of the mighty highway that runs down the pious center of America, often with Biblical wrath. But nobody has done it more succinctly than Jonathan Raban, revisiting the Midwestern states inundated by the river's recent massive floods. Here's how his article begins:

> Flying to Minneapolis from the West, you see it as a theological problem.
>
> The great flat farms of Minnesota are laid out in a ruled grid, as empty of surprises as a sheet of graph paper. Every gravelled path, every ditch has been projected along the latitude and longitude lines of the township-and-range-survey system. The farms are square, the fields are square, the houses are square; if you could pluck their roofs off from over people's heads, you'd see families sitting at square tables in the dead center of square rooms. Nature has been stripped, shaven, drilled, punished and repressed in this right-angled, right-thinking Lutheran country. It makes you ache for the sight of a rebellious curve or the irregular, dappled colour of a field where a careless farmer has allowed corn and soybeans to cohabit.
>
> But there are no careless farmers on this flight path. The landscape is open to your inspection—as to God's—as an enormous advertisement for the awful rectitude of the peo-

ple. There are no funny goings-on down here, it says; we are plain upright folk, fit candidates for heaven.

Then the river enters the picture—a broad serpentine shadow that sprawls unconformably across the checkerboard. Deviously winding, riddled with black sloughs and green cigar-shaped islands, the Mississippi looks as if it had been put here to teach the god-fearing Midwest a lesson about stubborn and unregenerate nature. Like John Calvin's bad temper, it presents itself as the wild beast in the heart of the heartland.

When people who live on the river attribute a gender to the Mississippi, they do so without whimsy, and nearly always they give it their own sex. "You better respect the river, or he'll do you in," growls the lockmaster. "She's mean—she's had a lot of people from round here," says the waitress at the lunch counter. When Eliot wrote that the river is within us (as the sea is all about us), he was nailing something true in an everyday way about the Mississippi. People do see its muddy turmoil as a bodying-forth of their own turbulent inner selves. When they boast to strangers about their river's wantonness, its appetite for trouble and destruction, its floods and drownings, there's a note in their voices that says, *I have it in me to do that . . . I know how it feels.*

What could be luckier for a nonfiction writer than to live in America? The country is unendingly various and surprising. Whether the locale you write about is urban or rural, east or west, every place has a look, a population and a set of cultural assumptions unlike any other place. Find those distinctive traits. The following three passages describe parts of America that could hardly be more different. Yet in each case the writer has given us so many precise images that we feel we are there. The first excerpt, from "Halfway to Dick and Jane: A Puerto Rican Pilgrimage," by Jack Agueros, describes the Hispanic neighborhood of the writer's boyhood in New York, a place where different principalities could exist within a single block:

> Every classroom had ten kids who spoke no English. Black, Italian, Puerto Rican relations in the classroom were good, but we all knew we couldn't visit one another's neighborhoods. Sometimes we could not move too freely within our own blocks. On 109th, from the lamp post west, the Latin Aces, and from the lamp post east, the Senecas, the "club" I belonged to. The kids who spoke no English became known as the Marine Tigers, picked up from a popular Spanish song. The *Marine Tiger* and the *Marine Shark* were two ships that sailed from San Juan to New York and brought over many, many migrants from the island.
>
> The neighborhood had its boundaries. Third Avenue and east, Italian. Fifth Avenue and west, black. South, there was a hill on 103rd Street known locally as Cooney's Hill. When you got to the top of the hill, something strange happened: America began, because from the hill south was where the "Americans" lived. Dick and Jane were not dead; they were alive and well in a better neighborhood.
>
> When, as a group of Puerto Rican kids, we decided to go swimming in Jefferson Park Pool, we knew we risked a fight and a beating from the Italians. And when we went to La Milagrosa Church in Harlem, we knew we risked a fight and a beating from the blacks. But when we went over Cooney's Hill, we risked dirty looks, disapproving looks, and questions from the police like "What are you doing in this neighborhood?" and "Why don't you kids go back where you belong?"
>
> Where we belonged! Man, I had written compositions about America. Didn't I belong on the Central Park tennis courts, even if I didn't know how to play? Couldn't I watch Dick play? Weren't these policemen working for me too?

Go from there to a small town in East Texas, just across the border from Arkansas. This piece by Prudence Mackintosh ran in *Texas Monthly,* a magazine I enjoy for the aliveness with which she and her fellow Texas writers take me—a resident of mid-Manhattan—to every corner of their state.

> I gradually realized that much of what I had grown up believing was Texan was really Southern. The cherished myths of Texas had little to do with my part of the state. I knew dogwood, chinaberry, crape myrtle, and mimosa, but no bluebonnets or Indian paintbrush. Although the Four States Fair and Rodeo was held in my town, I never really learned to ride a horse. I never knew anyone who wore cowboy hats or boots as anything other than a costume. I knew farmers whose property was known as Old Man So-and-so's place, not ranches with their cattle brands arched over entrance gates. Streets in my town were called Wood, Pine, Olive, and Boulevard, not Guadalupe and Lavaca.

Go still farther west—to Muroc Field, in California's Mojave Desert, the one place in America that was hard and desolate enough, as Tom Wolfe explains in the brilliant early chapters of *The Right Stuff,* for the Army Air Force to use when it set out a generation ago to break the sound barrier.

> It looked like some fossil landscape that had long since been left behind by the rest of territorial evolution. It was full of huge dry lake beds, the biggest being Rogers Lake. Other than sagebrush the only vegetation was Joshua trees, twisted freaks of the plant world that looked like a cross between cactus and Japanese bonsai. They had a dark petrified green color and horribly crippled branches. At dusk the Joshua trees stood out in silhouette on the fossil wasteland like some arthritic nightmare. In the summer the temperature went up

to 110 degrees as a matter of course, and the dry lake beds were covered in sand, and there would be windstorms and sandstorms right out of a Foreign Legion movie. At night it would drop to near freezing, and in December it would start raining, and the dry lakes would fill up with a few inches of water, and some sort of putrid prehistoric shrimps would work their way up from out of the ooze, and sea gulls would come flying in a hundred miles or more from the ocean, over the mountains, to gobble up these squirming little throwbacks. A person had to see it to believe it. . . .

When the wind blew the few inches of water back and forth across the lake beds, they became absolutely smooth and level. And when the water evaporated in the spring, and the sun baked the ground hard, the lake beds became the greatest natural landing fields ever discovered, and also the biggest, with miles of room for error. That was highly desirable, given the nature of the enterprise at Muroc.

Besides the wind, sand, tumbleweed, and Joshua trees, there was nothing at Muroc except for two quonset-style hangars, side by side, a couple of gasoline pumps, a single concrete runway, a few tarpaper shacks, and some tents. The officers stayed in the shacks marked "barracks," and lesser souls stayed in the tents and froze all night and fried all day. Every road into the property had a guardhouse on it manned by soldiers. The enterprise the Army had undertaken in this godforsaken place was the development of supersonic jet and rocket planes.

Practice writing this kind of travel piece, and just because I call it a travel piece I don't mean you have to go to Moscow or Mombasa. Go to your local mall, or bowling alley, or day-care center. But whatever place you write about, go there often enough to isolate the qualities that make it distinctive. Usually this will be some combination of the place and the people who inhabit it. If it's your local bowling alley it will be a mixture of the atmosphere inside and the regular patrons. If it's a foreign city it will be a mixture of the ancient culture and the present populace. Try to find it.

A master of this feat of detection was the English author V. S. Pritchett, one of the best and most versatile of nonfiction writers. Consider what he squeezes out of a visit to Istanbul:

> Istanbul has meant so much to the imagination that the reality shocks most travelers. We cannot get the sultans out of our minds. We half expect to find them still cross-legged and jeweled on their divans. We remember tales of the harem. The truth is that Istanbul has no glory except its situation. It is a city of steep, cobbled, noisy hills. . . .
>
> Mostly the shops sell cloth, clothes, stockings, shoes, the Greek traders rushing out, with cloth unrolled, at any potential customer, the Turks passively waiting. Porters shout; everyone shouts; you are butted by horses, knocked sideways by loads of bedding, and, through all this, you see one of the miraculous sights of Turkey—a demure youth carrying a brass tray suspended on three chains, and in the exact center of the tray a small glass of red tea. He never spills it; he maneuvers it through chaos to his boss, who is sitting on the doorstep of his shop.
>
> One realizes there are two breeds in Turkey: those who carry and those who sit. No one sits quite so relaxedly, expertly, beatifically as a Turk; he sits with every inch of his body; his very face sits. He sits as if he inherited the art from generations of sultans in the palace above Seraglio Point. Nothing he likes better than to invite you to sit with him in his shop or in his office with half a dozen other sitters: a few polite inquiries about your age, your marriage, the sex of your children, the number of your relations, and where and how you live, and then, like the other sitters, you clear your throat

with a hawk that surpasses anything heard in Lisbon, New York or Sheffield, and join the general silence.

I like the phrase "his very face sits"—just four short words, but they convey an idea so fanciful that they take us by surprise. They also tell us a great deal about Turks. I'll never be able to visit Turkey again without noticing its sitters. With one quick insight Pritchett has caught a whole national trait. This is the essence of good writing about other countries. Distill the important from the immaterial.

The English (as Pritchett reminds me) have long excelled at a distinctive form of travel writing—the article that's less notable for what a writer extracts from a place than for what the place extracts from him. New sights touch off thoughts that otherwise wouldn't have entered the writer's mind. If travel is broadening, it should broaden more than just our knowledge of how a Gothic cathedral looks or how the French make wine. It should generate a whole constellation of ideas about how men and women work and play, raise their children, worship their gods, live and die. Certainly the books by Britain's desert-crazed scholar-adventurers in Arabia, like T. E. Lawrence, Freya Stark and Wilfred Thesiger, who chose to live among the Bedouin, derive much of their strange power from the reflections born of surviving in so harsh and minimal an environment.

So when you write about a place, try to draw the best out of it. But if the process should work in reverse, let it draw the best out of you. One of the richest travel books written by an American is *Walden,* though Thoreau only went a mile out of town.

Finally, however, what brings a place alive is human activity: people doing the things that give a locale its character. More than 30 years later I still remember reading James Baldwin's dynamic account, in *The Fire Next Time,* of being a boy preacher in a Harlem church. I still carry with me what it *felt* like to be in that sanctuary on a Sunday morning, because Baldwin pushed himself beyond mere description into a higher literary region of sounds and rhythms, of shared faith and shared emotions:

> The church was very exciting. It took a long time for me to disengage myself from this excitement, and on the blindest, most visceral level, I never really have, and never will. There is no music like that music, no drama like the drama of the saints rejoicing, the sinners moaning, the tambourines racing, and all those voices coming together and crying holy unto the Lord. There is still, for me, no pathos quite like the pathos of those multicolored, worn, somehow triumphant and transfigured faces, speaking from the depths of a visible, tangible continuing despair of the goodness of the Lord. I have never seen anything to equal the fire and excitement that sometimes, without warning, fill a church, causing the church, as Leadbelly and so many others have testified, to "rock." Nothing that has happened to me since equals the power and the glory that I sometimes felt when, in the middle of a sermon, I knew that I was somehow, by some miracle, really carrying, as they said, "the Word"—when the church and I were one. Their pain and their joy were mine, and mine were theirs—and their cries of "Amen!" and "Hallelujah!" and "Yes, Lord!" and "Praise His name!" and "Preach it, brother!" sustained and whipped on my solos until we all became equal, wringing wet, singing and dancing, in anguish and rejoicing, at the foot of the altar.

Never be afraid to write about a place that you think has had every last word written about it. It's not your place until *you* write about it. I set myself that challenge when I decided to write a book, *American Places,* about 15 heavily touristed, cliché sites that have become American icons or that represent a powerful idea about American ideals and aspirations.

Nine of my sites were super-icons: Mount Rushmore, Niagara Falls, the Alamo, Yellowstone Park, Pearl Harbor, Mount Vernon, Concord & Lexington, Disneyland, and Rockefeller Center. Five were places that embody a distinctive idea about America: Hannibal, Missouri, Mark Twain's boyhood town, which he used to create twin myths of the Mississippi River and an ideal childhood; Appomattox, where the Civil War ended; Kitty Hawk, where the Wright brothers invented flight, symbolic of America as a nation of genius-tinkerers; Abilene, Kansas, Dwight D. Eisenhower's prairie town, symbolic of the values of small-town America; and Chautauqua, the upstate New York village that hatched most of America's notions of self-improvement and adult education. Only one of my shrines was new: Maya Lin's Civil Rights Memorial, in Montgomery, Alabama, to the men and women and children who were killed during the civil rights movement in the South. Except for Rockefeller Center, I had never visited any of those places and knew nothing of their history.

My method was not to ask tourists gazing up at Mount Rushmore, "What do you feel?" I know what they would have said: something subjective ("It's fabulous!") and therefore not useful to me as information. Instead I went to the custodians of these sites and asked: Why do *you* think two million people a year come to Mount Rushmore? Or three million to the Alamo? Or one million to Concord bridge? Or a quarter million to Hannibal? What kind of quest are all these people on? My purpose was to enter into the intention of each place: to find out what *it* was trying to be, not what *I* might have expected or wanted it to be.

By interviewing local men and women—park rangers, curators, librarians, merchants, old-timers, Daughters of the Republic of Texas, ladies of the Mount Vernon Ladies Association—I tapped into one of the richest veins waiting for any writer who goes looking for America: the routine eloquence of people who work at a place that fills a need for someone else. Here are things that custodians at three sites told me:

MOUNT RUSHMORE: "In the afternoon when the sunlight throws the shadows into that socket," one of the rangers, Fred Banks, said, "you feel that the eyes of those four men are looking right at you, no matter where you move. They're peering right into your *mind,* wondering what you're thinking, making you feel guilty: 'Are you doing your part?'"

KITTY HAWK: "Half the people who come to Kitty Hawk are people who have some tie to aviation, and they're looking for the roots of things," says superintendent Ann Childress. "We periodically have to replace certain photographs of Wilbur and Orville Wright because their faces get rubbed out—visitors want to touch them. The Wrights were everyday guys, barely out of high school in their education, and yet they did something extraordinary, in a very short time, with minimal funds. They succeeded wildly—they changed how we all live—and I think, 'Could *I* be so inspired and work so diligently to create something of such magnitude?'"

YELLOWSTONE PARK: "Visiting national parks is an American family tradition," said ranger George B. Robinson, "and the one park everyone has heard of is Yellowstone. But there's also a hidden reason. I think people have an innate need to reconnect with the places from which they have evolved. One of the closest bonds I've noticed here is the bond between the very young and the very old. They're nearer to their origins."

The strong emotional content of the book was mainly supplied by what I got other people to say. *I* didn't need to wax emotional or patriotic. Beware of waxing. If you're writing about places that are sacred or meaningful, leave the waxing to someone else. One fact that I learned soon after I got to Pearl Harbor is that the battleship *Arizona,* sunk by the Japanese on December 7, 1941, continues to leak as much as a gallon of oil every day. When I later interviewed superintendent Donald Magee he recalled that upon taking the job he reversed a bureaucratic fiat prohibiting children under 45 inches tall from visiting the Arizona Memorial. Their behavior, it had been decreed, could "negatively impact the experience" for other tourists.

"I don't think children are too young to appreciate what that ship represents," Magee told me. "They'll remember it if they see the leaking oil—if they see that the ship is still bleeding."

14

Writing About Yourself

The Memoir

Of all the subjects available to you as a writer, the one you know best is yourself: your past and your present, your thoughts and your emotions. Yet it's probably the subject you try hardest to avoid.

Whenever I'm invited to visit a writing class in a school or a college, the first thing I ask the students is: "What are your problems? What are your concerns?" Their answer, from Maine to California, is the same: "We have to write what the teacher wants." It's a depressing sentence.

"That's the last thing any good teacher wants," I tell them. "No teacher wants twenty-five copies of the same person, writing about the same topic. What we're all looking for—what we want to see pop out of your papers—is individuality. We're look-ing for whatever it is that makes you unique. Write about what you know and what you think."

They can't. They don't think they have permission. I think they get that permission by being born.

Middle age brings no release. At writers' conferences I meet women whose children have grown up and who now want to sort out their lives through writing. I urge them to write in per-sonal detail about what is closest to them. They protest. "We have to write what editors want," they say. In other words, "We have to write what the teacher wants." Why do they think they need permission to write about the experiences and feelings they know best—their own?

Jump still another generation. I have a journalist friend who has spent a lifetime writing honorably, but always out of second-hand sources, explicating other people's events. Over the years I've often heard him mention his father, a minister who took many lonely liberal stands in a conservative Kansas town, and obviously that's where my friend got his own strong social con-science. A few years ago I asked him when he was going to start writing about the elements in his life that were really important to him, including his father. One of these days, he said. But the day was always put off.

When he turned 65 I began to pester him. I sent him some memoirs that had moved me, and finally he agreed to spend his mornings writing in that retrospective vein. Now he can hardly believe what a liberating journey he is embarked on: how much he is discovering about his father that he never understood, and about his own life. But when he describes his journey he always says, "I never had the nerve before," or "I was always afraid to try." In other words, "I didn't think I had permission."

Why not? Wasn't America the land of the "rugged individual-ist"? Let's get that lost land and those lost individualists back. If you're a writing teacher, make your students believe in the validity of their lives. If you're a writer, give yourself permission to tell us who you are.

By "permission" I don't mean "permissive." I have no patience with sloppy workmanship—the let-it-all-hang-out verbiage of the '60s. To have a decent career in this country it's important to be able to write decent English. But on the question of who you're writing *for*, don't be eager to please. If you consciously write *for* a teacher or *for* an editor, you'll end up not writing for anybody. If you write for yourself, you'll reach the people you want to write *for*.

Writing about one's life is naturally related to how long one has lived. When students say they have to write what the teacher wants, what they often mean is that they don't have anything to say—so meager is their after-school existence, bounded largely by television and the mall, two artificial versions of reality. Still, at any age, the physical act of writing is a powerful search mechanism. I'm often amazed, dipping into my past, to find some forgotten incident clicking into place just when I need it. Your memory is almost always good for material when your other wells go dry.

Permission, however, is a two-edged instrument, and nobody should use it without posting a surgeon general's warning: EXCESSIVE WRITING ABOUT YOURSELF CAN BE HAZARDOUS TO THE HEALTH OF THE WRITER AND THE READER. A thin line separates ego from egotism. Ego is healthy; no writer can go far without it. Egotism, however, is a drag, and this chapter is not intended as a license to prattle just for therapy. Again, the rule I suggest is: Make sure every component in your memoir is doing useful work. Write about yourself, by all means, with confidence and with pleasure. But see that all the details—people, places, events, anecdotes, ideas, emotions—are moving your story steadily along.

Which brings me to memoir as a form. I'll read almost anybody's memoir. For me, no other nonfiction form goes so deeply to the roots of personal experience—to all the drama and pain and humor and unexpectedness of life. The books I remember most vividly from my first reading of them tend to be memoirs: books such as André Aciman's *Out of Egypt,* Michael J. Arlen's *Exiles,* Russell Baker's *Growing Up,* Vivian Gornick's *Fierce Attachments,* Pete Hamill's *A Drinking Life,* Moss Hart's *Act One,* John Houseman's *Run-Through,* Mary Karr's *The Liars' Club,* Frank McCourt's *Angela's Ashes,* Vladimir Nabokov's *Speak, Memory,* V. S. Pritchett's *A Cab at the Door,* Eudora Welty's *One Writer's Beginnings,* and Leonard Woolf's *Growing.*

What gives them their power is the narrowness of their focus. Unlike autobiography, which spans an entire life, memoir assumes the life and ignores most of it. The memoir writer takes us back to some corner of his or her past that was unusually intense—childhood, for instance—or that was framed by war or some other social upheaval. Baker's *Growing Up* is a box within a box. It's the story of a boy growing up, set inside the story of a family battered by the Depression; it takes its strength from its historical context. Nabokov's *Speak, Memory,* the most elegant memoir I know, invokes a golden boyhood in czarist St. Petersburg, a world of private tutors and summer houses that the Russian Revolution would end forever. It's an act of writing frozen in a unique time and place. Pritchett's *A Cab at the Door* recalls a childhood that was almost Dickensian; his grim apprenticeship to the London leather trade seems to belong to the 19th century. Yet Pritchett describes it without self-pity and even with a certain merriment. We see that his childhood was inseparably joined to the particular moment and country and class he was born into—and was an organic part of the wonderful writer he grew up to be.

Think narrow, then, when you try the form. Memoir isn't the summary of a life; it's a window into a life, very much like a photograph in its selective composition. It may look like a casual and even random calling up of bygone events. It's not; it's a deliberate construction. Thoreau wrote seven different drafts of

Walden in eight years; no American memoir was more painstak-ingly pieced together. To write a good memoir you must become the editor of your own life, imposing on an untidy sprawl of half-remembered events a narrative shape and an organizing idea. Memoir is the art of inventing the truth.

One secret of the art is detail. Any kind of detail will work—a sound or a smell or a song title—as long as it played a shaping role in the portion of your life you have chosen to distill. Con-sider sound. Here's how Eudora Welty begins *One Writer's Beginnings,* a deceptively slender book packed with rich remembrance:

> In our house on North Congress Street, in Jackson, Mis-sissippi, where I was born, the oldest of three children, in 1909, we grew up to the striking of clocks. There was a mis-sion-style oak grandfather clock standing in the hall, which sent its gong-like strokes through the living room, dining room, kitchen, and pantry, and up the sounding board of the stairwell. Through the night, it could find its way into our ears; sometimes, even on the sleeping porch, midnight could wake us up. My parents' bedroom had a smaller striking clock that answered it. Though the kitchen clock did nothing but show the time, the dining room clock was a cuckoo clock with weights on long chains, on one of which my baby brother, after climbing on a chair to the top of the china closet, once succeeded in suspending the cat for a moment. I don't know whether or not my father's Ohio family, in having been Swiss back in the 1700s before the first three Welty brothers came to America, had anything to do with this; but we all of us have been time-minded all our lives. This was good at least for a future fiction writer, being able to learn so penetratingly, and almost first of all, about chronology. It was one of a good many things I learned almost without knowing it; it would be there when I needed it.

My father loved all instruments that would instruct and fascinate. His place to keep things was the drawer in the "library table" where lying on top of his folded maps was a telescope with brass extensions, to find the moon and the Big Dipper after supper in our front yard, and to keep appointments with eclipses. There was a folding Kodak that was brought out for Christmas, birthdays, and trips. In the back of the drawer you could find a magnifying glass, a kaleidoscope, and a gyroscope kept in a black buckram box, which he would set dancing for us on a string pulled tight. He had also supplied himself with an assortment of puzzles composed of metal rings and intersecting links and keys chained together, impossible for the rest of us, however patiently shown, to take apart; he had an almost childlike love of the ingenious.

In time, a barometer was added to our dining room wall; but we really didn't need it. My father had the country boy's accurate knowledge of the weather and its skies. He went out and stood on our front steps first thing in the morning and took a look at it and a sniff. He was a pretty good weather prophet.

"Well, I'm *not*," my mother would say with enormous self-satisfaction. . . .

So I developed a strong meteorological sensibility. In years ahead when I wrote stories, atmosphere took its influential role from the start. Commotion in the weather and the inner feelings aroused by such a hovering disturbance emerged connected in dramatic form.

Notice how much we learn instantly about Eudora Welty's beginnings—the kind of home she was born into, the kind of man her father was. She has rung us into her Mississippi girl-hood with the chiming of clocks up and down the stairs and even out onto the sleeping porch.

For Alfred Kazin, smell is a thread that he follows back to his boyhood in the Brownsville section of Brooklyn. From my first encounter with Kazin's *A Walker in the City*, long ago, I remember it as a sensory memoir. The following passage is not only a good example of how to write with your nose; it shows how memoir is nourished by a writer's ability to create a sense of place—what it was that made his neighborhood and his heritage distinctive:

It was the darkness and emptiness of the streets I liked most about Friday evening, as if in preparation for that day of rest and worship which the Jews greet "as a bride"—that day when the very touch of money is prohibited, all work, all travel, all household duties, even to the turning on and off of a light—Jewry had found its way past its tormented heart to some ancient still center of itself. I waited for the streets to go dark on Friday evening as other children waited for the Christmas lights. . . . When I returned home after three, the warm odor of a coffee cake baking in the oven, and the sight of my mother on her hands and knees scrubbing the linoleum on the dining room floor, filled me with such tenderness that I could feel my senses reaching out to embrace every single object in our household. . . .

My great moment came at six, when my father returned from work, his overalls smelling faintly of turpentine and shellac, white drops of silver paint still gleaming on his chin. Hanging his overcoat in the long dark hall that led into our kitchen, he would leave in one pocket a loosely folded copy of the New York *World;* and then everything that beckoned to me from that other hemisphere of my brain beyond the East River would start up from the smell of fresh newsprint and the sight of the globe on the front page. It was a paper that carried special associations for me with Brooklyn Bridge. They published the *World* under the green dome on Park

Row overlooking the bridge; the fresh salt air of New York harbor lingered for me in the smell of paint and damp newsprint in the hall. I felt that my father brought the outside straight into our house with each day's copy of the *World*.

Kazin would eventually cross the Brooklyn Bridge and become the dean of American literary critics. But the literary genre that has been at the center of his life is not the usual stuff of literature: the novel, or the short story, or the poem. It's memoir, or what he calls "personal history"—specifically, such "personal American classics," discovered when he was a boy, as Walt Whitman's Civil War diary *Specimen Days* and his *Leaves of Grass*, Thoreau's *Walden* and especially his Journals, and *The Education of Henry Adams*. What excited Kazin was that Whitman, Thoreau and Adams wrote themselves into the landscape of American literature by daring to use the most intimate forms—journals, diaries, letters and memoirs—and that he could also make the same "cherished connection" to America by writing personal history and thereby place himself, the son of Russian Jews, in the same landscape.

You can use your own personal history to cross your own Brooklyn Bridge. Memoir is the perfect form for capturing what it's like to be a newcomer in America, and every immigrant son and daughter brings a distinctive voice from his or her culture. The following passage by Enrique Hank Lopez, "Back to Bachimba," is typical of the powerful tug of the abandoned past, of the country left behind, which gives the form so much of its emotion.

> I am a *pocho* from Bachimba, a rather small Mexican village in the state of Chihuahua, where my father fought with the army of Pancho Villa. He was, in fact, the only private in Villa's army.

Pocho is ordinarily a derogatory term in Mexico (to define it succinctly, a *pocho* is a Mexican slob who has pretensions of being a gringo sonofabitch), but I use it in a very special sense. To me that word has come to mean "uprooted Mexican," and that's what I have been all my life. Though my entire upbringing and education took place in the United States, I have never felt completely American; and when I am in Mexico, I sometimes feel like a displaced gringo with a curiously Mexican name—Enrique Preciliano Lopez y Martinez de Sepulveda de Sapien. One might conclude that I'm either a schizo-cultural Mexican or a cultured schizoid American.

In any event, the schizoing began a long time ago, when my father and many of Pancho Villa's troops fled across the border to escape the oncoming *federales* who eventually defeated Villa. My mother and I, traveling across the hot desert plains in a buckboard wagon, joined my father in El Paso, Texas, a few days after his hurried departure. With more and more Villistas swarming into El Paso every day, it became apparent that jobs would be exceedingly scarce and insecure, so my parents packed our few belongings and we took the first available bus to Denver. My father had hoped to move to Chicago because the name sounded so Mexican, but my mother's meager savings were hardly enough to buy tickets for Colorado.

There we moved into a ghetto of Spanish-speaking residents who chose to call themselves Spanish-Americans and resented the sudden migration of their brethren from Mexico, whom they sneeringly called *surumatos* (slang for "southerners"). . . . We *surumatos* began huddling together in a sub-neighborhood within the larger ghetto, and it was there that I became painfully aware that my father had been the only private in Pancho Villa's army. Most of my friends were the sons of captains, colonels, majors, and even generals, though a few fathers were admittedly mere sergeants and corporals. . . . My chagrin was accentuated by the fact that Pancho Villa's exploits were a constant topic of conversation in our household. My entire childhood seems to be shadowed by his presence. At our dinner table, almost every night, we would listen to endlessly repeated accounts of this battle, that stratagem, or some great act of Robin Hood kindness by *el centauro del norte*. . . .

As if to deepen our sense of *Villismo,* my parents also taught us "Adelita" and *"Se llevaron el cañón para Bachimba"* ("They took the cannon to Bachimba"), the two most famous songs of the Mexican revolution. Some twenty years later (during my stint at Harvard Law School), while strolling along the Charles River, I would find myself softly singing *"Se Llevaron el cañón para Bachimba, para Bachimba, para Bachimba"* over and over again. That's all I could remember of that poignant rebel song. Though I had been born there, I had always regarded "Bachimba" as a fictitious, made-up, Lewis Carroll kind of name. So that eight years ago, when I first returned to Mexico, I was literally stunned when I came to a crossroad south of Chihuahua and saw an old road marker: "Bachimba 18km." Then it really exists—I shouted inwardly—Bachimba is a real town! Swinging onto the narrow, poorly paved road, I gunned the motor and sped toward the town I'd been singing about since infancy.

For Maxine Hong Kingston, a daughter of Chinese immigrants in Stockton, California, shyness and embarrassment were central to the experience of being a child starting school in a strange land. In this passage, aptly called "Finding a Voice," from her book *The Woman Warrior,* notice how vividly Kingston recalls both facts and feelings from those traumatic early years in America:

When I went to kindergarten and had to speak English for the first time, I became silent. A dumbness—a shame—still

cracks my voice in two, even when I want to say "hello" casu-
ally, or ask an easy question in front of the check-out counter,
or ask directions of a bus driver. I stand frozen. . . .

During the first silent year I spoke to no one at school,
did not ask before going to the lavatory, and flunked kindergarten. My sister also said nothing for three years, silent in
the playground and silent at lunch. There were other quiet
Chinese girls not of our family, but most of them got over it
sooner than we did. I enjoyed the silence. At first it did not
occur to me I was supposed to talk or to pass kindergarten. I
talked at home and to one or two of the Chinese kids in
class. I made motions and even made some jokes. I drank
out of a toy saucer when the water spilled out of the cup,
and everybody laughed, pointed at me, so I did it some
more. I didn't know that Americans don't drink out of
saucers. . . .

It was when I found out I had to talk that school became a
misery, that the silence became a misery. I did not speak and
felt bad each time that I did not speak. I read aloud in first
grade, though, and heard the barest whisper with little
squeaks come out of my throat. "Louder," said the teacher,
who scared the voice away again. The other Chinese girls did
not talk either, so I knew the silence had to do with being a
Chinese girl.

That childhood whisper is now an adult writer's voice that
speaks to us with wisdom and humor, and I'm grateful to have
that voice in our midst. Nobody but a Chinese-American woman
could have made me feel what it's like to be a Chinese girl
plunked down in an American kindergarten and expected to be
an American girl. Memoir is one way to make sense of the cultural differences that can be a painful fact of daily life in
America. Consider the quest for identity described by Lewis P.
Johnson in the following essay, "For My Indian Daughter."

Johnson, who grew up in Michigan, is a great-grandson of the last recognized chief of the Potawatomi Ottawas:

> One day when I was 35 or thereabouts I heard about an Indian powwow. My father used to attend them and so with great curiosity and a strange joy at discovering a part of my heritage, I decided the thing to do to get ready for the big event was to have my friend make me a spear in his forge. The steel was fine and blue and iridescent. The feathers on the shaft were bright and proud.
>
> In a dusty state fairground in southern Indiana, I found white people dressed as Indians. I learned they were "hobbyists," that is, it was their hobby and leisure pastime to masquerade as Indians on weekends. I felt ridiculous with my spear, and I left.
>
> It was years before I could tell anyone of the embarrassment of this weekend and see any humor in it. But in a way it was that weekend, for all its stillness, that was my awakening. I realized I didn't know who I was. I didn't have an Indian name. I didn't speak the Indian language. I didn't know the Indian customs. Dimly I remembered the Ottawa word for dog, but it was a baby word, *kahgee,* not the full word, *muhkahgee,* which I was later to learn. Even more hazily I remembered a naming ceremony (my own). I remembered legs dancing around me, dust. Where had that been? Who had I been? "Suwaukquat," my mother told me when I asked, "where the tree begins to grow."
>
> That was 1968, and I was not the only Indian in the country who was feeling the need to remember who he or she was. There were others. They had powwows, real ones, and eventually I found them. Together we researched our past, a search that for me culminated in the Longest Walk, a march on Washington in 1978. Maybe because I now know what it means to be Indian, it surprises me that others don't. Of

course there aren't very many of us left. The chances of an average person knowing an average Indian in an average life-time are pretty slim.

The crucial ingredient in memoir is, of course, people. Sounds and smells and songs and sleeping porches will take you just so far. Finally you must summon back the men and women and children who notably crossed your life. What was it that made them memorable—what turn of mind, what crazy habits? A typical odd bird from memoir's vast aviary is John Mortimer's father, a blind barrister, as recalled by the son in *Clinging to the Wreckage*, a memoir that manages the feat of being both tender and hilarious. Mortimer, a lawyer himself and a prolific author and playwright, best known for *Rumpole of the Bailey*, writes that when his father became blind he "insisted on continuing with his legal practice as though nothing had happened" and that his mother thereupon became the person who would read his briefs to him and make notes on his cases.

She became a well-known figure in the Law Courts, as well known as the Tipstaff or the Lord Chief Justice, leading my father from Court to Court, smiling patiently as he tapped the paved floors with his clouded malacca cane and shouted abuse either at her or at his instructing solicitor, or at both of them at the same time. From early in the war, when they set-tled permanently in the country, my mother drove my father fourteen miles a day to Henley Station and took him up in the train. Ensconced in a corner seat, dressed like Winston Churchill, in a black jacket and striped trousers, bow-tie worn with a wing-collar, boots and spats, my father would require her to read in a loud and clear voice the evidence in the divorce case that would be his day's work. As the train ground to a halt around Maidenhead the first-class carriage would fall silent as my mother read out the reports of Private Investigators on adulterous behavior which they had observed in detail. If she dropped her voice over descriptions of stained bed-linen, male and female clothing found scattered about, or misconduct in motor cars, my father would call out, "Speak up, Kath!" and their fellow travelers would be treated to another thrilling installment.

But the most interesting character in a memoir, we hope, will turn out to be the person who wrote it. What did that man or woman learn from the hills and valleys of life? Virginia Woolf was an avid user of highly personal forms—memoirs, journals, diaries, letters—to clarify her thoughts and emotions. (How often we start writing a letter out of obligation and only discover in the third paragraph that we have something we really want to say to the person we're writing to.) What Virginia Woolf intimately wrote during her lifetime has been immensely helpful to other women wrestling with similar angels and demons. Acknowledging that debt in a 1989 review of a book about Woolf's abused girlhood, Kennedy Fraser begins with a memoir of her own that seizes our attention with its honesty and vulnerability:

> There was a time when my life seemed so painful to me that reading about the lives of other women writers was one of the few things that could help. I was unhappy, and ashamed of it; I was baffled by my life. For several years in my early thirties, I would sit in my armchair reading books about these other lives. Sometimes when I came to the end, I would sit down and read the book through from the beginning again. I remember an incredible intensity about all this, and also a kind of furtiveness—as if I were afraid that someone might look through the window and find me out. Even now, I feel I should pretend that I was reading only these women's fiction or their poetry—their lives as they chose to present them, alchemized as art. But that would be a lie. It

was the private messages I really liked—the journals and letters, and autobiographies and biographies whenever they
seemed to be telling the truth. I felt very lonely then, self
absorbed, shut off. I needed all this murmured chorus, this
continuum of true-life stories, to pull me through. They were
like mothers and sisters to me, these literary women, many of
them already dead; more than my own family, they seemed to
stretch out a hand. I had come to New York when I was
young, as so many come, in order to invent myself. And, like
many modern people—modern women, especially—I had
catapulted out of my context. . . . The successes [of the writ-
ers] gave me hope, of course, yet it was the desperate bits I
liked best. I was looking for directions, gathering clues. I was
especially grateful for the secret, shameful things about these
women—the pain: the abortions and misalliances, the pills
they took, the amount they drank. And what had made them
live as lesbians, or fall in love with homosexual men, or men
with wives?

The best gift you have to offer when you write personal history is the gift of yourself. Give yourself permission to write
about yourself, and have a good time doing it.

1 5

⚬⚬⚬

Science and Technology

Take a class of writing students in a liberal arts college and assign them to write about some aspect of science, and a pitiful moan will go around the room. "No! Not science!" the moan says. The students have a common affliction: fear of science. They were told at an early age by a chemistry or a physics teacher that they don't have "a head for science."

Take an adult chemist or physicist or engineer and ask him or her to write a report, and you'll see something close to panic. "No! Don't make us write!" they say. They also have a common affliction: fear of writing. They were told at an early age by an English teacher that they don't have "a gift for words."

Both are unnecessary fears to lug through life, and in this chapter I'd like to help you ease whichever one is yours. The chapter is based on a simple principle: writing is not a special language owned by the English teacher. Writing is thinking on paper. Anyone who thinks clearly can write clearly, about anything at all. Science, demystified, is just another nonfiction subject. Writing, demystified, is just another way for scientists to transmit what they know.

Of the two fears, mine has been fear of science. I once flunked a chemistry course taught by a woman who had become a legend with three generations of students; the legend was that she could teach chemistry to anybody. Even today I'm not much farther along than James Thurber's grandmother, who, as he recalled her in *My Life and Hard Times,* thought that "electricity was dripping invisibly all over the house" from wall sockets. But as a writer I've learned that scientific and technical material can be made accessible to the layman. It's just a matter of putting one sentence after another. The "after," however, is crucial. Nowhere else must you work so hard to write sentences that form a linear sequence. This is no place for fanciful leaps or implied truths. Fact and deduction are the ruling family.

The science assignment that I give to students is a simple one. I just ask them to describe how something works. I don't care about style or any other graces. I only want them to tell me, say, how a sewing machine does what it does, or how a pump operates, or why an apple falls down, or how the eye tells the brain what it sees. Any process will do, and "science" can be defined loosely to include technology, medicine and nature.

A tenet of journalism is that "the reader knows nothing." As tenets go, it's not flattering, but a technical writer can never forget it. You can't assume that your readers know what you assume everybody knows, or that they still remember what was once explained to them. After hundreds of demonstrations I'm still not sure I could get into one of those life jackets that airline flight attendants have shown me: something about "simply" putting my arms through the straps, "simply" pulling two toggle knobs sharply downward (or is it sideways?) and "simply" blow-ing it up—but not too soon. The only step I'm confident I could perform is to blow it up too soon.

Describing how a process works is valuable for two reasons. It forces you to make sure *you* know how it works. Then it forces you to take the reader through the same sequence of ideas and deductions that made the process clear to you. I've found it to be a breakthrough for many students whose thinking was disorderly. One of them, a bright Yale sophomore still spraying the page with fuzzy generalities at midterm, came to class in a high mood and asked if he could read his paper on how a fire extinguisher works. I was sure we were in for chaos. But his piece moved with simplicity and logic. It clearly explained how three different kinds of fires are attacked by three different kinds of fire extinguishers. I was elated by his overnight change into a writer who had learned to write sequentially, and so was he. By the end of his junior year he had written a how-to book that sold better than any book *I* had written.

Many other fuzzy students put themselves through the same cure and have written with clarity ever since. Try it. For the principle of scientific and technical writing applies to all non-fiction writing. It's the principle of leading readers who know nothing, step by step, to a grasp of subjects they didn't think they had an aptitude for or were afraid they were too dumb to understand.

Imagine science writing as an upside-down pyramid. Start at the bottom with the one fact a reader must know before he can learn any more. The second sentence broadens what was stated first, making the pyramid wider, and the third sentence broadens the second, so that you can gradually move beyond fact into significance and speculation—how a new discovery alters what was known, what new avenues of research it might open, where the research might be applied. There's no limit to how wide the pyramid can become, but your readers will understand the broad implications only if they start with one narrow fact.

A good example is an article by Harold M. Schmeck, Jr., which ran on page 1 of the *New York Times.*

> WASHINGTON—There was a chimpanzee in California with a talent for playing ticktacktoe. Its trainers were delighted with this evidence of learning, but they were even more impressed by something else. They found they could tell from the animal's brain whether any particular move would be right or wrong. It depended on the chimpanzee's state of attention. When the trained animal was properly attentive, he made the right move.

Well, that's a reasonably interesting fact. But why is it worth page 1 of the *Times?* Paragraph 2 tells me:

> The significant fact was that scientists were able to recognize that state. By elaborate computer analysis of brain wave signals they were learning to distinguish what might be called "states of mind."

But hadn't this been possible before?

> This was far more ambitious than simply detecting gross states of arousal, drowsiness or sleep. It was a new step toward understanding how the brain works.

How is it a new step?

> The chimpanzee and the research team at the University of California at Los Angeles have graduated from the ticktacktoe stage, but the work with brain waves is continuing. It has already revealed some surprising insights to the brain's behavior during space flight. It shows promise of application to social and domestic problems on earth and even to improvements in human learning.

Good. I could hardly ask for a broader application of the research: space, human problems and the cognitive process. But is it an isolated effort? No indeed.

It is part of the large ferment of modern brain research in progress in laboratories throughout the United States and abroad. Involved are all manner of creatures from men and monkeys to rats and mice, goldfish, flatworms and Japanese quail.

I begin to see the total context. But what is the purpose?

The ultimate goal is to understand the human brain—that incredible three-pound package of tissue that can imagine the farthest reaches of the universe and the ultimate core of the atom but cannot fathom its own functioning. Each research project bites off a little piece of an immense puzzle.

So now I know where the chimp at U.C.L.A. fits into the spectrum of international science. Knowing this, I'm ready to learn more about his particular contribution.

In the case of the chimpanzee being taught to play ticktacktoe, even the trained eye could see nothing beyond the ordinary in the wavy lines being traced on paper to represent electrical waves from an animal's brain. But through analysis by computer it was possible to tell which traces showed that the animal was about to make the right move and which preceded a mistake.

An important key was the system of computer analysis developed largely by Dr. John Hanley. The state of mind that always foreshadowed a correct answer was one that might be described as trained attentiveness. Without the computer's ability to analyze the huge complexities of the recorded brain waves, the "signatures" of such states could not have been detected.

The article goes on for four columns to describe potential uses of the research—measuring causes of domestic tension, reducing drivers' rush-hour stress—and eventually it touches on work being done in many pockets of medicine and psychology. But it started with one chimpanzee playing ticktacktoe.

You can take much of the mystery out of science writing by helping the reader to identify with the scientific work being done. Again, this means looking for the human element—and if you have to settle for a chimpanzee, at least that's the next-highest rung on the Darwinian ladder.

One human element is yourself. Use your own experience to connect the reader to some mechanism that also touches his life. In the following article on memory, notice how the writer, Will Bradbury, gives us a personal handle with which to grab a complex subject:

> Even now I see the dark cloud of sand before it hits my eyes, hear my father's calm voice urging me to cry the sting away, and feel anger and humiliation burn in my chest. More than 30 years have passed since that moment when a playmate, fighting for my toy ambulance, tossed a handful of sand in my face. Yet the look of the sand and ambulance, the sound of my father's voice and the throb of my bruised feelings all remain sharp and clear today. They are the very first things I can remember, the first bits of visual, verbal and emotional glass imbedded in the mosaic I have come to know as *me* by what is certainly the brain's most essential function—memory.
>
> Without this miracle function that enables us to store and recall information, the brain's crucial systems for waking and

sleeping, for expressing how we feel about things and for performing complicated acts could do little more than fumble with sensory inputs of the moment. Nor would man have a real feeling of self, for he would have no gallery of the past to examine, learn from, enjoy and, when necessary, hide away in. Yet after thousands of years of theorizing, of reading and misreading his own behavioral quirks, man is just beginning to have some understanding of the mysterious process that permits him to break and store bits of passing time.

One problem has been to decide what memory is and what things have it. Linseed oil, for example, has a kind of memory. Once exposed to light, even if only briefly, it will change consistency and speed the *second* time it is exposed. It will "remember" its first encounter with the light. Electronic and fluidic circuits also have memory, of a more sophisticated kind. Built into computers, they are able to store and retrieve extraordinary amounts of information. And the human body has at least four kinds of memory. . . .

That's a fine lead. Who doesn't possess some cluster of vivid images that can be recalled from an inconceivably early age? The reader is eager to learn how such a feat of storage and retrieval is accomplished. The example of the linseed oil is just piquant enough to make us wonder what "memory" really is, and then the writer reverts to the human frame of reference, for it is man who has built the computer circuits and has four kinds of memory himself.

Another personal method is to weave a scientific story around someone else. That was the appeal of the articles called "Annals of Medicine" that Berton Roueché wrote for many years in *The New Yorker*. They are detective stories, almost always involving a victim—some ordinary person struck by a mystifying ailment—and a gumshoe obsessed with finding the villain. Here's how one of them begins:

At about 8 o'clock on Monday morning, Sept. 25, 1944, a ragged, aimless old man of 82 collapsed on the sidewalk on Dey Street, near the Hudson Terminal. Innumerable people must have noticed him, but he lay there alone for several minutes, dazed, doubled up with abdominal cramps, and in an agony of retching. Then a policeman came along. Until the policeman bent over the old man he may have supposed that he had just a sick drunk on his hands; wanderers dropped by drink are common in that part of town in the early morning. It was not an opinion that he could have held for long. The old man's nose, lips, ears and fingers were sky-blue.

By noon, eleven blue men have been admitted to nearby hospitals. But never fear: Dr. Ottavio Pellitteri, field epidemiologist, is on the scene and telephoning Dr. Morris Greenberg at the Bureau of Preventable Diseases. Slowly the two men piece together fragments of evidence that seem to defy medical history until the case is nailed down and the villain identified as a type of poisoning so rare that many standard texts on toxicology don't even mention it. Roueché's secret is as old as the art of storytelling. We are in on a chase and a mystery. But he doesn't start with the medical history of poisoning, or talk about standard texts on toxicology. He gives us a man—and not only a man but a blue one.

Another way to help your readers understand unfamiliar facts is to relate them to sights they *are* familiar with. Reduce the abstract principle to an image they can visualize. Moshe Safdie, the architect who conceived Habitat, the innovative housing complex at Montreal's Expo '67, explains in his book *Beyond Habitat* that man would build better than he does if he took the time to see how nature does the job, since "nature makes form, and form is a by-product of evolution":

One can study plant and animal life, rock and crystal formations, and discover the reasons for their particular form.

The nautilus has evolved so that when its shell grows, its head will not get stuck in the opening. This is known as gnomonic growth; it results in the spiral formation. It is, mathematically, the only way it can grow.

The same is true of achieving strength with a particular material. Look at the wings of a vulture, at its bone formation. A most intricate three-dimensional geometric pattern has evolved, a kind of space frame, with very thin bones that get thicker at the ends. The main survival problem for the vulture is to develop strength in the wing (which is under tremendous bending movement when the bird is flying) without building up weight, as that would limit its mobility. Through evolution the vulture has the most efficient structure one can imagine—a space frame in bone.

"For each aspect of life there are responses of form," Safdie writes, noting that the maple and the elm have wide leaves to absorb the maximum amount of sun for survival in a temperate climate, whereas the olive tree has a leaf that rotates because it must preserve moisture and can't absorb heat, and the cactus turns itself perpendicular to light. We can all picture a maple leaf and a cactus plant. With every hard principle, Safdie gives us a simple illustration:

> Economy and survival are the two key words in nature. Examined out of context, the neck of the giraffe seems uneconomically long, but it is economical in view of the fact that most of the giraffe's food is high on the tree. Beauty as we understand it, and as we admire it in nature, is never arbitrary.

Or take this article about bats, by Diane Ackerman. Most of us know only three facts about bats: they're mammals, we don't like them, and they've got some kind of radar that enables them to fly at night without bumping into things. Obviously anyone writing about bats must soon get around to explaining how that mechanism of "echo-location" works. In the following passage Ackerman gives us details so precise—and so easy to relate to what we know—that the process becomes a pleasure to read about:

It's not hard to understand echo-location if you picture bats as calling or whistling to their prey with high-frequency sounds. Most of us can't hear these. At our youngest and keenest of ear, we might detect sounds of 20,000 vibrations a second, but bats can vocalize at up to 200,000. They do it not in a steady stream but at intervals—20 or 30 times a second. A bat listens for the sounds to return to it, and when the echoes start coming faster and louder it knows that the insect it's stalking has flown nearer. By judging the time between echoes, a bat can tell how fast the prey is moving and in which direction. Some bats are sensitive enough to register a beetle walking on sand, and some can detect the movement of a moth flexing its wings as it sits on a leaf.

That's my idea of sensitive; I couldn't ask a writer to give me two more wonderful examples. But there's more to my admiration than gratitude. I also wonder: how many other examples of bat sensitivity did she collect—dozens? hundreds?—to be able to choose those two? Always start with too much material. Then give your reader just enough.

As the bat closes in, it may shout faster, to pinpoint its prey. And there's a qualitative difference between a steady, solid echo bouncing off a brick wall and the light, fluid echo from a swaying flower. By shouting at the world and listening to the echoes, bats can compose a picture of their landscape and the objects in it which includes texture, density, motion, distance, size and probably other features, too. Most bats really belt it out; we just don't hear them. This is an eerie thought when one stands in a silent grove filled with bats. They spend their whole lives yelling. They yell at their loved ones, they yell at their enemies, they yell at their dinner, they yell at the big, bustling world. Some yell faster, some slower, some louder, some softer. Long-eared bats don't need to yell; they can hear their echoes perfectly well if they whisper.

Another way of making science accessible is to write like a person and not like a scientist. It's the same old question of being yourself. Just because you're dealing with a scholarly discipline that's usually reported in a style of dry pedantry is no reason why you shouldn't write in good fresh English. Loren Eiseley was a naturalist who refused to be cowed by nature as he passed on to us, in *The Immense Journey*, not only his knowledge but his enthusiasms:

> I have long been an admirer of the octopus. The cephalopods are very old, and they have slipped, protean, through many shapes. They are the wisest of the mollusks, and I have always felt it to be just as well for us that they never came ashore, but—there are other things that have.
>
> There is no need to be frightened. It is true that some of the creatures are odd, but I find the situation rather heartening than otherwise. It gives one a feeling of confidence to see nature still busy with experiments, still dynamic, and not through or satisfied because a Devonian fish managed to end as a two-legged character with a straw hat. There are other things brewing and growing in the oceanic vat. It pays to know this. It pays to know there is just as much future as past. The only thing that doesn't pay is to be sure of man's own part in it.

Eiseley's gift is that he helps us to feel what it's like to be a scientist. The central transaction in his writing is the naturalist's love affair with nature, just as in Lewis Thomas's writing it's the cell biologist's love of the cell. "Watching television," Dr. Thomas wrote in his elegant book *Lives of a Cell*, "you'd think we lived at bay, in total jeopardy, surrounded on all sides by human-seeking germs, shielded against infection and death only by a chemical technology that enables us to keep killing them off. We explode clouds of aerosol, mixed for good luck with deodorants, into our noses, mouths, underarms, privileged crannies—even into the intimate insides of our telephones." But even at our most paranoid, he says, "we have always been a relatively minor interest of the vast microbial world. The man who catches a meningococcus is in considerably less danger for his life, even without chemotherapy, than the meningococci with the bad luck to catch a man."

Lewis Thomas was scientific proof that scientists can write as well as anybody else. It's not necessary to be a "writer" to write well. We think of Rachel Carson as a writer because she launched the environmental movement with a book, *Silent Spring*. But Carson wasn't a writer; she was a marine biologist who wrote well. She wrote well because she was a clear thinker and had a passion for her subject. Charles Darwin's *The Voyage of the Beagle* is not only a classic of natural history; it's a classic of literature, its sentences striding forward with vividness and vigor. If you're a student with a bent for science or technology, don't assume that the English department has a monopoly on "literature." Every scientific discipline has a fine literature of its own. Read the scientists who write well in fields that interest you—for example, Primo Levi (*The Periodic Table*), Peter Medawar (*Pluto's Republic*), Oliver Sacks (*The Man Who Mistook His Wife for a Hat*), Stephen Jay Gould (*The Panda's Thumb*), S. M. Ulam (*Adventures of a Mathematician*), Paul Davies (*God and the New Physics*), Freeman Dyson (*Weapons and Hope*)—and use them as models for your own writing. Imitate their linear style, their avoidance of technical jargon, their constant relating of an arcane process to something any reader can visualize.

Here's an article called "The Future of the Transistor," in *Scientific American,* by Robert W. Keyes, who holds a doctorate in physics and is a specialist in semiconductors and information-processing systems. About 98 percent of people who hold a doctorate in physics can't write their way out of a petri dish, but that's not because they can't. It's because they *won't.* They won't deign to learn to use the simple tools of the English language—precision instruments as refined as any that are used in a physics lab. This is Keyes's lead:

> I am writing this article on a computer that contains some 10 million transistors, an astounding number of manufactured items for one person to own. Yet they cost less than the hard disk, the keyboard, the display and the cabinet. Ten million staples, in contrast, would cost about as much as the entire computer. Transistors have become this cheap because during the past 40 years engineers have learned to etch ever more of them on a single wafer of silicon. The cost of a given manufacturing step can thus be spread over a growing number of units.
>
> How much longer can this trend continue? Scholars and industry experts have declared many times in the past that some physical limit exists beyond which miniaturization could not go. An equal number of times they have been confounded by the facts. No such limit can be discerned in the quantity of transistors that can be fabricated on silicon, which has proceeded through eight orders of magnitude in the 46 years since the transistor was invented.

Take one more look at the sequential style. You'll see a scientist leading you in logical steps, one sentence after another, along the path of the story he set out to tell. He is also enjoying himself and therefore writing enjoyably.

I've quoted from so many writers, writing about so many facets of the physical world, to show that they all come across first as people: men and women finding a common thread of humanity between themselves and their specialty and their readers. You can achieve the same rapport, whatever your subject. The principle of sequential writing applies to every field where the reader must be escorted over difficult new terrain. Think of all the areas where biology and chemistry are intertwined with politics, economics, ethics and religion: AIDS, abortion, asbestos, drugs, gene splicing, geriatrics, global warming, health care, nuclear energy, pollution, toxic waste, surrogate motherhood and dozens of others. Only through clear writing by experts can the rest of us make educated choices as citizens in these areas where we have little or no education.

I'll close with an example that sums up everything this chapter has been about. Reading in my morning paper about the National Magazine Awards for 1993, I saw that the winner in the highly prized category of reporting, edging out such heavyweights as *The Atlantic Monthly, Newsweek, The New Yorker* and *Vanity Fair*, was a magazine called *I.E.E.E. Spectrum*, which I had never heard of. It turned out to be the flagship magazine of the Institute of Electrical and Electronics Engineers, a professional association with 320,000 members. According to its editor, Donald Christiansen, the magazine was once full of integral signs and acronyms, its articles often unfathomable even to other engineers. "There are 37 different identifiable disciplines within I.E.E.E.," he said. "If you can't describe something in words, our own people can't understand each other."

In making his magazine accessible to 320,000 engineers, Christiansen also made it accessible to the general reader, as I found when I tracked down the award-winning article, "How Iraq Reverse-Engineered the Bomb," by Glenn Zorpette. It's as good a piece of investigative reporting as I've read—the best kind of nonfiction writing in the service of informed public knowledge.

Constructed like a detective story, it describes the efforts of the International Atomic Energy Agency (I.A.E.A.) to monitor the secret program whereby the Iraqis almost built an atomic bomb and to explain how they came so close. Thus the article is both a work of science history and a political document, one that's still hot, for Iraqi research was conducted—and presumably continues to this day—in violation of the I.A.E.A.'s disclosure rules; much of the bomb-making material was illicitly acquired from various industrial nations, including the United States. The *Spectrum* article focuses on a technique known as E.M.I.S. (electromagnetic isotope separation), which was being carried out at a research complex south of Baghdad called Al Tuwaitha:

> The EMIS program surprised not only the IAEA, but the Western intelligence agencies. With this technique a stream of uranium ions is deflected by electromagnets in a vacuum chamber. The chamber and its associated equipment are called a calutron. The heavier U–238 ions are deflected less than the U–235 ions, and this slight difference is used to separate out the fissile U–235. However, "what in theory is a very efficient procedure is in practice a very, very messy affair," said Leslie Thorne, who recently retired as field activities manager on the IAEA action team. Invariably, some U–238 ions remain mixed with the U–235, and ion streams can be hard to control.

O.K. That's very clear. But *why* is the process so messy? *Why* are the ion streams hard to control? The writer obliges. He never forgets where he left his readers in the previous paragraph and what they want to know next.

> The two different isotopic materials accumulate in cup-shaped graphite containers. But their accumulation in the two

containers can be thrown off wildly by small variations in the power to, and temperature of, the electromagnets. Thus in practice the materials tend to spatter all over the inside of the vacuum chamber, which must be cleaned after every few dozen hours of operation.

That's anybody's idea of messy. But has this process, nevertheless, ever worked?

Hundreds of magnets and tens of millions of watts are needed. During the Manhattan Project, for example, the Y–12 EMIS facility at Oak Ridge in Tennessee used more power than Canada, plus the entire U.S. stockpile of silver; the latter was used to wind the many electromagnets required (copper was needed elsewhere in the war effort). Mainly because of such problems, U.S. scientists believed that no country would ever turn to EMIS to produce the relatively large amounts of enriched material needed for atomic weapons. . . .

The discovery of the Iraqi EMIS program had much of the drama of a good spy novel. The first clue apparently came in the clothing of U.S. hostages held by Iraqi forces at Tuwaitha. After the hostages were released, their clothes were analyzed by intelligence experts, who found infinitesimal samples of nuclear materials with isotopic concentrations producible only in a calutron. . . .

"Suddenly we found a live dinosaur," said Demetrios Perricos, deputy head of the IAEA's Iraq action team.

Even in the midst of such high technology the writer never loses the human ingredient. This isn't a story about "science"; it's a story about people doing science—a gang of clandestine bomb-makers and a team of high-tech cops. The quote about the dinosaur is pure gold, a metaphor we can all understand.

Even a child knows that dinosaurs aren't around anymore.

With the inevitability of good detective work, the article builds to the outcome that has been the whole point of the investigation: the discovery that Iraq, "not limiting itself to producing weapons-grade materials, was concurrently struggling to build a deliverable weapon around the material, a daunting task known as weaponization." First we are told what options exist for anyone attempting that task:

> The two basic types of atomic bombs are gun devices and implosion weapons. The latter are much more difficult to design and build, but provide higher explosive yields for a given amount of fissile material. IAEA investigators have found no evidence that Iraq was actively pursuing a gun device; it is clear, they say, that they concentrated their money and resources on an implosion device, and had even started work on fairly advanced implosion designs.

What's an implosion device? Read on:

> In an implosion device the fissile material is physically compressed by the force of a shock wave created with conventional explosives. Then, at just the right instant, neutrons are released, initiating the ultrafast fission chain reaction—an atomic blast. Thus the main elements of an implosion device are a firing system, an explosive assembly, and the core. The firing system includes vacuum-tube-based, high-energy discharge devices called krytons that are capable of releasing enough energy to detonate the conventional explosive. The explosive assembly includes "lenses" that precisely focus the spherical, imploding shock wave on the fissile core, within which is a neutronic initiator. The IAEA had amassed ample evidence that the Iraqis had made progress in each of these areas.

Speaking of compression, that paragraph is a gem of tight linear writing, successively explaining the implosion device and its three main elements. But how (we now want to know) was the I.A.E.A.'s evidence amassed?

> Iraq's attempts to import krytons from CSI Technologies, Inc., San Marcos, Calif., made news in March 1990, when two Iraqis were arrested at London's Heathrow airport after an 18-month "sting" operation involving U.S. and British Customs. Several years before that, however, Iraq did manage to get weapons-quality capacitors from other U.S. concerns, and also produced its own capacitors. . . .

I rest my case—or, rather, I let *Spectrum* rest it for me. If a scientific subject of that complexity can be made that clear and robust, in good English, with only a few technical words, which are quickly explained (kryton) or can be quickly looked up (fissile), *any* subject can be made clear and robust by all you writers who think you're afraid of science and all you scientists who think you're afraid of writing.

16

Business Writing

Writing in Your Job

If you have to do any writing in your job, this chapter is for you. Just as in science writing, anxiety is a big part of the problem, and humanity and clear thinking are a big part of the solution.

Although this is a book about writing, it's not just for writers. Its principles apply to everyone who is expected to do some writing as part of his or her daily employment. The memo, the business letter, the administrative report, the financial analysis, the marketing proposal, the note to the boss, the fax, the e-mail, the Post-it—all the pieces of paper that circulate through your office every day are forms of writing. Take them seriously. Countless careers rise or fall on the ability or the inability of employees to state a set of facts, summarize a meeting or present an idea coherently.

Most people work for institutions: businesses, banks, insurance firms, law firms, government agencies, school systems, nonprofit organizations and other entities. Many of those people are managers whose writing goes out to the public: the president addressing the stockholders, the banker explaining a change in procedure, the school principal writing a newsletter to parents. Whoever they are, they tend to be so afraid of writing that their sentences lack all humanity—and so do their institutions. It's hard to imagine that these are real places where real men and women come to work every morning.

But just because people work for an institution, they don't have to write like one. Institutions can be warmed up. Administrators can be turned into human beings. Information can be imparted clearly and without pomposity. You only have to remember that readers identify with people, not with abstractions like "profitability," or with Latinate nouns like "utilization" and "implementation," or with inert constructions in which nobody can be visualized doing something: "pre-feasibility studies are in the paperwork stage."

Nobody has made the point better than George Orwell in his translation into modern bureaucratic fuzz of this famous verse from Ecclesiastes:

> I returned and saw under the sun, that the race is not to the swift, nor the battle to the strong, neither yet bread to the wise, nor yet riches to men of understanding, nor yet favor to men of skill; but time and chance happeneth to them all.

Orwell's version goes:

> Objective consideration of contemporary phenomena compels the conclusion that success or failure in competitive activities exhibits no tendency to be commensurate with innate capacity, but that a considerable element of the unpredictable must invariably be taken into account.

First notice how the two passages look. The one at the top invites us to read it. The words are short and have air around them; they convey the rhythms of human speech. The second one is clotted with long words. It tells us instantly that a ponderous mind is at work. We don't want to go anywhere with a mind that expresses itself in such suffocating language. We don't even start to read.

Also notice what the two passages say. Gone from the second one are the short words and vivid images of everyday life—the race and the battle, the bread and the riches—and in their place have waddled the long and flabby nouns of generalized meaning. Gone is any sense of what one person did ("I returned") or what he realized ("saw") about one of life's central mysteries: the capriciousness of fate.

Let me illustrate how this disease infects the writing that most people do in their jobs. I'll use school principals as my first example, not because they are the worst offenders (they aren't) but because I happen to have such an example. My points, however, are intended for all the men and women who work in all the organizations where language has lost its humanity and nobody knows what the people in charge are talking about.

My encounter with the principals began when I got a call from Ernest B. Fleishman, superintendent of schools in Greenwich, Connecticut. "We'd like you to come and 'dejargonize' us," he said. "We don't think we can teach students to write unless all of us at the top of the school system clean up our own writing." He said he would send me some typical materials that had originated within the system. His idea was for me to analyze the writing and then conduct a workshop.

What appealed to me was the willingness of Dr. Fleishman and his colleagues to make themselves vulnerable; vulnerability has a strength of its own. We decided on a date, and soon a fat envelope arrived. It contained various internal memos and mimeographed newsletters that had been mailed to parents from the town's 16 elementary, junior and senior high schools.

The newsletters had a cheery and informal look. Obviously the system was making an effort to communicate warmly with its families. But even at first glance certain chilly phrases caught my eye ("prioritized evaluative procedures," "modified departmentalized schedule"), and one principal promised that his school would provide "enhanced positive learning environments." Just as obviously the system wasn't communicating as warmly as it thought it was.

I studied the principals' material and divided it into good and bad examples. On the appointed morning in Greenwich I found 40 principals and curriculum coordinators assembled and eager to learn. I told them I could only applaud them for submitting to a process that so threatened their identity. In the national clamor over why Johnny can't write, Dr. Fleishman was the first adult in my experience who admitted that youth has no monopoly on verbal sludge.

I told the principals that we want to think of the men and women who run our children's schools as people not unlike ourselves. We are suspicious of pretentiousness, of all the fad words that the social scientists have coined to avoid making themselves clear to ordinary mortals. I urged them to be natural. How we write and how we talk is how we define ourselves.

I asked them to listen to how they were defining themselves to the community. I had made copies of certain bad examples, changing the names of the schools and the principals. I explained that I would read some of the examples aloud. Later we would see if they could turn what they had written into plain English. This was my first example:

Dear Parent:
    We have established a special phone communication system to provide additional opportunities for parent input.

During this year we will give added emphasis to the goal of communication and utilize a variety of means to accomplish this goal. Your inputs, from the unique position as a parent, will help us to plan and implement an educational plan that meets the needs of your child. An open dialogue, feedback and sharing of information between parents and teachers will enable us to work with your child in the most effective manner.

DR. GEORGE B. JONES
Principal

That's the kind of communication I don't want to receive, unique though my parent inputs might be. I want to be told that the school is going to make it easier for me to telephone the teachers and that they hope I'll call often to discuss how my children are getting along. Instead the parent gets junk: "special phone communication system," "added emphasis to the goal of communication," "plan and implement an educational plan." As for "open dialogue, feedback and sharing of information," they are three ways of saying the same thing.

Dr. Jones is clearly a man who means well, and his plan is one we all want: a chance to pick up the phone and tell the principal what a great kid Johnny is despite that unfortunate incident in the playground last Tuesday. But Dr. Jones doesn't sound like a person I want to call. In fact, he doesn't sound like a person. His message could have been tapped out by a computer. He is squandering a rich resource: himself.

Another example I chose was a "Principal's Greeting" sent to parents at the start of the school year. It consisted of two paragraphs that were very different:

Fundamentally, Foster is a good school. Pupils who require help in certain subjects or study skills areas are receiving special attention. In the school year ahead we seek to provide enhanced positive learning environments. Children, and staff, must work in an atmosphere that is conducive to learning. Wide varieties of instructional materials are needed. Careful attention to individual abilities and learning styles is required. Cooperation between school and home is extremely important to the learning process. All of us should be aware of desired educational objectives for every child.

Keep informed about what is planned for our children this year and let us know about your own questions and about any special needs your child may have. I have met many of you in the first few weeks. Please continue to stop in to introduce yourself or to talk about Foster. I look forward to a very productive year for all of us.

DR. RAY B. DAWSON
Principal

In the second paragraph I'm being greeted by a person; in the first I'm hearing from an educator. I like the real Dr. Dawson of Paragraph 2. He talks in warm and comfortable phrases: "Keep informed," "let us know," "I have met," "Please continue," "I look forward."

By contrast, Educator Dawson of Paragraph 1 never uses "I" or even suggests a sense of "I." He falls back on the jargon of his profession, where he feels safe, not stopping to notice that he really isn't telling the parent anything. What are "study skills areas," and how do they differ from "subjects"? What are "enhanced positive learning environments," and how do they differ from "an atmosphere that is conducive to learning"? What are "wide varieties of instructional materials": pencils, textbooks, filmstrips? What exactly are "learning styles"? What "educational objectives" are "desired"?

The second paragraph, in short, is warm and personal; the other is pedantic and vague. That was a pattern I found repeatedly. Whenever the principals wrote to notify the parents of some human detail, they wrote with humanity:

> It seems that traffic is beginning to pile up again in front of the school. If you can possibly do so, please come to the rear of the school for your child at the end of the day.

> I would appreciate it if you would speak with your children about their behavior in the cafeteria. Many of you would be totally dismayed if you could observe the manners of your children while they are eating. Check occasionally to see if they owe money for lunch. Sometimes children are very slow in repaying.

But when the educators wrote to explain how they proposed to do their educating, they vanished without a trace:

> In this document you will find the program goals and objectives that have been identified and prioritized. Evaluative procedures for the objectives were also established based on acceptable criteria.

> Prior to the implementation of the above practice, students were given very little exposure to multiple choice questions. It is felt that the use of practice questions correlated to the unit that a student is presently studying has had an extremely positive effect as the test scores confirm.

After I had read various good and bad examples, the principals began to hear the difference between their true selves and their educator selves. The problem was how to close the gap. I recited my four articles of faith: clarity, simplicity, brevity and humanity. I explained about using active verbs and avoiding "concept nouns." I told them not to use the special vocabulary of education as a crutch; almost any subject can be made accessible in good English.

These were all basic tenets, but the principals wrote them down as if they had never heard them before—and maybe they hadn't, or at least not for many years. Perhaps that's why bureaucratic prose becomes so turgid, whatever the bureaucracy. Once an administrator rises to a certain level, nobody ever points out to him again the beauty of a simple declarative sentence, or shows him how his writing has become swollen with pompous generalizations.

Finally our workshop got down to work. I distributed my copies and asked the principals to rewrite the more knotty sentences. It was a grim moment. They had met the enemy for the first time. They scribbled on their pads and scratched out what they had scribbled. Some didn't write anything. Some crumpled their paper. They began to look like writers. An awful silence hung over the room, broken only by the crossing out of sentences and the crumpling of paper. They began to sound like writers.

As the day went on, they slowly relaxed. They began to write in the first person and to use active verbs. For a while they still couldn't loose their grip on long words and vague nouns ("parent communication response"). But gradually their sentences became human. When I asked them to tackle "Evaluative procedures for the objectives were also established based on acceptable criteria," one of them wrote: "At the end of the year we will evaluate our progress." Another wrote: "We will see how well we have succeeded."

That's the kind of plain talk a parent wants. It's also what stockholders want from their corporation, what customers want from their bank, what the widow wants from the agency that's handling her social security. There is a deep yearning for human contact and a resentment of bombast. Recently I got a "Dear Customer" letter from the company that supplies my computer needs. It began: "Effective March 30 we will be migrating our end user order entry and supplies referral processing to a new telemarketing center." I finally figured out that they had a new 800 number and that the end user was me. Any organization that won't take the trouble to be both clear and personal in its writing will lose friends, customers and money. Let me put it another way for business executives: a shortfall will be experienced in anticipated profitability.

Here's an example of how companies throw away their humanity with pretentious language. It's a "customer bulletin" distributed by a major corporation. The sole purpose of a customer bulletin is to give helpful information to a customer. This one begins: "Companies are increasingly turning to capacity planning techniques to determine when future processing loads will exceed processing capabilities." That sentence is no favor to the customer; it's congealed with Orwellian nouns like "capacity" and "capabilities" that convey no procedures that a customer can picture. What *are* capacity planning techniques? Whose capacity is being planned? By whom? The second sentence says: "Capacity planning adds objectivity to the decision-making process." More dead nouns. The third sentence says: "Management is given enhanced decision participation in key areas of information system resources."

The customer has to stop after every sentence and translate it. The bulletin might as well be in Hungarian. He starts with the first sentence—the one about capacity planning techniques. Translated, that means "It helps to know when you're giving your computer more than it can handle." The second sentence—"Capacity planning adds objectivity to the decision-making process"—means you should know the facts before you decide. The third sentence—the one about enhanced decision participation—means "The more you know about your system, the better it will work." It could also mean several other things.

But the customer isn't going to keep translating. Soon he's

going to look for another company. He thinks, "If these guys are so smart, why can't they tell me what they do? Maybe they're *not* so smart." The bulletin goes on to say that "for future cost avoidance, productivity has been enhanced." That seems to mean the product will be free—all costs have been avoided. Next the bulletin assures the customer that "the system is delivered with functionality." That means it works. I would hope so.

Finally, at the end, we get a glimmer of humanity. The writer of the bulletin asks a satisfied customer why he chose this system. The man says he chose it because of the company's reputation for service. He says: "A computer is like a sophisticated pencil. You don't care how it works, but if it breaks you want someone there to fix it." Notice how refreshing that sentence is after all the garbage that preceded it: in its language (comfortable words), in its details that we can visualize (the pencil), and in its humanity. The writer has taken the coldness out of a technical process by relating it to an experience we're all familiar with: waiting for the repairman when something breaks. I'm reminded of a sign I saw in the New York subway that proves that even a huge municipal bureaucracy can talk to its constituents humanely: "If you ride the subway regularly you may have seen signs directing you to trains you've never heard of before. These are only new names for very familiar trains."

Still, plain talk will not be easily achieved in corporate America. Too much vanity is on the line. Managers at every level are prisoners of the notion that a simple style reflects a simple mind. Actually a simple style is the result of hard work and hard thinking; a muddled style reflects a muddled thinker or a person too arrogant, or too dumb, or too lazy to organize his thoughts. Remember that what you write is often the only chance you'll get to present yourself to someone whose business or money or good will you need. If what you write is ornate, or pompous, or fuzzy, that's how you'll be perceived. The reader has no other choice.

I learned about corporate America by venturing out into it, after Greenwich, to conduct workshops for some major corporations, which also asked to be dejargonized. "We don't even understand our own memos anymore," they told me. I worked with the men and women who write the vast amounts of material these companies generate for internal and external consumption. The internal material consists of house organs and newsletters whose purpose is to tell employees what's happening at their "facility" and to give them a sense of belonging. The external material includes the glossy magazines and annual reports that go to stockholders, the speeches delivered by executives, the releases sent to the press, and the consumer manuals that explain how the product works. I found almost all of it lacking in human juices and much of it impenetrable.

Typical of the sentences in the newsletters was this one:

> Announced concurrently with the above enhancements were changes to the System Support Program, a program product which operates in conjunction with the NCP. Among the additional functional enhancements are dynamic reconfiguration and inter-systems communications.

There's no joy for the writer in such work, and certainly none for the reader. It's language out of *Star Trek*, and if I were an employee I wouldn't be cheered—or informed—by these efforts to raise my morale. I would stop reading them. I told the corporate writers they had to find the people behind the fine achievements being described. "Go to the engineer who conceived the new system," I said, "or to the designer who designed it, or to the technician who assembled it, and get them to tell you in their own words how the idea came to them, or how they put it together, or how it will be used by real people in the real world." The way to warm up any institution is to locate the missing "I." Remember: "I" is the most interesting element in any story.

The writers explained that they often did interview the engineer but couldn't get him to talk English. They showed me some typical quotes. The engineers spoke in an arcane language studded with acronyms ("Sub-system support is available only with VSAG or TNA"). I said that the writers had to keep going back to the engineer until he finally made himself intelligible. They said the engineer didn't *want* to be made intelligible: if he spoke too simply he would look like a jerk to his peers. I said that their responsibility was to the facts and to the reader, not to the vanity of the engineer. I urged them to believe in themselves as writers and not to relinquish control. They replied that this was easier said than done in hierarchical corporations, where approval of written reports is required at a succession of higher levels. I sensed an undercurrent of fear: do things the company way and don't risk your job trying to make the company human.

High executives were equally victimized by wanting to sound important. One corporation had a monthly newsletter to enable "management" to share its concerns with middle managers and lower employees. Prominent in every issue was a message of exhortation from the division vice-president, whom I'll call Thomas Bell. Judging by his monthly message, he was a pompous ass, saying nothing and saying it in inflated verbiage.

When I mentioned this, the writers said that Thomas Bell was actually a diffident man and a good executive. They pointed out that he doesn't write the message himself; it's written for him. I said that Mr. Bell was being done a disservice—that the writers should go to him every month (with a tape recorder, if necessary) and stay there until he talked about his concerns in the same language he would use when he got home and talked to Mrs. Bell.

What I realized was that most executives in America don't write what appears over their signature or what they say in their speeches. They have surrendered the qualities that make them unique. If they and their institutions seem cold, it's because they acquiesce in the process of being pumped up and dried out. Preoccupied with their high technology, they forget that some of the most powerful tools they possess—for good and for bad—are words.

If you work for an institution, whatever your job, whatever your level, be yourself when you write. You will stand out as a real person among the robots, and your example might even persuade Thomas Bell to write his own stuff.

17

Sports

As an addict of the sports pages in my boyhood, I learned about the circuit clout before I learned about the electrical circuit. I learned that a hurler (or twirler) who faces left when he toes the slab is a southpaw or a portsider. Southpaws were always lanky, portsiders always chunky, though I've never heard "chunky" applied to anything else except peanut butter (to distinguish it from "creamy"), and I have no idea what a chunky person would look like. When hurlers fired the old horsehide, a batsman would try to solve their slants. If he succeeded he might rap a sharp bingle to the outfield, garnering a win for the home contingent, or at least knotting the count. If not, he might bounce into a twin killing, snuffing out a rally and dimming his team's hopes in the flag scramble.

I could go on, mining every sport for its lingo and extracting from the mother lode a variety of words found nowhere else in the mother tongue. I could write of hoopsters and pucksters, grapplers and matmen, strapping oarsmen and gridiron greats. I could rhapsodize about the old pigskin—more passionately than any pig farmer—and describe the frenzied bleacherites caught up in the excitement of the autumn classic. I could, in short, write sports English instead of good English, as if they were two different languages. They're not. Just as in writing about science or any other field, there's no substitute for the best.

What, you might ask, is wrong with "southpaw"? Shouldn't we be grateful for a word so picturesque? Why isn't it a relief to have twirlers and circuit clouts instead of the same old pitchers and home runs? The answer is that these words have become even cheaper currency than the coins they were meant to replace. They come flooding automatically out of the typewriter of every scribe (sportswriter) in every press box.

The man who first thought of "southpaw" had a right to be pleased. I like to think he allowed himself the small smile that is the due of anyone who invents a good novelty. But how long ago was that? The color that "southpaw" added to the language has paled with decades of repetition, along with the hundreds of other idioms that form the fabric of daily sportswriting. There is a weariness about them. We read the articles to find out who won, but we don't read them with enjoyment.

The best sportswriters know this. They avoid the exhausted synonyms and strive for freshness elsewhere in their sentences. You can search the columns of Red Smith and never find a batsman bouncing into a twin killing; Smith wasn't afraid to let a batter hit into a double play. But you will find hundreds of unusual words—good English words—chosen with precision and fitted into situations where no other sportswriter would put them. They please us because the writer cared about using fresh imagery in a journalistic form where his competitors settled for the same old stuff. That's why Red Smith was still king of his field after half a century of writing, and why his competitors had long since been sent—as they would be the first to say—to the showers.

I can still remember many phrases in Red Smith's columns that took me by surprise with their humor and originality. Smith was a devout angler, and it was a pleasure to watch him bait his hook and come up with that slippery fish, a sports commissioner, gasping for air. "In most professional sports the bottom has just about dropped out of the czar business," he wrote in 1971, noting that the cupidity of team owners has a tendency to outrun the courage of the sport's monitors. "The first and toughest of the [baseball] overlords was Kenesaw Mountain Landis, who came to power in 1920 and ruled with a heavy hand until his death in 1944. But if baseball started with Little Caesar, it wound up with Ethelred the Unready." Red Smith was the daily guardian of our perspective, a writer who kept us honest. But that was largely because he was writing good English. His style was not only graceful; it was strong enough to carry strong convictions.

What keeps most sportswriters from writing good English is the misapprehension that they shouldn't be trying to. They have been reared on so many clichés that they assume they are the required tools of the trade. They also have a dread of repeating the word that's easiest for the reader to visualize—batter, runner, golfer, boxer—if a synonym can be found. And usually, with exertion, it can. This excerpt from a college newspaper is typical:

Bob Hornsby extended his skein yesterday by toppling Dartmouth's Jerry Smithers, 6–4, 6–2, to lead the netmen to victory over a surprisingly strong foe. The gangling junior put his big serve to good use in keeping the Green captain off balance. The Memphis native was in top form as he racked up the first four games, breaking the Indian's service twice in the first four games. The Exeter graduate faltered and the Hanover mainstay rallied to cop three games. But the racquet ace was not to be denied, and the Yankee's attempt to knot the first stanza at 4–4 failed when he was passed by a crosscourt volley on the sixth deuce point. The redhead was simply too determined, and. . .

What ever became of Bob Hornsby? Or Jerry Smithers? Hornsby has been metamorphosed within one paragraph into the gangling junior, the Memphis native, the Exeter graduate, the racquet ace and the redhead, and Smithers turns up as the Green captain, the Indian, the Hanover mainstay and the Yankee. Readers don't know them in these various disguises—or care. They only want the clearest picture of what happened. Never be afraid to repeat the player's name and to keep the details simple. A set or an inning doesn't have to be recycled into a stanza or a frame just to avoid redundancy. The cure is worse than the ailment.

Another obsession is with numbers. Every sports addict lives with a head full of statistics, cross-filed for ready access, and many a baseball fan who flunked simple arithmetic in school can perform prodigies of instant calculation in the ballpark. Still, some statistics are more important than others. If a pitcher wins his 20th game, if a golfer shoots a 61, if a runner runs the mile in 3:48, please mention it. But don't get carried away:

AUBURN, Ala., Nov. 1 (UPI)—Pat Sullivan, Auburn's sophomore quarterback, scored two touchdowns and passed for two today to hand Florida a 38–12 defeat, the first of the season for the ninth-ranked Gators.

John Reaves of Florida broke two Southeastern Conference records and tied another. The tall sophomore from Tampa, Fla., gained 369 yards passing, pushing his six-game season total to 2,115. That broke the S.E.C. season record of 2,012 set by the 1966 Heisman trophy winner, in 10 games.

Reaves attempted 66 passes—an S.E.C. record—and tied the record of 33 completions set this fall by Mississippi's Archie Manning.

Fortunately for Auburn, nine of Reaves's passes were intercepted—breaking the S.E.C. record of eight interceptions suffered by Georgia's Zeke Bratkowski against Georgia Tech in 1951.

Reaves's performance left him only a few yards short of the S.E.C. season total offense record of 2,187 set by Georgia's Frank Sinkwich in 11 games in 1942. And his two touchdown passes against Auburn left him only one touchdown pass short of the S.E.C. season record of 23 set in 1950 by Kentucky's Babe Parilli. . . .

Those are the first five paragraphs of a six-paragraph story that was prominently displayed in my New York newspaper, a long way from Auburn. It has a certain mounting hilarity—a figure freak amok at his typewriter. But can anybody read it? And does anybody care? Only Zeke Bratkowski—finally off the hook.

Sports is one of the richest fields now open to the nonfiction writer. Many authors better known for "serious" books have done some of their most solid work as observers of athletic combat. John McPhee's *Levels of the Game,* George Plimpton's *Paper Lion* and George F. Will's *Men at Work*—books about tennis, pro football and baseball—take us deeply into the lives of the players. In mere detail they have enough information to keep any fan happy. But what makes them special is their humanity. Who is this strange bird, the winning athlete, and what engines keep him going? One of the classics in the literature of baseball is "Hub Fans Bid Kid Adieu," John Updike's account of Ted Williams's final game, on September 28, 1960, when the 42-year-old "Kid," coming up for his last time at bat in Fenway Park, hit one over the wall. But before that Updike has distilled the essence of "this brittle and temperamental player":

. . . of all team sports, baseball, with its graceful intermittences of action, its immense and tranquil field sparsely settled with poised men in white, its dispassionate mathematics, seems to me best suited to accommodate, and be ornamented by, a loner. It is essentially a lonely game. No other player visible to my generation has concentrated within himself so much of the sport's poignance, has so assiduously refined his natural skills, has so constantly brought to the plate that intensity of competence that crowds the throat with joy.

What gives the article its depth is that it's the work of a writer, not a sportswriter. Updike knows there's not much more to say about Williams's matchless ability at the plate: the famous swing, the eyes that could see the stitches on a ball arriving at 90 miles an hour. But the mystery of the man is still unsolved, even on the final day of his career, and that's where Updike steers our attention, suggesting that baseball was suited to such a reclusive star because it's a lonely game. Baseball lonely? Our great American tribal rite? Think about it, Updike says.

Something in Updike made contact with something in Williams: two solitary craftsmen laboring in the glare of the crowd. Look for this human bond. Remember that athletes are men and women who become part of our lives during the season, acting out our dreams or filling some other need for us, and we want that bond to be honored. Hold the hype and give us heroes who are believable.

Even Babe Ruth was ushered down from the sanitized slopes of Olympus and converted into a real person, with appetites as big as his girth, in Robert Creamer's fine biography *Babe*. The same qualities would go into Creamer's later book, *Stengel*. Until then readers willingly settled for the standard version of Casey Stengel as an aging pantaloon who mangled the language and somehow managed to win 10 pennants. Creamer's Stengel is far more interesting: a complex man who was nobody's fool and whose story is very much the story of baseball itself, stretching back to 19th-century rural America.

Honest portraiture is only one of many new realities in what used to be a fairy-tale world. Sport is now a major frontier of social change, and some of the nation's most vexing issues—drug abuse, violence, women's rights, minorities in management, television contracts—are being played out in our stadiums, grandstands and locker rooms. If you want to write about America, this is one place to pitch your tent. Take a hard look at such stories as the financial seduction of school and college athletes. It's far more than a sports story. It's the story of our values and our priorities in the education of our children. King Football and King Basketball sit secure on their throne. How many coaches get paid more than the college president, the school principal and the teachers?

Money is the looming monster in American sport, its dark shadow everywhere. Salaries of obscene magnitude swim through the sports section, which now seems to contain as much financial news as the financial section. How much money a player earned for winning a golf or tennis tournament is mentioned in the lead of the story, ahead of the score. Big money has also brought big emotional trouble. Much of today's sports reporting has nothing to do with sport. First we have to be told whose feelings are hurt because he's being booed by fans who think a $6 million player ought to bat higher than .225 and run after fly balls hit in his direction. In tennis the pot of gold is huge and the players are strung as tightly as their high-tech racquets—millionaires quick to whine and to swear at the referee and the linesmen. In football and basketball the pay is sky-high, and so are the sulks.

The ego of the modern athlete has in turn rubbed off on the modern sportswriter. I'm struck by how many sportswriters now think *they* are the story, their thoughts more interesting than the game they were sent to cover. I miss the days when reporters had the modesty to come right out and say who won. Today that news can be a long time in arriving. Half the sportswriters think they are Guy de Maupassant, masters of the exquisitely delayed lead. The rest think they are Sigmund Freud, privy to the athlete's psychic needs and wounded sensibilities. Some also practice orthopedics and arthroscopic surgery on the side, quicker than the team physician to assess what the magnetic resonance imaging scan revealed or didn't reveal about the pitcher's torn or perhaps not torn rotator cuff. "His condition is day-to-day," they conclude. Whose condition isn't?

The would-be Maupassants specialize in episodes that took place earlier, which they gleaned by hanging around the clubhouse in search of "color." No nugget is too trivial or too boring if it can be cemented into that baroque edifice, the lead. The following example is one that I'll invent, but every fan will recognize the genre:

Two weeks ago Bernie Williams' grandmother had a dream. She told him she dreamed he and some of his Yankee teammates went to a Chinese restaurant for dinner. When it came time for dessert, Bernie asked the waiter to bring him a fortune cookie. "Sometimes those things can really tell it to you straight," his grandmother said he told Derek Jeter. Unwrapping the paper message, Bernie saw the words: "You will soon do something powerful to confound your enemies."

Maybe Bernie was thinking of his grandmother's dream last night at Yankee Stadium when he stepped to the plate to face the Orioles' Mike Mussina. He was 0-for-12 against Mussina in 1997 and was mired in his longest slump of the season. Nobody had to tell him the fans were on his case; he had heard the boos. This would be the perfect moment to confound his enemies. It was the bottom of the eighth, two men were on, and the Orioles were leading, 3–1. Time was running out. Could that fortune cookie be trying to tell him something?

Working the count full, Williams got a waist-high slider from Mussina and crunched it. The ball rose in a high arc, and you knew just by watching Bernie that he thought the ball might carry to the left-field seats. A strong wind was swirling into the Stadium, but Bernie's "something powerful" was not to be denied, and when Mariano Rivera shut down the O's in the top of the ninth, the scoreboard said Yankees 4, Baltimore 3. Thanks, Granny.

The would-be Freuds are no less eager to swagger before settling down. "Somebody should have told Jimmy Connors he was into mortality denial before he took the court yesterday against a foe 20 years his junior," they write, experts in human motivation, using words like "predictably futile"—no proper part of a reporter's vocabulary—to show their superiority over an athlete having an inferior day. "Last night the Mets took the field determined to find another ridiculous way to lose," the reporter covering that team for my local paper kept telling me, typically, during a recent lean season, using sarcasm instead of fact. The Mets did no such thing; no athlete sets out to lose. If you want to write about sports, remember that the men and women you're writing about are doing something immensely difficult, and they have their pride. You, too, are doing a job that has its codes of honor. One of them is that you are not the story.

Red Smith had no patience with self-important sportswriting. He said it was always helpful to remember that baseball is a game that little boys play. That also goes for football and basketball and hockey and tennis and most other games. The little boys—and girls—who once played those games grow up to be readers of the sports pages, and in their imagination they are still young, still on the field and the court and the rink, still playing those games. What they want to know when they open their newspaper is how the players played and how the game came out. Please tell us.

One new role for the sportswriter is to let us know what it feels like to actually perform a sport: to be a marathon runner or a soccer goalie, a skier or a golfer or a gymnast. The historic moment is ripe—popular interest in how far the body can be pushed has never been higher. Americans are jogging, not walking, toward the millennium, keeping fit on fitness machines, calibrating every nuance of weight gain and weight loss, pulmonary intake and cardiac stress. For a nonfiction writer these weekend warriors provide a whole new readership: sports fans who are also recreational sportsmen, eager to be put inside the head of athletes at the top of their form.

High speed, a central thrill of many sports, is typical of the sensations that ordinary mortals can only try to imagine. As the owner of cars that tend to shake at 65 miles per hour, I've never come close to knowing how it feels to drive a racing car. I needed a writer, Lesley Hazleton, to strap me into the seat of a Formula One vehicle. "Whenever I drive fast," she writes, "there is an awareness that I am in transgression of the laws of nature, moving faster than my body was designed to move." This awareness doesn't truly begin, Hazleton says, until a driver experiences the g-force, an outside force that "works on you with such pressure that it seems as though your body is moved first and your insides follow after":

> Race drivers contend with g-forces so great that they are subject to three or four times the normal force of gravity. From a standing start, a Formula One car will reach a hundred miles an hour in just under three seconds. And in that first second the driver's head is pushed back so violently that his face distends, giving him a ghostly smile.
>
> Within another second he has changed gears twice, and each time he does so, the acceleration force smashes him back into the seat again. After three seconds, accelerating upward from a hundred miles an hour toward two hundred, his peripheral vision is completely blurred. He can only see straight ahead. The 800-horsepower engine is screaming at 130 decibels, and each piston completes four combustion

cycles 10,000 times a minute, which means that the vibration
he feels is at that rate.

His neck and shoulder muscles are under immense strain,
trying to keep his eyes level as the g-force pushes his head
from side to side in the corners. The strong acceleration
makes blood pool in his legs so that less is delivered to the
heart, which means that there's less cardiac output, forcing
the pulse rate up. Formula One drivers' pulses are often up to
180, even 200, and they stay at 85 percent of that maximum
for almost the entire length of a two-hour race.

Breathing quickens as the muscles call for more blood—
speed literally takes your breath away—and the whole body
goes into emergency stance. A two-hour emergency. The
mouth goes dry, the eyes dilate as the car travels the length
of a football field for every normal heartbeat. The brain processes information at an astonishingly rapid rate, since the
higher the speed, the less the reaction time. Reactions have
to be not only quick but also extraordinarily precise, no matter how great the physical strain. Split seconds may be mere
slivers of time, but they are also the difference between winning and losing a race, or between entering and avoiding a
crash.

In short, a Formula One driver has to be almost preternat-
urally alert under conditions of maximum physical pressure.
Obviously, the adrenaline is pumping.... But in addition to
the physical fitness of top athletes, he needs that chess
player's mind as he assimilates telemetry data, calculates over-
taking points, and executes a racing strategy. All of which is
why speed is so dangerous for most of us: we simply have neither the physical nor the mental stamina to handle it.

Psychologically, what happens in a race is still more complex. The muscles, the brain chemicals, the laws of physics,
the vibration, the conditions of the race—all these combine to
generate a high level of excitement and tension in the body,

making the driver feel absolutely clearheaded and alert. And high.

Although Hazleton keeps using "his"—his muscles, his eyes, his legs—the pronoun for her article should be "her." Amid all the erosions in sports and sports journalism today, she represents one huge gain: the emergence of women as fine athletes, often on turf previously monopolized by men, and as reporters with equal access to male locker rooms and the other routine rights of journalism. Consider the many kinds of progress—both in performance and in attitude—embodied in the following piece by one of those writers, Janice Kaplan, which ran in 1984:

To understand how good women have become in sports, you have to understand how bad they were just a decade ago. In the early '70s the debate wasn't how much women could do athletically, but whether a normal woman should be athletic at all.

Marathoning, for example, was said to be bad for children, for the elderly and for women. The formidable Boston Marathon was officially closed to women until 1972. That year Nina Kuscsik battled sexism and a mid-race bout with diarrhea to become the first winner of the women's division. Those of us who knew about it felt a surge of pride, mixed with a tinge of embarrassment. Pride, because Kuscsik's victory proved that women could run 26 miles after all. Embarrassment, because her time of three hours and ten minutes was more than 50 minutes slower than the best men's times. Fifty minutes. That's an eternity in racing lingo. The obvious explanation was that women had rarely run marathons before and lacked training and experience. An obvious explanation—but who really believed it?

Flash ahead to this year. For the first time, the women's marathon will be an Olympic event. One of the top competitors is likely to be Joan Benoit, who holds the current women's world record—two hours and 22 minutes. In the dozen years since the first woman raced in Boston, the best women's times have improved by about 50 minutes. Another eternity.

Men's times in the marathon have meanwhile improved by only a few minutes, so this dramatic progress should begin to answer the question of training vs. hormones: Are women slower and weaker than men because of built-in biological differences—or because of cultural bias and the fact that we haven't been given a chance to prove what we can do?... Whether the gap between men and women will ever be totally closed seems almost beside the point. What matters is that women are doing what they never dreamed they could do—taking themselves and their bodies seriously.

A pivotal event in this revolution of altered consciousness was the mid–1970s tennis match between Billie Jean King and Bobby Riggs. "It was billed as the battle of the sexes," Kaplan recalls in another article, "and it was."

There has probably never been a sporting event that was less about sports and more about social issues. The big issue in this match was women: where we belonged and what we could do. Forget Supreme Court decisions and ERA votes; we looked to two athletes to settle the issues of equality for women in a way that really mattered. In sports, all is writ large and writ in concrete. There is a winner and a loser; there is no debate.

For many women there was a sense of personal triumph in Billie Jean's victory. It seemed to release an energy in women all over the country. Young women demanded—and got—a greater role in college sports. Prize money for women in many professional sports soared. Little girls began playing

Little League, joining boys' teams, proving that the physiological differences between males and females aren't as great as they were once imagined.

American sport has always been interwoven with social history, and the best writers are men and women who make the connection. "It wasn't my idea for basketball to become tax-shelter show biz," Bill Bradley writes in *Life on the Run,* a chronicle of his seasons with the New York Knicks. Ex-Senator Bradley's book is a good example of the new sportswriting because it ponders some of the destructive forces that are altering American sport—the greed of owners, the worship of stars, the inability to accept defeat:

> After Van's departure I realized that no matter how kind, friendly and genuinely interested the owners may be, in the end most players are little more than depreciable assets to them.
> Self-definition comes from external sources, not from within. While their physical skill lasts, professional athletes are celebrities—fondled and excused, praised and believed. Only toward the end of their careers do the stars realize that their sense of identity is insufficient.
> The winning team, like the conquering army, claims everything in its path and seems to say that only winning is important. Yet victory has very narrow meanings and can become a destructive force. The taste of defeat has a richness of experience all its own.

Bradley's book is also an excellent travel journal, catching the fatigue and loneliness of the professional athlete's nomadic life—the countless night flights and bus rides, the dreary days and endless waits in motel rooms and terminals: "In the airports that have become our commuter stations we see so many dramatic personal moments that we are callused. To some, we live romantic lives. To me, every day is a struggle to stay in touch with life's subtleties."

Those are the values to look for when you write about sport: people and places, time and transition. Here's an enjoyable list of the kind of people every sport comes furnished with. It's from the obituary of G. F. T. Ryall, who covered thoroughbred racing for *The New Yorker*, under the pen name Audax Minor, for more than half a century, until a few months before he died at 92. The obituary said that Ryall "came to know *everyone* connected with racing—owners, breeders, stewards, judges, timers, mutuel clerks, Pinkertons, trainers, cooks, grooms, handicappers, hot-walkers, starters, musicians, jockeys and their agents, touts, high-rolling gamblers and tinhorns."

Hang around the track and the stable, the stadium and the rink. Observe closely. Interview in depth. Listen to old-timers. Ponder the changes. Write well.

1 8

⊸≈≈⊸

Writing About
the Arts

Critics and Columnists

The arts are all around us, a daily enrichment of our lives, whether we perform them ourselves—acting, dancing, painting, writing poetry, playing an instrument—or seek them out in concert halls and theaters and museums and galleries. We also want to read about the arts: to be kept in touch with the cultural currents of the day, wherever art is being made.

Some of the writing that accomplishes that job is journalistic—the interview with the new symphony orchestra conductor, the tour of the new museum with its architect or its curator—and it calls for the same methods as the other forms discussed in this book. Writing about how the new museum got designed and financed and built is no different in principle from explaining how the Iraqis almost built an atomic bomb.

But to write about the arts from the inside—to appraise a new work, to evaluate a performance, to recognize what's good and what's bad—calls for a special set of skills and a special body of knowledge. It's necessary, in short, to be a critic—which, at some point in his or her career, almost every writer wants to be. Small-town reporters dream of the moment when their editor will summon them to cover the pianist or the ballet troupe or the repertory company that has been booked into the local auditorium. They will trot out the hard-won words of their college education—"intuit" and "sensibility" and "Kafkaesque"—and show the whole county that they know a *glissando* from an *entrechat*. They will discern more symbolism in Ibsen than Ibsen thought of.

This is part of the urge. Criticism is the stage on which journalists do their fanciest strutting. It's also where reputations for wit are born. The American vernacular is rich in epigrams ("She ran the gamut of emotions from A to B") minted by people like Dorothy Parker and George S. Kaufman, who became famous partly by minting them, and the temptation to make a name at the expense of some talentless ham is too strong for all but the most saintly. I particularly like Kaufman's hint that Raymond Massey in *Abe Lincoln in Illinois* was overplaying the title role: "Massey won't be satisfied until he's assassinated."

True wit, however, is rare, and a thousand barbed arrows fall at the feet of the archer for every one that flies. It's also too facile an approach if you want to write serious criticism, for, by no accident, the only epigrams that have survived are cruel ones. It's far easier to bury Caesar than to praise him—and that goes for Cleopatra, too. But to say why you think a play is *good*, in words that don't sound banal, is one of the hardest chores in the business.

So don't be deluded that criticism is an easy route to glory. Nor does the job carry as much power as is widely supposed.

Probably only the daily drama critic of the *New York Times* can make or break the product. Music critics have almost no power, writing about a cluster of sounds that have vanished into the air and will never be heard in the same way again, and literary critics haven't kept the best-seller list from becoming a nesting ground for authors like Danielle Steel, whose sensibility they don't intuit.

A distinction should therefore be made between a "critic" and a "reviewer." Reviewers write for a newspaper or a popular magazine, and what they cover is primarily an industry—the output of, for instance, the television industry, the motion-picture industry and, increasingly, the publishing industry in its flood of cookbooks, health books, how-to books, "as told to" books, "gift books" and other such items of merchandise. As a reviewer your job is more to report than to make an aesthetic judgment. You are the deputy for the average man or woman who wants to know: "What is the new TV series about?" "Is the movie too dirty for the kids?" "Will the book really improve my sex life or tell me how to make a chocolate mousse?" Think what you would want to know if *you* had to spend the money for the movie, the baby-sitter and the long-promised dinner at a good restaurant. Obviously you will make your review plainer and less sophisticated than if you were judging a new production of Chekhov.

Yet I suggest several conditions that apply to both good reviewing and good criticism.

One is that critics should like—or, better still, love—the medium they are reviewing. If you think movies are dumb, don't write about them. The reader deserves a movie buff who will bring along a reservoir of knowledge, passion and prejudice. It's not necessary for the critic to like every film; criticism is only one person's opinion. But he should go to every movie wanting to like it. If he is more often disappointed than pleased, it's because the film has failed to live up to its best possibilities. This is far different from the critic who prides himself on hating everything. He becomes tiresome faster than you can say "Kafkaesque."

Another rule is: don't give away too much of the plot. Tell readers just enough to let them decide whether it's the kind of story they tend to enjoy, but not so much that you'll kill their enjoyment. One sentence will often do the trick. "This is a picture about a whimsical Irish priest who enlists the help of three orphan boys dressed as leprechauns to haunt a village where a mean widow has hidden a crock of gold." I couldn't be flailed into seeing that movie—I've had my fill of "the little people" on stage and screen. But there are legions who don't share that crotchet of mine and would flock to the film. Don't spoil their pleasure by revealing every twist of the narrative, especially the funny part about the troll under the bridge.

A third principle is to use specific detail. This avoids dealing in generalities, which, being generalities, mean nothing. "The play is always fascinating" is a typical critic's sentence. But *how* is it fascinating? Your idea of fascinating is different from someone else's. Cite a few examples and let your readers weigh them on their own fascination scale. Here are excerpts from two reviews of a film directed by Joseph Losey. (1) "In its attempts to be civilized and restrained it denies its possibilities for vulgarity and mistakes bloodlessness for taste." The sentence is vague, giving us a whiff of the movie's mood but no image we can visualize. (2) "Losey pursues a style that finds portents in lampshades and meanings in table settings." The sentence is precise—we know just what kind of arty filmmaking this is. We can almost see the camera lingering with studied sluggishness over the family crystal.

In book reviewing this means allowing the author's words to do their own documentation. Don't say that Tom Wolfe's style is gaudy and unusual. Quote a few of his gaudy and unusual sentences and let the reader see how quirky they are. In reviewing a play, don't just tell us that the set is "striking." Describe its various levels, or how it is ingeniously lit, or how it helps the actors to make their entrances and exits as a conventional set would not. Put your readers in your theater seat. Help them to see what you saw.

A final caution is to avoid the ecstatic adjectives that occupy such disproportionate space in every critic's quiver—words like "enthralling" and "luminous." Good criticism needs a lean and vivid style to express what you observed and what you think. Florid adjectives smack of the panting prose with which *Vogue* likes to disclose its latest chichi discovery: "We've just heard about the most utterly enchanting little beach at Cozumel!"

So much for reviewing and the simpler rules of the game. What is criticism?

Criticism is a serious intellectual act. It tries to evaluate serious works of art and to place them in the context of what has been done before in that medium or by that artist. This doesn't mean that critics must limit themselves to work that aims high; they may select some commercial product like *L.A. Law* to make a point about American society and values. But on the whole they don't want to waste their time on peddlers. They see themselves as scholars, and what interests them is the play of ideas in their field.

Therefore if you want to be a critic, steep yourself in the literature of the medium you hope to make your specialty. If you want to be a theater critic, see every possible play—the good and the bad, the old and the new. Catch up on the past by reading the classics or seeing them in revival. Know your Shakespeare and Shaw, your Chekhov and Molière, your Arthur Miller and Tennessee Williams, and know how they broke new ground. Learn about the great actors and directors and how their methods differed. Know the history of the American musical: the particular contribution of Jerome Kern and the Gershwin brothers and Cole Porter, of Rodgers and Hart and Hammerstein, of

Frank Loesser and Stephen Sondheim, of Agnes de Mille and Jerome Robbins. Only then can you place every new play or musical within an older tradition and tell the pioneer from the imitator.

I could make the same kind of list for every art. A film critic who reviews a new Robert Altman picture without having seen Altman's earlier films isn't much help to the serious moviegoer. A music critic should know not only his Bach and Palestrina, his Mozart and Beethoven, but his Schoenberg and Ives and Philip Glass—the theoreticians and mavericks and experimenters.

Obviously I'm now assuming a more urbane body of readers. As a critic you can presuppose certain shared areas of knowledge with the men and women you are writing for. You don't have to tell them that William Faulkner was a Southern novelist. What you *do* have to do, if you are assessing the first novel of a Southern author and weighing Faulkner's influence, is to generate a provocative idea and throw it onto the page, where your readers can savor it. They may disagree with your point—that's part of their intellectual fun. But they have enjoyed the turn of your mind and the journey that took you to your conclusion. We like good critics as much for their personality as for their opinions.

There's no medium like the movies to give us the pleasure of traveling with a good critic. The shared territory is so vast. Movies are intertwined with our daily lives and attitudes, our memories and myths—four different lines from *Casablanca* have made it into *Bartlett's Familiar Quotations*—and we count on the critic to make those connections for us. A typical service that the critic provides is to freeze briefly for our inspection the stars who shoot across the screen in film after film, sometimes arriving from a galaxy previously unknown to stargazers. Molly Haskell, reviewing *A Cry in the Dark*, in which Meryl Streep plays an Australian woman convicted of killing her baby on a camping trip, ponders Streep's "delight in disguise—in bizarre wigs, unorthodox getups and foreign accents—and in playing women who are outside the normal range of audience sympathy." Putting this in a historical context, as good critics should, she writes:

> The aura of the old stars radiated out of a sense of self, a core identity projected into every role. However varied the performances of Bette Davis, or Katharine Hepburn, or Margaret Sullavan, we always felt we were in the presence of something knowable, familiar, constant. They had recognizable voices, ways of reading a line, even certain expressions that remained constant from film to film. Comics could do imitations of them, and you either responded to them, unambivalently, or you didn't. Streep, chameleon-like, undercuts this response by never staying in one place long enough for you to get a fix on her.
>
> Bette Davis, stretching the bounds of type, went in for costume *(The Virgin Queen)* and period *(The Old Maid)*, but she was always Bette Davis, and no one would have thought to want it otherwise. Like Streep, she even dared to play unlikable, morally ambiguous heroines, her greatest being the wife of the plantation owner in *The Letter* who murders her treacherous lover in cold blood, then refuses to repent. The difference is that Davis fused with the role, poured her own passion and intensity into it. Her heroine is as icily proud and implacable as Medea—which may be why members of the Academy denied her the Oscar she deserved in favor of sweeter and tamer Ginger Rogers for *Kitty Foyle*—but Davis makes us respond to the fire within. It's hard to imagine an actress like Streep, who remains at a safe distance from her roles, rising to such heights. . . or falling to such depths.

The passage deftly connects Hollywood past and Hollywood present, leaving us to fathom the postmodern cool of Meryl

Streep but also telling us everything we need to know about Bette Davis. By extension it tells us about a whole generation of grand dragons who reigned with Davis in the golden age of the star system—the likes of Joan Crawford and Barbara Stanwyck—and who didn't mind being hated on the screen as long as they were loved at the box office.

Turning to another medium, here's an excerpt from *Living-Room War*, by Michael J. Arlen, a collection of columns of television criticism that Arlen wrote in the mid–1960s.

Vietnam is often referred to as "television's war," in the sense that this is the first war that has been brought to the people preponderantly by television. People indeed look at television. They really look at it. They look at Dick Van Dyke and become his friend. They look at thoughtful Chet Huntley and find him thoughtful, and at witty David Brinkley and find him witty. They look at Vietnam. They look at Vietnam, it seems, as a child kneeling in the corridor, his eye to the keyhole, looks at two grownups arguing in a locked room—the aperture of the keyhole small; the figures shadowy, mostly out of sight; the voices indistinct, isolated threats without meaning; isolated glimpses, part of an elbow, a man's jacket (who is the man?), part of a face, a woman's face. Ah, she is crying. One sees the tears. (The voices continue indistinctly.) One counts the tears. Two tears. Three tears. Two bombing raids. Four seek-and-destroy missions. Six administration pronouncements. Such a fine-looking woman. One searches in vain for the other grownup, but, ah, the keyhole is so small, he is somehow never in the line of sight. Look! There is General Ky. Look! There are some planes returning safely to the *Ticonderoga*. I wonder (sometimes) what it is that the people who run television think about the war, because *they* have given us this keyhole view; we have given them the airwaves, and now, at this crucial time, they have given back to us this keyhole view—and I wonder if they truly think that those isolated glimpses of elbow, face, a swirl of dress (who *is* that other person anyway?) are all that we children can stand to see of what is going on inside the room.

This is criticism at its best: stylish, allusive, disturbing. It disturbs us—as criticism often should—because it jogs a set of beliefs and forces us to reexamine them. What holds our attention is the metaphor of the keyhole, so exact and yet so mysterious. But what remains is a fundamental question about how the country's most powerful medium told the people about the war they were fighting—and escalating. The column ran in 1966, when most Americans still supported the Vietnam war. Would they have turned against it sooner if TV had widened the keyhole, had shown us not only the "swirl of dress" but the severed head and the burning child? It's too late now to know. But at least one critic was keeping watch. Critics should be among the first to notify us when the truths we hold to be self-evident cease to be true.

Some arts are harder to catch in print than others. One is dance, which consists of movement. How can a writer freeze all the graceful leaps and pirouettes? Another is music. It's an art that we receive through our ears, yet writers are stuck with describing it in words that we will see. At best they can only partly succeed, and many a music critic has built a long career by hiding behind a hedge of Italian technical terms. He will find just a shade too much *rubato* in a pianist, a tinge of shrillness in a soprano's *tessitura*.

But even in this world of evanescent notes a good critic can make sense of what happened by writing good English. Virgil Thomson, the music critic of the *New York Herald Tribune* from 1940 to 1954, was an elegant practitioner. A composer himself, an erudite and cultivated man, he never forgot that his readers were real people, and he wrote with a zest that swept them along, his style alive with pleasant surprises. He was also fearless; during his tenure no sacred cow could safely graze. He never forgot that musicians are real people, and he didn't hesitate to shrink the giants to human scale:

It is extraordinary how little musicians discuss among themselves Toscanini's rightness or wrongness about matters of speed and rhythm and the tonal amenities. Like other musicians, he is frequently apt about these and as frequently in error. What seems to be more important is his unvarying ability to put over a piece. He quite shamelessly whips up the tempo and sacrifices clarity and ignores a basic rhythm, just making the music, like his baton, go round and round, if he finds his audience's attention tending to waver. No piece has to mean anything specific; every piece has to provoke from its hearers a spontaneous vote of acceptance. This is what I call the "wow technique."

No *rubatos* or *tessituras* there, and no blind hero worship. Yet the paragraph catches the essence of what made Toscanini great: an extra helping of show biz. If his fans are offended to think that the essence contained so coarse an ingredient, they can continue to admire the Maestro for his "lyrical colorations" or "orchestral *tuttis.*" I'll go along with Thomson's diagnosis, and so, I suspect, would the Maestro.

One lubricant in criticism is humor. It allows the critic to come at a work obliquely and to write a piece that is itself an entertainment. But the column should be an organic piece of writing, not just a few rabbit punches of wit. James Michener's books have long defied reviewers to say anything bad about them; by their earnestness they are unassailable. Reviewing *The Covenant,* however, John Leonard ambushed Michener by the roundabout route of metaphor:

What must be said for James A. Michener is that he wears you down. He numbs you into acquiescence. Page after page of pedestrian prose marches, like a defeated army, across the optic tract. It is a Great Trek from platitude to piety. The mind, between the ears, might as well be the South African veld after one of the devastations of Mzilikazi or the "scorched earth" policy of the British during the Boer War. No bird sings and the antelope die of thirst.

And yet Mr. Michener is as sincere as shoes. In *The Covenant,* as in *Hawaii* and *Centennial* and *Chesapeake,* he takes the long view. He begins 15,000 years ago and he stops at the end of 1979. He is going to make us understand South Africa whether we want to or not. Like the Dutchmen whose point of view he often presents with a grim sense of fair play, he is stubborn; he endures his own bad weather; he drives the cattle of his facts until they drop.

After 300 pages or so the reader—this reader anyway— submits with a sigh. Of course, if we are going to spend a week with a book, the book should be written by Proust or Dostoyevsky, not stapled together from file cards by Mr. Michener. But there is no turning back. This is less fiction than it is drudgery; we are lashed on by the pedagogue who rides our shoulders. Maybe learning will be good for us.

Learn we do. Mr. Michener doesn't cheat. His personal covenant is not with God, but with the encyclopedia. If, 15,000 years ago in the African bush, the San used poison arrows, he will describe those arrows and name the source of the poison.

How should a good piece of criticism start? You must make an immediate effort to orient your readers to the special world they are about to enter. Even if they are broadly educated men and women they need to be told or reminded of certain facts. You can't just throw them in the water and expect them to swim easily. The water needs to be warmed up.

This is particularly true of literary criticism. So much has gone before—all writers are part of a long stream, whether they decide to swim with the current or to hurl themselves against it. No poet of this century was more innovative and influential than T. S. Eliot. Yet his 100th birthday in 1988 passed with surprisingly little public attention, as Cynthia Ozick noted at the start of a critical essay in *The New Yorker,* pointing out that today's college students have almost no knowledge of the poet's "mammoth prophetic presence" for her generation: "[To us], in a literary period that resembled eternity, T. S. Eliot. . . seemed pure zenith, a colossus, nothing less than a permanent luminary, fixed in the firmament like the sun and the moon."

How adroitly Ozick warms up the waters, beckoning us to return to the literary landscape of her own college years and thereby understand her amazement at the tale of near oblivion she is about to unfold.

The doors to Eliot's poetry were not easily opened. His lines and themes were not readily understood. But the young flung themselves through those portals, lured by unfamiliar enchantments and bound by pleasurable ribbons of ennui. "April is the cruellest month"—Eliot's voice, with its sepulchral cadences, came spiraling out of student phonographs— "breeding/ Lilacs out of the dead land, mixing/ Memory and desire." That tony British accent—flat, precise, steady, unemotive, surprisingly high-pitched, bleakly passive—coiled through awed English Departments and worshipful dormitories, rooms where the walls had pinup Picassos, and where Pound and Eliot and *Ulysses* and Proust jostled one another higgledy-piggledy in the rapt late adolescent breast. The voice was, like the poet himself, nearly sacerdotal; it was impersonal, winding and winding across the country's campuses like a spool of blank robotic woe. "Shantih shantih shantih," "not with a bang but a whimper," "an old man in a dry month," "I shall wear the bottoms of my trousers rolled": these were the devout chants of the literarily passionate in the forties and fifties, who in their own first verses piously copied Eliot's tone—its restraint, gravity, mystery, its invasive remoteness and immobilized, disjointed despair.

The paragraph is brilliant in its remembered detail, its scholarly fastidiousness, its conjuring back of Eliot himself as a huge physical presence on campuses across America. As readers we are transported back to the high priest's highest moment—a perfect launch for the descent that lies ahead. Many scholars didn't like Ozick's essay; they thought she had exaggerated the poet's fall from renown. But for me that merely validated her piece. Literary criticism that doesn't stir a few combative juices is hardly worth writing, and there are few spectator sports as enjoyable as a good academic brawl.

Today, criticism has many first cousins in journalism: the newspaper or magazine column, the personal essay, the editorial, and the essay-review, in which a critic digresses from a book or a cultural phenomenon into a larger point. (Gore Vidal has brought a high impudence and humor to the form.) Many of the same principles that govern good criticism go into these columns. A political columnist, for example, must love politics and its ancient, tangled threads.

But what is common to all the forms is that they consist of personal opinion. Even the editorial that uses "we" was obviously written by an "I." What is crucial for you as the writer is to express your opinion firmly. Don't cancel its strength with last-minute evasions and escapes. The most boring sentence in the daily newspaper is the last sentence of the editorial, which says "It is too early to tell whether the new policy will work" or "The effectiveness of the decision remains to be seen." If it's too early to tell, don't bother us with it, and as for what remains to be seen, *everything* remains to be seen. Take your stand with conviction.

Many years ago, when I was writing editorials for the *New York Herald Tribune,* the editor of the page was a huge and choleric man from Texas named L. L. Engelking. I respected him because he had no pretense and hated undue circling around a subject. Every morning we would all meet to discuss what editorials we would like to write for the next day and what position we would take. Frequently we weren't quite sure, especially the writer who was an expert on Latin America.

"What about that coup in Uruguay?" the editor would ask.

"It could represent progress for the economy," the writer would reply, "or then again it might destabilize the whole political situation. I suppose I could mention the possible benefits and then—"

"Well," the man from Texas would break in, "let's not go peeing down both legs."

It was a plea he made often, and it was the most inelegant advice I ever received. But over a long career of writing reviews and columns and trying to make a point I felt strongly about, it was also probably the best.

Humor

Humor is the secret weapon of the nonfiction writer. It's secret because so few writers realize that humor is often their best tool—and sometimes their only tool—for making an important point.

If this strikes you as a paradox, you're not alone. Writers of humor live with the knowledge that many of their readers don't know what they are trying to do. I remember a reporter calling to ask how I happened to write a certain parody in *Life*. At the end he said, "Should I refer to you as a humorist? Or have you also written anything serious?"

The answer is that if you're trying to write humor, almost everything you do is serious. Few Americans understand this. We dismiss our humorists as triflers because they never settled down to "real" work. The Pulitzer Prizes go to authors like Ernest Hemingway and William Faulkner, who are (God knows) serious and are therefore certified as men of literature. The prizes seldom go to people like George Ade, H. L. Mencken, Ring Lardner, S. J. Perelman, Art Buchwald, Jules Feiffer,

Woody Allen and Garrison Keillor, who seem to be just fooling around.

They're not just fooling around. They are as serious in purpose as Hemingway or Faulkner—a national asset in forcing the country to see itself clearly. Humor, to them, is urgent work. It's an attempt to say important things in a special way that regular writers aren't getting said in a regular way—or if they are, it's so regular that nobody is reading it.

One strong editorial cartoon is worth a hundred solemn editorials. One *Doonesbury* comic strip by Garry Trudeau is worth a thousand words of moralizing. One *Catch–22* or *Dr. Strangelove* is more powerful than all the books and movies that try to show war "as it is." Those two works of comic invention are still standard points of reference for anyone trying to warn us about the military mentality that could blow us all up tomorrow. Joseph Heller and Stanley Kubrick heightened the truth about war just enough to catch its lunacy, and we recognize it as lunacy. The joke is no joke.

This heightening of some crazy truth—to a level where it will be seen as crazy—is the essence of what serious humorists are trying to do. Here's one example of how they go about their mysterious work.

One day in the 1960s I realized that half the girls and women in America were suddenly wearing hair curlers. It was a weird new blight, all the more puzzling because I couldn't understand when the women took the curlers out. There was no evidence that they ever did—they wore them to the supermarket and to church and on dates. So what was the wonderful event they were saving the wonderful hairdo for?

I tried for a year to think of a way to write about this phenomenon. I could have said "It's an outrage" or "Have these women no pride?" But that would have been a sermon, and sermons are the death of humor. The writer must find some comic device—satire, parody, irony, lampoon, nonsense—that he can use to disguise his serious point. Very often he never finds it, and the point doesn't get made.

Luckily, my vigil was at last rewarded. I was browsing at a newsstand and saw four magazines side by side: *Hairdo, Celebrity Hairdo, Combout* and *Pouf.* I bought all four—to the alarm of the news dealer—and found a whole world of journalism devoted solely to hair: life from the neck up, but not including the brain. The magazines had diagrams of elaborate roller positions and columns in which a girl could send her roller problem to the editors for their advice. That was what I needed. I invented a magazine called *Haircurl* and wrote a series of parody letters and replies. The piece ran in *Life* and it began like this:

Dear Haircurl:

I am 15 and am considered pretty in my group. I wear baby pink rollers, jumbo size. I have been going steady with a certain boy for 2½ years and he has never seen me without my rollers. The other night I took them off and we had a terrible fight. "Your head looks small," he told me. He called me a dwarf and said I had misled him. How can I win him back?

HEARTSICK
Speonk, N.Y.

Dear Heartsick:

You have only yourself to blame for doing something so stupid. The latest "Haircurl" survey shows that 94% of American girls now wear rollers in their hair 21.6 hours a day and 359 days a year. You tried to be different and you lost your fella. Take our advice and get some super-jumbo rollers (they come in your favorite baby pink shade, too) and your head will look bigger than ever and twice as lovely. Don't ever take them off again.

Dear Haircurl:

My boyfriend likes to run his fingers through my hair. The trouble is he keeps getting them pinched in my rollers. The other night a terribly embarrassing episode happened. We were at the movies and somehow my boyfriend got two of his fingers caught (it was right where the medium roller meets the clip-curl) and couldn't get them out. I felt very conspicuous leaving the theater with his hand still in my hair, and going home on the bus several people gave us "funny looks." Fortunately I was able to reach my stylist at home and he came right over with his tools and got poor Jerry loose. Jerry was very mad and said he's not going to date me again until I get some rollers that don't have this particular habit. I think he is being unfair, but he "means business." Can you help me?

FRANTIC
Buffalo

Dear Frantic Buffalo:

We're sorry to have to tell you that no rollers have yet been developed that do not occasionally catch the fingers of boys who tousle. The roller industry, however, is working very hard on the problem, as this complaint frequently comes up. Meanwhile why not ask Jerry to wear mittens? That way you'll be happy and he'll be safe.

There were many more, and perhaps I even made a small contribution to Lady Bird Johnson's "beautification" program. But the point is this: once you've read that article you can never look at hair curlers in the same way again. You've been jolted by humor into looking with a fresh eye at something bizarre in our daily environment that was previously taken for granted. The subject here isn't important—hair curlers won't be the ruin of our society. But the method will work for subjects that *are* important, or for almost any subject, if you can find the right comic frame.

Over the last five years of the old *Life*, 1968–1972, I used humor to get at a number of unlikely subjects, such as the excesses of military power and nuclear testing. One column was on the petty squabbling over the shape of the table at the Vietnam peace conference in Paris. The situation had become so outrageous after nine weeks that it could be approached only through ridicule, and I described various efforts to get peace at my own dinner table by changing its shape every night, or by lowering the chairs of different people to give them less "status," or by turning their chairs around so the rest of us wouldn't have to "recognize" them. It was exactly what was happening in Paris.

What made those pieces work was that they stuck close to the form they were parodying. Humor may seem to be an act of gross exaggeration. But the hair curler letters wouldn't succeed if we didn't recognize them as a specific journalistic form, both in their style and in their mentality. Control is vital to humor. Don't use comical names like Throttlebottom. Don't make the same kind of joke two or three times—readers will enjoy themselves more if you make it only once. Trust the sophistication of readers who *do* know what you're doing, and don't worry about the rest.

The columns that I wrote for *Life* made people laugh. But they had a serious purpose, which was to say: "Something crazy is going on here—some erosion in the quality of life, or some threat to life itself, and yet everyone assumes it's normal." Today the outlandish becomes routine overnight. The humorist is trying to say that it's still outlandish.

I remember a cartoon by Bill Mauldin during the student turmoil of the late 1960s, when infantrymen and tanks were summoned to keep peace at a college in North Carolina and undergraduates at Berkeley were dispersed by a helicopter spraying them with Mace. The cartoon showed a mother pleading with her son's draft board: "He's an only child—please get him off the campus." It was Mauldin's way of pinning down this particular lunacy, and he was right on target—in fact, at the center of the bull's-eye, as the killing of four students at Kent State University proved not long after his cartoon appeared.

The targets will change from week to week, but there will never be a dearth of new lunacies and dangers for the humorist to fight. Lyndon Johnson, in the years of his disastrous war in Vietnam, was brought down partly by Jules Feiffer and Art Buchwald. Senator Joseph McCarthy and Vice-President Spiro Agnew were brought down partly by Walt Kelly in the comic strip *Pogo*. H. L. Mencken brought down a whole galaxy of hypocrites in high places, and "Boss" Tweed of Tammany Hall was partly toppled by the cartoons of Thomas Nast. Mort Sahl, a comic, was the only person who stayed awake during the Eisenhower years, when America was under sedation and didn't want to be disturbed. Many people regarded Sahl as a cynic, but he thought of himself as an idealist. "If I criticize somebody," he said, "it's because I have higher hopes for the world, something good to replace the bad. I'm not saying what the Beat Generation says: 'Go away because I'm not involved.' I'm here and I'm involved."

"I'm here and I'm involved": make that your creed if you want to write serious humor. Humorists operate on a deeper current than most people suspect. They must be willing to go against the grain, to say what the populace and the President may not want to hear. Art Buchwald and Garry Trudeau perform an act of courage every week. They say things that need to be said that a regular columnist couldn't get away with. What saves them is that politicians are not known for humor and are therefore even more befuddled by it than the general public.

But humor has many uses besides the topical. They aren't as urgent, but they help us to look at far older problems of the heart, the home, the family, the job and all the other frustrations of just getting from morning to night. I once interviewed Chic Young, creator of *Blondie,* when he had been writing and drawing that daily and Sunday comic strip for 40 years, or 14,500 strips. It was the most popular of all strips, reaching 60 million readers in every corner of the world, and I asked Young why it was so durable.

"It's durable because it's simple," he said. "It's built on four things that everybody does: sleeping, eating, raising a family and making money." The comic variations on those four themes are as numerous in the strip as they are in life. Dagwood's efforts to get money from his boss, Mr. Dithers, have their perpetual counterweight in Blondie's efforts to spend it. "I try to keep Dagwood in a world that people are used to," Young told me. "He never does anything as special as playing golf, and the people who come to the door are just the people that an average family has to deal with."

I cite Young's four themes to remind you that most humor, however freakish it may seem, is based on fundamental truths. Humor is not a separate organism that can survive on its own frail metabolism. It's a special angle of vision granted to certain writers who already write good English. They aren't writing about life that's essentially ludicrous; they are writing about life that's essentially serious, but their eye falls on areas where serious hopes are mocked by some ironic turn of fate—"the strange incongruity," as Stephen Leacock put it, "between our aspiration and our achievement." E. B. White made the same point. "I don't like the word 'humorist,'" he said. "It seems to me misleading. Humor is a by-product that occurs in the serious work of some and not others. I was more influenced by Don Marquis than by Ernest Hemingway, by Perelman than by Dreiser."

Therefore I suggest several principles for the writer of humor. Master the craft of writing good "straight" English; humorists from Mark Twain to Russell Baker are, first of all, superb writers. Don't search for the outlandish and scorn what seems too ordinary; you will touch more chords by finding what's funny in what you know to be true. Finally, don't strain for laughs; humor is built on surprise, and you can surprise the reader only so often.

Unfortunately for writers, humor is elusive and subjective. No two people think the same things are funny, and a piece that one magazine will reject as a dud is often published by another that finds it a jewel. The reasons for rejection are equally elusive. "It just doesn't work," editors say, and there's not much they can add. Occasionally such a piece can be made to work— it has some flaw that can be repaired. Mortality, however, is high. "Humor can be dissected, as a frog can," E. B. White once wrote, "but the thing dies in the process and the innards are discouraging to any but the pure scientific mind."

I'm no fancier of dead frogs, but I wanted to see if at least a few lessons could be learned by poking about in the innards, and when I was teaching at Yale I decided, one year, to teach a course in humor writing. I warned my students that possibly it couldn't be done and that we might end up killing the thing we loved. Luckily, humor not only didn't die; it bloomed in the desert of solemn term papers, and I repeated the course the following year. Let me briefly reconstruct our journey.

"I hope to point out that American humor has an honorable literature," I wrote in a memo for prospective students, "and to consider the influence of certain pioneers on their successors. . . . Although the line between 'fiction' and 'nonfiction' is fuzzy in humor, I see this as a nonfiction course: what you write will be based on external events. I'm not interested in 'creative writing,' flights of pure imagination and pointless whimsy."

I began by reading excerpts from early writers to show that a humorist can employ a wide range of literary forms, or invent new ones. We started with George Ade's "Fables in Slang," the first of which appeared in 1897 in the *Chicago Record,* where

Ade was a reporter. "He was just sitting unsuspectingly in front of a sheet of paper," Jean Shepherd writes in a fine introduction to his anthology, *The America of George Ade,* "when the innocent idea came to him to write something in fable form, using the language and the clichés of the moment. In other words, slang. To let people know that he knew better than to use slang in writing, he decided to capitalize all suspicious words and phrases. He was mortally afraid people would think he was illiterate."

He needn't have worried; by 1900 the Fables were so popular that he was earning $1,000 a week. Here's "The Fable of the Subordinate Who Saw a Great Light":

> Once there was an Employé who was getting the Nub End of the Deal. He kicked on the long Hours and the small Salary, and helped to organize a Clerks' Protective Association. He was for the Toiler as against the Main Squeeze.
>
> To keep him simmered down, the Owners gave him an Interest. After that he began to perspire when he looked at the Pay-Roll, and it did seem to him that a lot of big, lazy Lummixes were standing around the shop doing the Soldier Act. He learned to snap his Fingers every time the Office Boy giggled. As for the faithful old Book-Keeper who wanted an increase to $9 and a week's Vacation in the Summer, the best he got was a little Talk about Contentment being a Jewel.
>
> The saddest moment of the Day for him was when the whole Bunch knocked off at 6 o'clock in the Evening. It seemed a Shame to call 10 Hours a Full Day. As for the Saturday Half-Holiday Movement, that was little better than Highway Robbery. Those who formerly slaved alongside of him in the Galleys had to address him as Mister, and he had them numbered the same as Convicts.
>
> One day an Underling ventured to remind the Slave-Driver that once he had been the Friend of the Salaried Minion.

"Right you are," said the Boss. "But when I plugged for the lowly Wage-Earner I never had been in the Directors' Office to see the beautiful Tableau entitled 'Virtue copping out the Annual Dividend.' I don't know that I can make the situation clear to you, so I will merely remark that all those who get on our side of the Fence are enabled to catch a new Angle on this Salary Question."

Moral: *For Educational Purposes, every Employé should be taken into the Firm.*

The universal truth in that hundred-year-old gem is still true today, as it is in almost all the Fables. "Ade was my first influence as a humorist," S. J. Perelman told me. "He had a social sense of history. His pictures of Hoosier life at the turn of the century are more documentary than any of those studies on how much people paid for their coal. His humor was rooted in a perception of people and places. He had a cutting edge and an acerbic wit that no earlier American humorist had."

From Ade I proceeded to Ring Lardner, author of the classic line "Shut up, he explained," partly to demonstrate that dramatic dialogue is another form that can serve the humorist. I'm a pushover for Lardner's nonsense plays, which he presumably wrote just to amuse himself. But he was also lampooning the holy conventions of playwriting, in which yards of italic type are used to establish what's happening onstage. Act I of Lardner's *I Gaspiri (The Upholsterers)* consists of ten lines of dialogue, none of it involving the listed characters, and nine lines of irrelevant italic, concluding with "The curtain is lowered for seven days to denote the lapse of a week." In his career Lardner would put humor to powerful use in many literary forms, such as the baseball novel, *You Know Me, Al.* His ear was perfectly tuned to American piety and self-delusion.

Next I resurrected *Archy and Mehitabel,* by Don Marquis, to show that this influential humorist also used an unorthodox medium—doggerel—for his message. Marquis, a columnist for the *New York Sun,* stumbled on a novel solution to the newspaperman's brutal problem of meeting a deadline and presenting his material in orderly prose, just as Ade stumbled on the fable. In 1916 he created the cockroach Archy, who banged out free verse on Marquis's typewriter at night, minus capital letters because he wasn't strong enough to press the shift key. Archy's poems, describing his friendship with a cat named Mehitabel, are of a philosophical bent that one wouldn't guess from their ragged appearance. No formal essay could more thoroughly deflate the aging actors who bemoan the current state of the theater than Marquis does in "The Old Trouper," a long poem in which Archy describes Mehitabel's meeting with an old theater cat named Tom:

> i come of a long line
> of theatre cats
> my grandfather
> was with forrest
> he had it he was a real trouper. . .

Marquis was using the cat to leaven his impatience with a type of bore he knew well. It's a universal impatience, whatever the category of old-timer, just as it's a universal trait of old-timers to complain that their field has gone to the dogs. Marquis achieves one of the classic functions of humor: to deflect anger into a channel where we can laugh at frailty instead of railing against it.

The next writers on my tour were Donald Ogden Stewart, Robert Benchley and Frank Sullivan, who greatly broadened the possibilities of "free association" humor. Benchley added a dimension of warmth and vulnerability that wasn't present in humorists like Ade and Marquis, who ducked into impersonal forms like fable and doggerel, where they could hide. Nobody is better than Benchley at diving headlong into his subject:

St. Francis of Assisi (unless I am getting him mixed up with St. Simeon Stylites, which might be very easy to do as both their names begin with "St.") was very fond of birds, and often had his picture taken with them sitting on his shoulders and pecking at his wrists. That was all right, if St. Francis liked it. We all have our likes and dislikes, and I have more of a feeling for dogs.

Perhaps they were all just paving the way for S. J. Perelman. If so, Perelman gratefully acknowledged the debt. "You must learn by imitation," he said. "I could have been arrested for imitating Lardner in my pieces in the late 1920s—not the content, but the manner. These influences gradually fall away."

His own influence hasn't been so easily shed. At his death in 1979 he had been writing steadily for more than half a century, putting the language through breathtaking loops, and the woods are still full of writers and comics who were drawn into the gravitational pull of his style and never quite got back out. It doesn't take a detective to see Perelman's hand not only in writers like Woody Allen but in the BBC's *Goon Show* and *Monty Python,* in the radio skits of Bob and Ray, and in the glancing wit of Groucho Marx—an influence more easily traceable because Perelman wrote several of the Marx Brothers' early movies.

What he created was an awareness that when the writer's mind works by free association it can ricochet from the normal to the absurd and, by the unexpectedness of its angle, demolish whatever trite idea had been there before. Onto this element of constant surprise he grafted the dazzling wordplay that was his trademark, a rich and recondite vocabulary, and an erudition based on reading and travel.

But even that mixture wouldn't have sustained him if he hadn't had a target. "All humor must be *about* something—it must touch concretely on life," he said, and although readers savoring his style may lose sight of his motive, some form of pomposity lies in ruins at the end of a Perelman piece, just as grand opera never quite recovered from the Marx Brothers' *A Night at the Opera* or banking from W. C. Fields's *The Bank Dick*. He was seldom at a loss for charlatans and knaves, especially in the worlds of Broadway, Hollywood, advertising and merchandising.

I still remember the teenage moment when I first got hit by one of Perelman's sentences. His sentences were unlike any I had ever seen, and they fractured me:

> The whistle shrilled and in a moment I was chugging out of Grand Central's dreaming spires. I had chugged only a few feet when I realized that I had left without the train, so I had to run back and wait for it to start. . . . With only two hours in Chicago I would be unable to see the city, and the thought drew me into a state of composure. I noted with pleasure that a fresh coat of grime had been given to the Dearborn Street station, though I was hardly vain enough to believe that it had anything to do with my visit.

> Women loved this impetual Irish adventurer who would rather fight than eat and vice-versa. One night he was chafing at The Bit, a tavern in Portsmouth, when he overheard a chance remark from a brawny gunner's mate in his cups. . . . The following morning the "Maid of Hull," a frigate of the line mounting 36 guns, out of Bath and into bed in a twinkling, dropped downstream on the tide, bound for Bombay, object matrimony. On her as passenger went my great-grandfather. . . . Fifty-three days later, living almost entirely on cameo brooches and the ptarmigan which fell to the ptrigger of his pfowling piece, he at last sighted the towers of Ishpeming, the Holy City of the Surds and Cosines, fanatical Mohammedan warrior sects.

My classroom survey ended with Woody Allen, the most cerebral practitioner of the trade. Allen's magazine pieces, now collected in several books, constitute a body of written humor unique for being both intellectual and hilarious, probing not only his well-known themes of death and anxiety but such over-bearing academic disciplines and literary forms as philosophy, psychology, drama, Irish poetry and the explication of texts ("Hassidic Tales"). "A Look at Organized Crime," a parody of all the articles ever written explaining the Mafia, is one of the fun-niest pieces I know, and "The Schmeed Memoirs"—the recol-lections of Hitler's barber—is the ultimate jab at the "good Ger-man" who was just doing his job:

> I have been asked if I was aware of the moral implications of what I was doing. As I told the tribunal at Nuremberg, I did not know that Hitler was a Nazi. The truth was that for years I thought he worked for the phone company. When I finally did find out what a monster he was, it was too late to do anything, as I had made a down payment on some furniture. Once, toward the end of the war, I did contemplate loosening the Führer's neck-napkin and allowing some tiny hairs to get down his back, but at the last minute my nerve failed me.

The brief excerpts in this chapter can convey only a glimmer of the vast output and artistry of these giants. But I wanted my students to know that they were working within a long tradition of serious intent and considerable nerve, one that is still alive in the work of such writers as Ian Frazier, Garrison Keillor, Fran Lebowitz, Nora Ephron, Calvin Trillin and Mark Singer. Singer is the current star in a long lineage of *New Yorker* writers—St. Clair McKelway, Robert Lewis Taylor, Lillian Ross, Wolcott Gibbs—who used deadpan humor to assassinate such public nuisances as Walter Winchell, leaving hardly a mark where their stiletto broke the skin.

Singer's lethal potion is concocted of hundreds of outlandish facts and quotes—he is a tenacious reporter—and a style that barely suppresses his own amusement. It works particularly well on the egregious buccaneers of the late 1990s who have long tried the patience of the citizenry, as proved by his profile in *The New Yorker* of the developer Donald Trump. Noting that Trump "had aspired to and achieved the ultimate luxury, an existence unmolested by the rumbling of a soul," Singer describes a visit to Mar-a-Lago, the Palm Beach spa converted by Trump from the 118-room Hispano-Moorish-Venetian mansion built in the 1920s by Marjorie Merriweather Post and E. F. Hutton:

> Evidently, Trump's philosophy of wellness is rooted in a belief that prolonged exposure to exceptionally attractive young spa attendants will instill in the male clientele a will to live. Accordingly, he limits his role to a pocket veto of key hiring decisions. While giving me a tour of the main exercise room, where Tony Bennett, who does a couple of gigs at Mar-a-Lago each season and had been designated an "artist-in-residence," was taking a brisk walk on a treadmill, Trump introduced me to "our resident physician, Dr. Ginger Lee Southall"—a recent chiropractic-college graduate. As Dr. Ginger, out of earshot, manipulated the sore back of a grateful member, I asked Trump where she had done her training. "I'm not sure," he said. "Baywatch Medical School? Does that sound right? I'll tell you the truth. Once I saw Dr. Ginger's photograph, I didn't really need to look at her résumé or anyone else's. Are you asking, 'Did we hire her because she trained at Mount Sinai for fifteen years?' The answer is no. And I'll tell you why: because by the time she's spent fifteen years at Mount Sinai, we don't want to look at her."

Of all the current humorists, Garrison Keillor has the surest eye for social change and the most inventive mind for making his point obliquely. Again and again he gives us the pleasure of finding an old genre dressed up in new clothes. America's current hostility to cigarette smokers is a trend that any alert writer might have noticed and written about with due sobriety. This approach, however, is pure Keillor:

> The last cigarette smokers in America were located in a box canyon south of Donner Pass in the High Sierra by two federal tobacco agents in a helicopter who spotted the little smoke puffs just before noon. One of them, the district chief, called in the ground team by air-to-ground radio. Six men in camouflage outfits, members of a crack anti-smoking joggers unit, moved quickly across the rugged terrain, surrounded the bunch in their hideout, subdued them with tear gas, and made them lie face down on the gravel in the hot August sun. There were three females and two males, all in their mid-forties. They had been on the run since the adoption of the Twenty-eighth Amendment.

The genre that's in Keillor's head has been a staple of American newspapers since the Dillinger era of the 1930s, and his enjoyment of that form, with its echoes of gangsters and G-men, of stakeouts and shootouts, is obvious in his writing.

Another situation that Keillor obviously enjoyed having found a perfect framework for was the Bush administration's bailout of the savings-and-loan industry. This is how his piece "How the Savings and Loans Were Saved" begins:

> The President was playing badminton in Aspen the day vast hordes of barbaric Huns invaded Chicago, and a reporter whose aunt lives in Evanston shouted to him as he headed for the clubhouse, "The Huns are wreaking carnage in Chicago, Mr. President! Any comment?"
> Mr. Bush, though caught off guard by news of the inva-

sion, said, "We're following that whole Hun situation very closely, and right now it looks encouraging, but I'm hoping we can get back to you in a few hours with something more definite." The President appeared concerned but relaxed and definitely chin-up and in charge.

The piece goes on to describe how rapacious barbarians swarmed into the city, "burned churches and performing-arts centers and historic restorations, and dragged away monks, virgins and associate professors. . . to be sold into slavery" and seized the savings-and-loan offices, provoking no action by President Bush, however, because "exit polling at shopping malls showed that people thought he was handling it O.K."

> The President decided not to interfere with the takeover attempts in the savings-and-loan industry and to pay the hundred and sixty-six billion dollars, not as a ransom of any type but as ordinary government support, plain and simple, nothing irregular about it, and the Huns and the Vandals rode away, carrying their treasure with them, and the Goths sailed away up Lake Michigan.

Keillor's satire left me full of admiration—first for an act of humor so original, but also for expressing the citizen outrage I hadn't found a way to express. All I had been able to muster was helpless anger that my grandchildren in their old age would still be paying for Bush's rescue of the industry that the greedy hordes had plundered.

But there's no law that says humor has to make a point. Pure nonsense is a joy forever, as Keats didn't quite say. I love to see a writer flying high, just for the hell of it. The following two excerpts, from recent pieces by Ian Frazier and John Updike, are 100 percent off-the-wall; nothing written during America's earlier golden ages was any funnier. Frazier's piece is called "Dating Your Mom," and it begins like this:

In today's fast-moving, transient, rootless society, where people meet and make love and part without ever really touching, the relationship every guy already has with his own mother is too valuable to ignore. Here is a grown, experienced, loving woman—one you do not have to go to a party or a singles bar to meet, one you do not have to go to great lengths to get to know. There are hundreds of times when you and your mother are thrown together naturally, without the tension that usually accompanies courtship—just the two of you, alone. All you need is a little presence of mind to take advantage of these situations. Say your mom is driving you downtown in the car to buy you a new pair of slacks. First, find a nice station on the car radio, one that she likes. Get into the pleasant lull of freeway driving—tires humming along the pavement, air conditioner on max. Then turn to look at her across the front seat and say something like, "You know, you've really kept your shape, Mom, and don't think I haven't noticed." Or suppose she comes into your room to bring you some clean socks. Take her by the wrist, pull her close, and say, "Mom, you're the most fascinating woman I've ever met." Probably she'll tell you to cut out the foolishness, but I can guarantee you one thing: she will never tell your dad. Possibly she would find it hard to say, "Dear, Piper just made a pass at me," or possibly she is secretly flattered, but whatever the reason, she will keep it to herself until the day comes when she is no longer ashamed to tell the world of your love.

Updike's piece, "Glad Rags," though no less an act of bungee-jumping, bringing him within inches of the rocks at the bottom of the gorge, has a disturbing core of reality. Not only does it flirt with some of the nation's darker suppositions about J. Edgar Hoover; it deals with high-ranking Americans of recent memory—a sainted President and his cabinet. What makes it work, for all its seeming frivolity, is Updike's meticulous research. You can bet that all the details—names, dates and fashion terminology—are correct:

> To those of us who were alive and sartorially active at the time, it was saddening to read in the Boston *Globe* recently the allegation, by "New York socialite" Susan Rosenstiel, that in 1958 J. Edgar Hoover was parading around in a Plaza Hotel suite wearing women's clothes: "He was wearing a fluffy black dress, very fluffy, with flounces, and lace stockings and high heels, and a black curly wig." I was saddened to think that future generations, trying to grasp the peculiar splendor and excitement of high-echelon cross-dressing during Eisenhower's second term, will imagine that dowdy bit of black fluff, with its fussy flounces and matching wig, to have been *très à la mode,* when the truth is we all considered J. Edgar something of a frump.
>
> Ike, for instance, dear Ike with his infallible instincts, would never have let himself be caught in lace stockings, even though he did have the legs for them. I remember, within a month of Saint Laurent's 1958 collection for Dior, Ike coming out in a stunning cobalt-blue wool trapeze, with white open-backed heels and a false chignon. That very day, if memory serves, he had sent five thousand marines to Lebanon, and not a hair out of place. It was with this outfit—or was it a belted A-line from the previous year?—that he sported a flowered silk neck cloth, when scarves were still thought to be strictly for babushkas. He was very conservative as to hemlines, however; when Saint Laurent lifted skirts to the knee in 1959, the President waited three months for Congress to decide the issue, and then, losing all patience, switched to

Balenciaga with a stroke of his pen. Thenceforth, to the very end of his administration, he stuck with long-waisted day dresses in neutral duns and beiges.

John Foster Dulles, on the other hand, favored a slinky-pajama look and pastel pants suits with a touch of glimmer in the fabric. Oodles of bangles, upswept blond wigs, and pompommed mules. Despite his staunch anti-Communism, he was oddly partial to red, though I believe on good authority that Sherman Adams at least once took Foster aside and made the point that bright colors did not become a big-boned frame. Sherman, though he was undone by vicuña, lingers in my mind's eye as a creature of whimsical ostrich-feather boas and enchantments in lightly starched lemon voile. . . .

Enjoyment, finally, is what all humorists must convey—the idea that they are having a terrific time, and this notion of cranked-up audacity is what I wanted my Yale students to grapple with. At first I told them to write in one of the existing humor forms—satire, parody, lampoon, etc.—and not to use "I" or to write from their own experience. I assigned the same topic to the whole class, bringing in some absurdity I had noticed in the newspaper. The students jumped boldly into free association, surrealism and nonsense. They found that it was possible to slip off the chains of logic and have fun making a serious point within a given humor form. They were heavily under the influence of Woody Allen's non sequiturs ("For this the Rabbi bashes his head in, which, according to the Torah, is one of the most subtle methods of showing concern").

After about four weeks, fatigue set in. The students learned that they were capable of writing humor. But they had also learned how tiring it is to sustain a weekly act of comic invention, writing in other voices. It was time to slow down their metabolism—to start them writing in their own voice, about their own lives. I declared a moratorium on Woody Allen and said I would tell them when they could read him again. That day never came.

I adopted the Chic Young principle—stick to what you know—and began to read from writers who use humor as a vein that runs quietly through their work. One piece was E. B. White's "The Eye of Edna," in which White recalls waiting on his Maine farm for the arrival of Hurricane Edna while listening for several days to inane radio reports of its progress. It's a perfect essay, full of wisdom and gentle wit.

Another writer whose work I excavated was Stephen Leacock, a Canadian. I recalled him from my boyhood as hilarious but was afraid that, as often happens in looking up old friends, he would turn out to be merely "comical." His pieces, however, had survived the erosion of time, and one that I particularly remembered—"My Financial Career," in which he tries to open a bank account with $56—still seems the model piece of humor on how rattled we all become when dealing with banks, libraries and other uptight institutions. Rereading Leacock reminded me that another function of the humorist is to represent himself as the victim or dunce, helpless in most situations. It's therapy for readers, enabling them to feel superior to the writer, or at least to identify with a fellow victim. A humorist who deals with ordinary life never runs out of material, as Erma Bombeck enjoyably proved over many decades.

So that was the direction in which our Yale humor class began to move. Many of the students wrote about their families. We ran into problems, mainly of exaggeration, and gradually solved them, trying to achieve control, cutting the extra sentence that explains a funny point that is already implicit. A hard decision was to know how much exaggeration was allowable and how much was too much. One student wrote a funny piece about what a terrible cook his grandmother was. When I praised it he said she was really a very good cook. I said I was sorry to hear it—somehow the piece now seemed less funny. He asked if that made a difference. I said it didn't make a difference in this piece, since I had enjoyed it without knowing it was untrue, but that I thought he would last longer if he started from the truth rather than from invention—surely one secret of James Thurber's longevity as a major American humorist. In Thurber's "The Night the Bed Fell" we know that he has slightly enlarged the facts. But we also know that *something* happened to the bed that night in the attic.

In short, our class began by striving first for humor and hoping to wing a few truths along the way. We ended by striving for truth and hoping to add humor along the way. Ultimately we realized that the two are intertwined.

PART IV

Attitudes

20

The Sound of Your Voice

I wrote one book about baseball and one about jazz. But it never occurred to me to write one of them in sports English and the other in jazz English. I tried to write them both in the best English I could, in my usual style. Though the books were widely different in subject, I wanted readers to know that they were hearing from the same person. It was *my* book about baseball and *my* book about jazz. Other writers would write *their* book. My commodity as a writer, whatever I'm writing about, is me. And your commodity is you. Don't alter your voice to fit your subject. Develop one voice that readers will recognize when they hear it on the page, a voice that's enjoyable not only in its musical line but in its avoidance of sounds that would cheapen its tone: breeziness and condescension and clichés.

Let's start with breeziness.

There is a kind of writing that sounds so relaxed that you think you hear the author talking to you. E. B. White was probably its best practitioner, though many other masters of the style—James Thurber, V. S. Pritchett, Lewis Thomas—come to mind. I'm partial to it because it's a style that I've always tried to write myself. The common assumption is that the style is effortless. In fact the opposite is true: the effortless style is achieved by strenuous effort and constant refining. The nails of grammar and syntax are in place and the English is as good as the writer can make it.

Here's how a typical piece by E. B. White begins:

I spent several days and nights in mid-September with an ailing pig and I feel driven to account for this stretch of time, more particularly since the pig died at last, and I lived, and things might easily have gone the other way round and none left to do the accounting.

The sentence is so folksy that we imagine ourselves sitting on the porch of White's house in Maine. White is in a rocking chair, puffing on a pipe, and the words just tumble out in his story-teller's voice. But look at the sentence again. Nothing about it is accidental. It's a disciplined act of writing. The grammar is formal, the words are plain and precise, and the cadences are those of a poet. That's the effortless style at its best: a methodical act of composition that disarms us with its generated warmth. The writer sounds confident; he's not trying to ingratiate himself with the reader.

Inexperienced writers miss this point. They think that all they have to do to achieve a casual effect is to be "just folks"— good old Betty or Bob chatting over the back fence. They want to be a pal to the reader. They're so eager not to appear formal that they don't even try to write good English. What they write is the breezy style.

How would a breezy writer handle E. B. White's vigil with the pig? He might sound like this:

> Ever stay up late babysitting for a sick porker? Believe you me, a guy can lose a heckuva lot of shut-eye. I did that gig for three nights back in September and my better half thought I'd lost my marbles. (Just kidding, Pam!) Frankly, the whole deal kind of bummed me out. Because, you see, the pig up and died on me. To tell you the truth, I wasn't feeling in the pink myself, so I suppose it could have been yours truly and not old Porky who kicked the bucket. And you can bet your bottom dollar Mr. Pig wasn't going to write a book about it!

There's no need to labor all the reasons why this stuff is so terrible. It's crude. It's corny. It's verbose. It's contemptuous of the English language. It's condescending. (I stop reading writers who say "You see.") But the most pathetic thing about the breezy style is that it's harder to read than good English. In the writer's attempt to ease the reader's journey he has littered the path with obstacles: cheap slang, shoddy sentences, windy philosophizing. E. B. White's style is much easier to read. He knows that the tools of grammar haven't survived for so many centuries by chance; they are props the reader needs and subconsciously wants. Nobody ever stopped reading E. B. White or V. S. Pritchett because the writing was too good. But readers will stop reading you if they think you are talking down to them. Nobody wants to be patronized.

Write with respect for the English language at its best—and for readers at their best. If you're smitten by the urge to try the breezy style, read what you've written aloud and see if you like the sound of your voice.

Finding a voice that your readers will enjoy is largely a matter of taste. Saying that isn't much help—taste is a quality so intangible that it can't even be defined. But we know it when we meet it. A woman with taste in clothes delights us with her ability to turn herself out in a combination that's not only stylish and surprising, but exactly right. She knows what works and what doesn't.

For writers and other creative artists, knowing what *not* to do is a major component of taste. Two jazz pianists may be equally proficient. The one with taste will put every note to useful work in telling his or her story; the one without taste will drench us in ripples and other unnecessary ornaments. Painters with taste will trust their eye to tell them what needs to be on the canvas and what doesn't; a painter without taste will give us a landscape that's too pretty, or too cluttered, or too gaudy—anyway, too something. A graphic designer with taste knows that less is more: that design is the servant of the written word. A designer without taste will smother the writing in background tints and swirls and decorative frills.

I realize that I'm trying to pin down a matter that's subjective; one person's beautiful object is somebody else's kitsch. Taste can also change from one decade to another—yesterday's charm is derided today as junk, but it will be back in vogue tomorrow, certified again as charming. So why do I even raise the issue? Just to remind you that it exists. Taste is an invisible current that runs through writing, and you should be aware of it.

Sometimes, in fact, it's visible. Every art form has a core of verities that survive the fickleness of time. There must be something innately pleasing in the proportions of the Parthenon; Western man continues to let the Greeks of two thousand years ago design his public buildings, as anyone walking around Washington, D.C., soon discovers. The fugues of Bach have a timeless elegance that's rooted in the timeless laws of mathematics.

Does writing have any such guideposts for us? Not many; writing is the expression of every person's individuality, and we know what we like when it comes along. Again, however, much can be gained by knowing what to omit. Clichés, for instance. If a writer lives in blissful ignorance that clichés are the kiss of death, if in the final analysis he leaves no stone unturned to use them, we can infer that he lacks an instinct for what gives language its freshness. Faced with a choice between the novel and the banal, he goes unerringly for the banal. His voice is the voice of a hack.

Not that clichés are easy to stamp out. They are everywhere in the air around us, familiar friends just waiting to be helpful, ready to express complex ideas for us in the shorthand form of metaphor. That's how they became clichés in the first place, and even careful writers use quite a few on their first draft. But after that we are given a chance to clean them out. Clichés are one of the things you should keep listening for when you rewrite and read your successive drafts aloud. Notice how incriminating they sound, convicting you of being satisfied to use the same old chestnuts instead of making an effort to replace them with fresh phrases of your own. Clichés are the enemy of taste.

Extend the point beyond individual clichés to your larger use of language. Again, freshness is crucial. Taste chooses words that have surprise, strength and precision. Non-taste slips into the breezy vernacular of the alumni magazine's class notes—a world where people in authority are the top brass or the powers that be. What exactly is wrong with "the top brass"? Nothing—and everything. Taste knows that it's better to call people in authority what they are: officials, executives, chairmen, presidents, directors, managers. Non-taste reaches for the corny synonym, which has the further disadvantage of being imprecise; exactly *which* company officers are the top brass? Non-taste uses "umpteenth." And "zillions." Non-taste uses "period": "She said she didn't want to hear any more about it. Period."

But finally taste is a mixture of qualities that are beyond analyzing: an ear that can hear the difference between a sentence that limps and a sentence that lilts, an intuition that knows when a casual or a vernacular phrase dropped into a formal sentence will not only sound right but will seem to be the inevitable choice. (E. B. White was a master of that balancing act.) Does this mean that taste can be learned? Yes and no. Perfect taste, like perfect pitch, is a gift from God. But a certain amount can be acquired. The trick is to study writers who have it.

Never hesitate to imitate another writer. Imitation is part of the creative process for anyone learning an art or a craft. Bach and Picasso didn't spring full-blown as Bach and Picasso; they needed models. This is especially true of writing. Find the best writers in the fields that interest you and read their work aloud. Get their voice and their taste into your ear—their attitude toward language. Don't worry that by imitating them you'll lose your own voice and your own identity. Soon enough you will shed those skins and become who you are supposed to become.

By reading other writers you also plug yourself into a longer tradition that enriches you. Sometimes you will tap a vein of eloquence or racial memory that gives your writing a depth it could never attain on its own. Let me illustrate what I mean by a roundabout route.

Ordinarily I don't read the proclamations issued by state officials to designate important days of the year as important days of the year. But in 1976, when I was teaching at Yale, the governor of Connecticut, Ella Grasso, had the pleasant idea of reissuing the Thanksgiving Proclamation written 40 years earlier by Governor Wilbur Cross, which she called "a masterpiece of eloquence." I often wonder whether eloquence has vanished from American life, or whether we even still consider it a goal worth striving for. So I studied Governor Cross's words to see how they had weathered the passage of time, that cruel judge of the rhetoric of earlier generations. I was delighted to find that I agreed with Governor Grasso. It was a piece written by a master:

Time out of mind at this turn of the seasons when the hardy oak leaves rustle in the wind and the frost gives a tang

to the air and the dusk falls early and the friendly evenings
lengthen under the heel of Orion, it has seemed good to our
people to join together in praising the Creator and Preserver,
who has brought us by a way that we did not know to the end
of another year. In observance of this custom, I appoint
Thursday, the 26th of November, as a day of Public Thanksgiving for the blessings that have been our common lot and
have placed our beloved state with the favored regions of
earth—for all the creature comforts: the yield of the soil that
has fed us and the richer yield from labor of every kind that
has sustained our lives—and for all those things, as dear as
breath to the body, that quicken man's faith in his manhood,
that nourish and strengthen his word and act; for honor held
above price; for steadfast courage and zeal in the long, long
search after truth; for liberty and for justice freely granted by
each to his fellow and so as freely enjoyed; and for the crowning glory and mercy of peace upon our land—that we may
humbly take heart of these blessings as we gather once again
with solemn and festive rites to keep our Harvest Home.

Governor Grasso added a postscript urging the citizens of
Connecticut "to renew their dedication to the spirit of sacrifice
and commitment which the Pilgrims invoked during their first
harsh winter in the New World," and I made a mental note to
look at Orion that night. I was glad to be reminded that I was
living in one of the favored regions of earth. I was also glad to be
reminded that peace is not the only crowning glory to be thankful for; so is the English language when it is gracefully used for
the public good. The cadences of Jefferson, Lincoln, Churchill,
Roosevelt and Adlai Stevenson came rolling down to me. (The
cadences of Eisenhower, Nixon and Bush did not.)
I posted the Thanksgiving proclamation on a bulletin board
for my students to enjoy. From their comments I realized that
several of them thought I was being facetious. Knowing my

obsession with simplicity, they assumed that I regarded Governor Cross's message as florid excess.

The incident left me with several questions. Had I sprung Wilbur Cross's prose on a generation that had never been exposed to nobility of language as a means of addressing the populace? I couldn't recall a single attempt since John F. Kennedy's inaugural speech in 1961. (Mario Cuomo and Jesse Jackson have partly restored my faith.) This was a generation reared on television, where the picture is valued more than the word—where the word, in fact, is devalued, used as mere chatter, and often misused and mispronounced. It was also a generation reared on music—songs and rhythms meant primarily to be heard and felt. With so much noise in the air, was any American child being trained to listen? Was anyone calling attention to the majesty of a well-constructed sentence?

My other question raised a more subtle mystery: what is the line that separates eloquence from bombast? Why are we exalted by the words of Wilbur Cross and anesthetized by the speeches of most politicians and public officials who ply us with oratorical ruffles and flourishes?

Part of the answer takes us back to taste. A writer with an ear for language will reach for fresh imagery and avoid phrases that are trite. The hack will reach for those very clichés, thinking he will enrich his thoughts with currency that is, as he would put it, tried and true. Another part of the answer lies in simplicity. Writing that will endure tends to consist of words that are short and strong; words that sedate are words of three, four and five syllables, mostly of Latin origin, many of them ending in "ion" and embodying a vague concept. In Wilbur Cross's Thanksgiving Proclamation there are no four-syllable words and only ten three-syllable words, three of which are proper nouns he was stuck with. Notice how many of the governor's words are anything but vague: leaves, wind, frost, air, evening, earth, comforts, soil, labor, breath, body, justice, courage, peace, land, rites, home. They are homely words in the best sense—they catch the rhythm of the seasons and the dailiness of life. Also notice that all of them are nouns. After verbs, plain nouns are your strongest tools; they resonate with emotion.

But ultimately eloquence runs on a deeper current. It moves us with what it leaves unsaid, touching off echoes in what we already know from our reading, our religion and our heritage. Eloquence invites us to bring some part of ourselves to the transaction. It was no accident that Lincoln's speeches resounded with echoes of the King James Bible; he knew it almost by heart from his boyhood, and he had so soaked himself in its sonorities that his formal English was more Elizabethan than American. The Second Inaugural Address reverberates with Biblical phrases and paraphrases: "It may seem strange that any men should dare to ask a just God's assistance in wringing their bread from the sweat of other men's faces, but let us judge not, that we be not judged." The first half of the sentence borrows a metaphor from Genesis, the second half reshapes a famous command in Matthew, and "a just God" is from Isaiah.

If this speech affects me more than any other American document, it's not only because I know that Lincoln was killed five weeks later, or because I'm moved by all the pain that culminated in his plea for a reconciliation that would have malice toward none and charity for all. It's also because Lincoln tapped some of Western man's oldest teachings about slavery, clemency and judgment. His words carried stern overtones for the men and women who heard him in 1865, reared, as he was, on the Bible. But even in the late 1990s it's hard not to feel a wrath almost too ancient to grasp in Lincoln's notion that God might will the Civil War to continue "until all the wealth piled by the bondsman's two hundred and fifty years of unrequited toil shall be sunk, and until every drop of blood drawn with the lash shall be paid by another drawn with the sword, as was said three thousand years ago, so still it must be said 'the judgments of the Lord are true and righteous altogether.'"

Wilbur Cross's Thanksgiving Proclamation also echoes with truths that we know in our bones. To such mysteries as the changing of the seasons and the bounty of the earth we bring strong emotions of our own. Who hasn't looked with awe at Orion? To such democratic processes as "the long search after truth" and "liberty and justice freely granted" we bring fragments of our own searches after truth, our own grantings and receivings, in a nation where so many human rights have been won and so many still elude us. Governor Cross doesn't take our time to explain these processes, and I'm grateful to him for that. I hate to think how many clichés a hack orator would marshal to tell us far more—and nourish us far less.

Therefore remember the uses of the past when you tell your story. What moves us in writing that has regional or ethnic roots—Southern writing, African-American writing, Jewish-American writing—is the sound of voices far older than the narrator's, talking in cadences that are more than ordinarily rich. Toni Morrison, one of the most eloquent of black writers, once said: "I remember the language of the people I grew up with. Language was so important to them. All that power was in it. And grace and metaphor. Some of it was very formal and Biblical, because the habit is that when you have something important to say you go into parable, if you're from Africa, or you go into another level of language. I wanted to use language that way, because my feeling was that a black novel was not black because I wrote it, or because there were black people in it, or because it was about black things. It was the style. It had a certain style. It was inevitable. I couldn't describe it, but I could produce it."

Go with what seems inevitable in your own heritage. Embrace it and it may lead you to eloquence.

2 1

Enjoyment, Fear and Confidence

As a boy I never wanted to grow up to be a writer, or—God forbid—an author. I wanted to be a newspaperman, and the newspaper I wanted to be a man on was the *New York Herald Tribune*. Reading it every morning, I loved the sense of enjoyment it conveyed. Everyone who worked on the paper—editors, writers, photographers, make-up men—was having a wonderful time. The articles usually had an extra touch of gracefulness, or humanity, or humor—some gift of themselves that the writers and editors enjoyed making to their readers. I thought they were putting out the paper just for me. To be one of those editors and writers was my idea of the ultimate American dream.

That dream came true when I returned home from World War II and got a job on the *Herald Tribune* staff. I brought with me my belief that a sense of enjoyment is a priceless attribute for a writer or for a publication, and I was now in the same room with the men and women who had first put that idea in my head. The great reporters wrote with warmth and gusto, and the great critics and columnists like Virgil Thomson and Red Smith wrote with elegance and with a mirthful confidence in their opinions. On the "split page"—as the first page of the second section was called, when papers only had two sections—the political column of Walter Lippmann, America's most venerated pundit, ran above the one-panel cartoon by H. T. Webster, creator of "The Timid Soul," who was also an American institution. I liked the insouciance that presented on the same page two features so different in gravity. Nobody thought of hustling Webster off to the comics section. Both men were giants, part of the same equation.

Among those blithe souls a city-desk reporter named John O'Reilly, who was admired for his deadpan coverage of human-interest and animal-interest stories, managed to make whimsy a serious beat. I remember his annual article about the woolly bear, the caterpillar whose brown and black stripes are said to foretell by their width whether the coming winter will be harsh or mild. Every fall O'Reilly would drive to Bear Mountain Park with the photographer Nat Fein, best known for his Pulitzer Prize–winning shot of Babe Ruth's farewell at Yankee Stadium, to observe a sample of woolly bears crossing the road, and his article was written in mock-scientific museum-expedition style, duly portentous. The paper always ran the story at the bottom of page one under a three-column head, along with a cut of a woolly bear, its stripes none too distinct. In the spring O'Reilly would write a follow-up piece telling his readers whether the woolly bears had been right, and nobody blamed him—or them—if they hadn't. The point was to give everybody a good time.

I've made that *Herald Tribune* sense of enjoyment my credo as a writer and an editor. Writing is such lonely work that I try to keep myself cheered up. If something strikes me as funny in the act of writing, I throw it in just to amuse myself. If I think it's funny I assume that a few other people will find it funny, and that seems to me to be a good day's work. It doesn't bother me that a certain number of readers will not be amused; I know that a fair chunk of the population has no sense of humor—no idea that there are people in the world trying to entertain them.

When I was teaching at Yale I invited the humorist S. J. Perelman to talk to my students, and one of them asked him, "What does it take to be a comic writer?" He said, "It takes audacity and exuberance and gaiety, and the most important one is audacity." Then he said: "The reader has to feel that the writer is feeling good." The sentence went off in my head like a Roman candle: it stated the entire case for enjoyment. Then he added: "Even if he isn't." That sentence hit me almost as hard, because I knew that Perelman's life contained more than the usual share of depression and travail. Yet he went to his typewriter every day and made the English language dance. How could he not be feeling good? He cranked it up.

Writers have to jump-start themselves at the moment of performance, no less than actors and dancers and painters and musicians. There are some writers who sweep us along so strongly in the current of their energy—Norman Mailer, Tom Wolfe, Toni Morrison, William F. Buckley, Jr., Hunter Thompson, David Foster Wallace—that we assume that when they go to work the words just flow. Nobody thinks of the effort they make every morning to turn on the switch.

You also have to turn on the switch. Nobody is going to do it for you.

Unfortunately, an equally strong negative current—fear—is at work. Fear of writing gets planted in most Americans at an early age, usually at school, and it never entirely goes away. The blank piece of paper or the blank computer screen, waiting to be filled with our wonderful words, can freeze us into not writing any words at all, or writing words that are less than wonderful. I'm often dismayed by the sludge I see appearing on my screen if I approach writing as a task—the day's work—and not with some enjoyment. My only consolation is that I'll get another shot at those dismal sentences tomorrow and the next day and the day after. With each rewrite I try to force my personality onto the material.

Probably the biggest fear for nonfiction writers is the fear of not being able to bring off their assignment. With fiction it's a different situation. Because authors of fiction are writing about a world of their own invention, often in an allusive style that they have also invented (Thomas Pynchon, Don DeLillo), we have no right to tell them, "That's wrong." We can only say, "It doesn't work for me." Nonfiction writers get no such break. They are infinitely accountable: to the facts, to the people they interviewed, to the locale of their story and to the events that happened there. They are also accountable to their craft and all its perils of excess and disorder: losing the reader, confusing the reader, boring the reader, not keeping the reader engaged from beginning to end. With every inaccuracy of reporting and every misstep of craft we can say, "That's wrong."

How can you fight off all those fears of disapproval and failure? One way to generate confidence is to write about subjects that interest you and that you care about. The poet Allen Ginsberg, another writer who came to Yale to talk to my students, was asked if there was a moment when he consciously decided to become a poet. Ginsberg said, "It wasn't quite a choice—it was a realization. I was twenty-eight and I had a job as a market researcher. One day I told my psychiatrist that what I really wanted to do was to quit my job and just write poetry. And the psychiatrist said, 'Why not?' And I said, 'What would the American Psychoanalytical Association say?' And he said, 'There's no party line.' So I did."

We'll never know how big a loss that was for the field of market research. But it was a big moment for poetry. There's no party line: good advice for writers. You can be your own party line. Red Smith, delivering the eulogy at the funeral of a fellow sportswriter, said, "Dying is no big deal. Living is the trick." One of the reasons I admired Red Smith was that he wrote about sports for 55 years, with grace and humor, without succumbing to the pressure, which was the ruin of many sportswriters, that he ought to be writing about something "serious." He found in sportswriting what he wanted to do and what he loved doing, and because it was right for him he said more important things about American values than many writers who wrote about serious subjects—so seriously that nobody could read them.

Living is the trick. Writers who write interestingly tend to be men and women who keep themselves interested. That's almost the whole point of becoming a writer. I've used writing to give myself an interesting life and a continuing education. If you write about subjects you think you would enjoy knowing about, your enjoyment will show in what you write. Learning is a tonic.

That doesn't mean you won't be nervous when you go forth into unfamiliar terrain. As a nonfiction writer you'll be thrown again and again into specialized worlds, and you'll worry that you're not qualified to bring the story back. I feel that anxiety every time I embark on a new project. I felt it when I went to Bradenton to write my baseball book, *Spring Training*. Although I've been a baseball fan all my life, I had never done any sports reporting, never interviewed a professional athlete. Strictly, I had no credentials; any of the men I approached with my notebook—managers, coaches, players, umpires, scouts—could have asked, "What else have you written about baseball?" But nobody did. They didn't ask because I had another kind of credential: sincerity. It was obvious to those men that I really wanted to know how they did their work. Remember this when you enter new territory and need a shot of confidence. Your best credential is yourself.

Also remember that your assignment may not be as narrow as you think. Often it will turn out to touch some unexpected corner of your experience or your education, enabling you to broaden the story with strengths of your own. Every such reduction of the unfamiliar will reduce your fear.

That lesson was brought home to me in 1992 when I got a call from an editor at *Audubon* asking if I would write an article for the magazine. I said I wouldn't. I'm a fourth-generation New Yorker, my roots deep in the cement. "That wouldn't be right for me, or for you, or for *Audubon*," I told the editor. I've never accepted an assignment I didn't think I was suited for, and I'm quick to tell editors that they should look for someone else. The *Audubon* editor replied—as good editors should—that he was sure we could come up with something, and a few weeks later he called to say that the magazine had decided it was time for a new article on Roger Tory Peterson, the man who made America a nation of birdwatchers, his *Field Guide to the Birds* a best-seller since 1934. Was I interested? I said I didn't know enough about birds. The only one I can identify for sure is the pigeon, a frequent caller at my Manhattan windowsill.

I need to feel a certain rapport with the person I'll be writing about. The Peterson assignment wasn't one that I originated; it came looking for me. Almost every profile I've written has been of someone whose work I knew and had an affection for: such creative souls as the cartoonist Chic Young ("Blondie"), the songwriter Harold Arlen, the British actor Peter Sellers and the British travel writer Norman Lewis. My gratitude for the pleasure of their company over the years was a source of energy when I sat down to write. If you want your writing to convey enjoyment, write about people you respect. Writing to destroy and to scandalize can be as destructive to the writer as it is to the subject.

Something came up, however, that changed my mind about the *Audubon* offer. I happened to see a PBS television documentary called "A Celebration of Birds," which summed up Roger Tory Peterson's life and work. The film had so much beauty that I wanted to know more about him. What caught my attention was that Peterson was still going at full momentum at 84—painting four hours a day and photographing birds in habitats all over the world. That *did* interest me. Birds aren't my subject, but survivors are: how old people keep going. I remembered that Peterson lived in a Connecticut town not far from where our family goes in the summer. I could just drive over and meet him; if the vibrations weren't right, nothing would be lost except a gallon of gas. I told the *Audubon* editor that I would try something informal—"a visit with Roger Tory Peterson," not a major profile.

Of course it did turn into a major profile, 4,000 words long, because as soon as I saw Peterson's studio I realized that to think of him as an ornithologist, as I always had, was to miss the point of his life. He was above all an artist. It was his skill as a painter that had made his knowledge of birds accessible to millions and had given him his authority as a writer, editor and conservationist. I asked him about his early teachers and mentors—major American artists like John Sloan and Edmund Dickinson—and about the influence of the great bird painters James Audubon and Louis Agassiz Fuertes, and my story became an art story and a teaching story as well as a bird story, engaging many of my interests. It was also a survivor story; in his mid–80s Peterson was on a schedule that would tax a man of 50.

The moral for nonfiction writers is: think broadly about your assignment. Don't assume that an article for *Audubon* has to be strictly about nature, or an article for *Car & Driver* strictly about cars. Push the boundaries of your subject and see where it takes you. Bring some part of your own life to it; it's not your version of the story until you write it.

As for *my* version of the Peterson story, not long after it ran in *Audubon* my wife found a message on our home answering machine that said, "Is this the William Zinsser who writes about nature?" She thought it was hilarious, and it was. But in fact my article was received by the birding community as a definitive portrait of Peterson. I mention this to give confidence to all nonfiction writers: a point of craft. If you master the tools of the trade—the fundamentals of interviewing and of orderly construction—and if you bring to the assignment your general intelligence and your humanity, you can write about *any* subject. That's your ticket to an interesting life.

Still, it's hard not to be intimidated by the expertise of the expert. You think, "This man knows so much about his field, I'm too dumb to interview him. He'll think I'm stupid." The reason he knows so much about his field is because it's his field; you're a generalist trying to make his work accessible to the public. That means prodding him to clarify statements that are so obvious to him that he assumes they are obvious to everyone else. Trust your common sense to figure out what you need to know, and don't be afraid to ask a dumb question. If the expert thinks you're dumb, that's his problem.

Your test should be: is the expert's first answer sufficient? Usually it's not. I learned that when I signed up for a second expedition into Peterson territory. An editor at Rizzoli, the publisher of art books, called to say that the firm was preparing a coffee-table volume on "The Art and Photography of Roger Tory Peterson," with hundreds of color plates. An 8,000-word text was needed, and as the new Peterson authority I was asked to write it. Talk about hilarious.

I told the editor that I made it a point never to write the same story twice. I had written my *Audubon* article as carefully as I could the first time and wouldn't be able to rework it. He would be welcome, however, to acquire and reprint my article in his book. He agreed to that if I would write an additional 4,000 words—invisible weaving—that would deal mainly with Peterson's methods as an artist and a photographer.

That sounded interesting, and I went back to Peterson with a new set of questions, more technical than the ones I had put to him for *Audubon*. That audience had wanted to hear about a life. Now I was writing for readers who wanted to know how the artist created his art, and my questions got right down to process and technique. We began with painting.

"I call my work 'mixed media,'" Peterson told me, "because my main purpose is to instruct. I may start with transparent watercolors, then I go to gouache, then I give it a protective coat of acrylic, then I go over that with acrylics or a touch of pastel, or colored pencil, or pencil, or ink—anything that will do what I want."

I knew from my earlier interview that Peterson's first answer was seldom sufficient. He was a taciturn man, the son of Swedish immigrants, not given to amplitude. I asked him how his present technique differed from his previous methods.

"Right now I'm straddling," he said. "I'm trying to add more detail without losing the simplified effect." Then he stopped again.

But why did he feel that he needed more detail at this late point in his life?

"Over the years so many people have become familiar with the straight profile of my birds," he said, "that they've begun to want something more: the look of feathers, or a more three-dimensional feeling."

After we got through with painting we moved on to photography. Peterson recalled every bird-shooting camera he ever owned, starting at age 13 with a Primo #9, which used glass plates and had bellows, and ended with praise for such modern technology as auto-focus and the fill-in flash. Not being a photographer, I had never heard of auto-focus or the fill-in flash, but I only had to reveal my stupidity to learn why they are so helpful. Auto-focus: "If you can get the bird in your viewfinder the camera will do the rest." Fill-in flash: "Film never sees as much as you see. The human eye sees detail in the shadows, but the fill-in flash enables the camera to pick up that detail."

Technology, however, is only technology, Peterson reminded me. "Many people think good equipment makes it easy," he said. "They're deceived into thinking the camera does it all." He knew what he meant by that, but *I* needed to know why the camera doesn't do it all. When I pressed him with my "Why not?" and my "What else?" I got not just one answer but three:

"As a photographer, you bring your eye and a sense of composition to the process, and also warmth—you don't shoot pictures at high noon, for instance, or at the beginning or the end of the day. You're also mindful of the quality of light; a thin overcast can do nice things. Knowledge of the animal is also a tremendous help: anticipating what a bird will do. You can anticipate such activities as a feeding frenzy, when birds feed on fish traveling in small groups. Feeding frenzies are important to a photographer because one of the basic things birds do is eat, and they'll put up with you a lot longer if they're eating. In fact, they'll often ignore you."

So we proceeded, Mr. Expert and Mr. Stupid, until I had extracted many ideas that I found interesting. "I go halfway back to Audubon," Peterson said—*that* was interesting—"so I have a feeling for the changes that have taken place because of the environmental movement." In his boyhood, he recalled, every kid with a slingshot would shoot birds, and many species had been killed off or brought close to extermination by hunters who slaughtered them for their plumes, or to sell to restaurants, or for sport. The good news, which he had lived long enough to see, was that many species had made a comeback from their narrow escape, helped by a citizenry that now takes an active role in protecting birds and their habitats. Then he said: "The attitude of people towards birds has changed the attitude of birds towards people."

That was interesting. I'm struck by how often as a writer I say to myself, "That's interesting." If you find yourself saying it, pay attention and follow your nose. Trust your curiosity to connect with the curiosity of your readers.

What did Peterson mean about birds changing their attitudes?

"Crows are becoming tamer," he said. "Gulls have increased—they're the cleanup crew at garbage dumps. The Least Tern has taken to nesting on top of shopping malls; a few years ago there were a thousand pair on the roof of the Singing River Mall in Gautier, Mississippi. Mockingbirds are particularly fond of malls—they like the planting, especially the multiflora rose; its tiny hips are small enough for them to swallow. They also enjoy the bustle of shopping malls—they sit there and direct the traffic."

We had been talking for several hours in Peterson's studio. The studio was a small outpost of the arts and sciences—easels, paints, paintbrushes, paintings, prints, maps, cameras, photographic equipment, tribal masks, and shelves of reference books and journals—and at the end of my visit, as he was walking me out, I said, "Have I seen everything?" Often you'll get your best material after you put your pencil away, in the chitchat of leave-taking. The person being interviewed, off the hook after the hard work of making his or her life presentable to a stranger, thinks of a few important afterthoughts.

When I asked whether I had seen everything, Peterson said, "Would you like to see my collection of birds?" I said I certainly would. He led me down an outside staircase to a cellar door, which he unlocked, ushering me into a basement full of cabinets and drawers—the familiar furniture of scientific storage, reminiscent of every small college museum that never got modernized. Darwin might have used such drawers.

"I've got two thousand specimens down here that I use for research," he told me. "Most of them are around a hundred years old, and they're still useful." He pulled open a drawer and took out a bird and showed me the tag, which said ACORN

WOODPECKER, APRIL 10, 1882. "Think of it! This bird is 112 years old," he said. He opened some other drawers and gently held several other late Victorians for me to ponder—a link to the presidency of Grover Cleveland.

The Rizzoli book, with its stunning paintings and photographs, was published in 1995, and Peterson died a year later, his quest finally over, having sighted "scarcely more than 4,500" of the world's 9,000 species of birds. Did I enjoy the time I spent on the two articles? I can't really say I did; Peterson was too dour for that, not much fun. But I enjoyed having brought off a complicated story that took me outside my normal experience. I also had bagged a rare bird of my own, and when I put Peterson away in a drawer with my other collected specimens I thought: that was interesting.

—⊸⊸⊸—

The Tyranny of the Final Product

In the writing course called "People and Places" that I teach at the New School, in Manhattan, students often tell me they have an idea for an article that would be perfect for *New York*, or for *Sports Illustrated*, or for some other magazine. That's the last thing I want to hear. They can already picture their story in print: the headline, the layout, the photographs and, best of all, the byline. Now all they have to do is write it.

This fixation on the finished article causes writers a lot of trouble, deflecting them from all the earlier decisions that have to be made to determine its shape and voice and content. It's a very American kind of trouble. We are a culture that worships the winning result: the league championship, the high test score. Coaches are paid to win, teachers are valued for getting students into the best colleges. Less glamorous gains made along the way—learning, wisdom, growth, confidence, dealing with failure—aren't given the same respect because they can't be given a grade.

For writers the winning grade is the check. The question that professional authors get asked most often at writing conferences is "How can I sell my writing?" It's the only question I won't try to answer, partly because I'm not qualified—I have no idea what editors in today's market are looking for; I wish I did. But mainly it's because I have no interest in teaching writers how to sell. I want to teach them how to write. If the process is sound, the product will take care of itself, and sales are likely to follow.

That's the premise of my course at the New School. Better known by its original name, the New School for Social Research, it was founded in 1919 by liberal-minded scholars and has been one of the city's most vibrant colleges ever since. I like to teach there because I've always felt sympathetic to its historic role: to provide information that helps motivated adults to get on with their lives. I like arriving by subway for my evening class and being part of the rush of men and women entering the building and getting out of classes that have just ended.

I chose "people and places" as the focus of my course because together they are at the heart of expository writing. By concentrating on those two elements I thought I would be able to teach much of what nonfiction writers need to know: how to situate what they write in a particular place, and how to get the people who live in that place to talk about what makes it—or once made it—unique.

But I also wanted to conduct an experiment. As an editor and a teacher I've found that the most untaught and underestimated skill in nonfiction writing is how to organize a long article: how to put the jigsaw puzzle together. Writers are endlessly taught how to write a clear declarative sentence. But ask them to try something more extensive—an article or a book—and the sentences leach out all over the floor like marbles. Every editor of a lengthy manuscript knows that grim moment of irreversible chaos. The writer, his eye on the finish line, never gave enough thought to how to run the race.

I wondered if there was any way to wrest writers away from their infatuation with the completed act of writing. Suddenly I had a radical idea: I would teach a writing course in which no writing is required.

At our first session my class consisted—as it has ever since—of two dozen adults, ranging from their twenties to their sixties, mostly women. A few were journalists with small suburban newspapers and television stations and trade magazines. But on the whole they were people with everyday jobs who wanted to learn how to use writing to make sense of their lives: to find out who they were at that moment, who they once were, and what heritage formed them.

I devoted the first period to getting us all introduced and explaining some of the principles of writing about people and places. At the end I said: "Next week I want you to come here prepared to tell us about one place that's important to you that you'd like to write about. Tell us *why* you want to write about it and *how* you want to write about it." I've never been a teacher who likes to read student writing aloud unless it's unusually good; people are too vulnerable about what they have written. But I guessed that they wouldn't be self-conscious about what they were merely thinking. Thoughts haven't been committed to sacred paper; they can always be changed or rearranged or disowned. Still, I didn't know what to expect.

The first volunteer the following week was a young woman who said she wanted to write about her church, on upper Fifth Avenue, which had recently had a bad fire. Although the church was back in use, its walls were blackened and its wood was charred and it smelled of smoke. The woman found that unsettling, and she wanted to sort out what the fire meant to her as a parishioner and to the church. I asked her what she proposed to write. She said she might interview the minister, or the organist, or the firemen, or maybe the sexton, or the choirmaster.

"You've given us five good pieces by Francis X. Clines," I told her, referring to a *New York Times* reporter who writes local features warmly and well. "But they're not good enough for you, or for me, or for this course. I want you to go deeper. I want you to find some connection between yourself and the place you're writing about."

The woman asked what sort of piece I had in mind. I said I was reluctant to suggest one because the idea of the course was to think our way collectively to possible solutions. But since she was our first guinea pig I would give it a try. "When you go to church in the next few weeks," I said, "just sit there and think about the fire. After three or four Sundays the church is going to tell you what that fire means." Then I said: "God is going to tell that church to tell you what the fire means."

There was a small gasp in the classroom; Americans get squeamish at any mention of religion. But the students saw that I was serious, and from that moment they took my idea seriously, inviting the rest of us into their lives each week, telling us about some place that touched their interests or their emotions and trying to decide how to write about it. I would spend the first half of each class period teaching the craft and reading passages by nonfiction writers who had solved issues that the students were struggling with. The other half was our lab: a dissecting table of writers' organizational problems.

By far the biggest problem was compression: how to distill a coherent narrative from a tangled mass of facts and feelings and memories. "I want to write an article about the disappearance of small towns in Iowa," one woman told us, describing how the fabric of life in the Midwest had frayed since she was a girl on her grandparents' farm. It was a good American subject, valuable as social history. But nobody can write an article about the disappearance of small towns in Iowa; it would be all generalization and no humanity. The writer would have to write about *one* small town in Iowa and thereby tell her larger story, and even within that one town she would have to reduce her story still further: to one store, or one family, or one farmer. We talked about different approaches, and the writer gradually thought her story down to human scale.

Focus was another problem. Of all the possible stories that you might distill out of this place, which one is *your* story? One woman wanted to write about the house in Michigan where she grew up. Her mother had died, the house had been sold, and she was about to go home to help her father and her ten brothers and sisters dispose of the contents. Writing about the visit, she thought, would help her to understand her childhood in that large Catholic family, and she planned to start by interviewing all her brothers and sisters. I asked her if the story she wanted to write was her brothers' and sisters' story. No, she said, it was *her* story. In that case, I said, interviewing her brothers and sisters would be almost a complete waste of her time and energy. Only then did she begin to glimpse the proper shape of her story and prepare her mind for confronting the house and its possessions.

Another common problem had to do with voice and tense. A woman wanted to write about the public school she attended as a child in the Bronx, which she remembered vividly. She had recently visited the school, and now she didn't know what voice to use for her story. Should she write from the point of view of the girl who had been a pupil in the school, or as the woman she was today, bringing the wisdom of age to the credulities of childhood? That question has troubled everyone who ever tried to write a memoir: whose truth is the "right" truth? The question doesn't have one right answer, but it has to be settled in advance. Readers won't put up with vacillating between two perspectives and tones.

I was struck by how often my students' gropings led to a sudden revelation of the proper path, obvious to everyone in the room. A man would say that he wanted to try a piece about the town where he lived and would venture a possible approach: "I could write about X." X, however, was uninteresting, even to him, lacking any distinctiveness, and so were Y and Z, and so were P and Q and R, the writer continuing to dredge up fragments of his life, when, almost accidentally, he stumbled into M, a long-forgotten memory, seemingly unimportant but unassailably true, compressing into one incident everything that had made him want to write about the town in the first place. "There's your story," several people in the class would say, and it was. The student had been given time to find it.

That release from immediacy was what I wanted to get into the metabolism of my students. I told them that if they actually wrote their piece I would be glad to read it, even if they sent it to me after the course was over, but that that wasn't my primary interest. I was primarily interested in the process, not the product. At first that made them uneasy. This was America—they not only wanted validation; it was their national right. Quite a few came to me privately, almost furtively, as if letting me in on some shabby secret, and said, "You know, this is the only writing course I've ever taken that isn't market-driven." But after a while they found it liberating to be freed from a deadline, the monster of all their school and college and postgraduate years ("the paper is due on Friday"), insatiably demanding to be fed. They relaxed and enjoyed considering different ways of getting where they wanted to go. Some of those ways would work and some wouldn't. The right to fail was as liberating as the right to succeed.

Occasionally I've described this course to elementary and high school teachers at a workshop. I didn't particularly expect them to find it pertinent to their age group—adolescents with fewer memories and attachments than adults have. But they always pressed me for more details. When I asked why they were so interested they said, "You've given us a new timetable."

By which they meant that the traditional assigning of short-term papers may be a tradition that teachers have followed too unquestioningly for too long. They began to muse about writing assignments that would give their pupils more room and would be judged by different expectations.

I always remind my New School students that there are many good reasons for writing that have nothing to do with getting published. Writing for yourself is a powerful search mechanism: there's no better way to find out who you are and what you know and what you think. Writing for your children and your grandchildren—the family history or the personal or local memoir—is also satisfying.

My father, a businessman with no literary pretensions, wrote both a family history and a history of the family business, which he gave to each of his four children, his sons-in-law, his daughter-in-law and his 15 grandchildren. Pride of ancestry was not what got him going; the Zinssers, he said, "came over from Germany on the pickle boat." But the process of re-examining his German-American roots and his turn-of-the-century New York boyhood not only kept him engaged when he was an old man with few talents for self-amusement. His two histories also have considerable charm as social history. In my own older years I find myself dipping into them surprisingly often.

The methodology of my course—thinking of a particular place—is only a pedagogical device. My real purpose was to give writers a new mentality, one they could apply to whatever writing projects they might try thereafter, allowing as much time as they need for the journey. For one of my students, a lawyer in his late 30s, the journey took three years. One day in 1996 he called me to say that he had finally wrestled into submission the subject whose organizational problems he had presented to our class is 1993. Would I look at it?

What arrived was a 350-page manuscript. I'll admit that one part of me didn't want to receive a 350-page manuscript. But a larger part of me was delighted that the process I had set in motion had worked its way to a conclusion. I was also curious to see how the lawyer had solved his problems, because I remembered them well.

The place he wanted to write about, he told us, was the town in suburban Connecticut where he grew up, and his theme was soccer. Playing on the school team as a boy, he had formed close friendships with five other boys who loved the sport as much as he did, and he wanted to write about that bonding experience and his gratitude to soccer for providing it. That was a good writer's subject: a memoir.

So strong was the bond, the lawyer went on to say, that the six men were still bonded as midlife professionals in the northeast—they continued to see each other regularly—and he also wanted to write about that experience and about his gratitude for such lasting friendships. That was also a good subject: a personal essay.

But there was more. He also wanted to write about the state of soccer today. The texture of the sport he remembered had been eroded by social change, he explained. Among other losses, players no longer change in the locker room; they get into their uniform at home and drive to the field and then drive home again. The lawyer's idea was to volunteer as a soccer coach at his old school and to write about the contrast between the present and the past. That was still another good subject: investigative reporting.

I enjoyed hearing the lawyer's story. I was being taken into a world I knew nothing about, and his affection for that world was appealing. But I also knew that he was about to drive himself crazy, and I told him so. He couldn't fit all those stories under one small roof; he would have to choose one story. As it turned out, he did fit all those stories under one roof, but the house had to be greatly enlarged and the job took three years of his spare time.

After I had read his manuscript, which was called *The Autumn of Our Lives*, he asked me if it was good enough to submit to a publisher. Not yet, I told him; it was still one rewrite away. Maybe he just didn't want to make that kind of effort. He gave it some thought and said that, having traveled this far, he would probably give it one more shot. I have a feeling I'll see the book in print some day.

"But even if it never gets published," he said, "I'm glad I did it. I can't begin to describe how rewarding it has been to write about what soccer has meant in my life."

Two final words occur to me. One is quest, the other is intention.

The quest is one of the oldest themes in storytelling, an act of faith we never get tired of hearing about. Looking back, I notice that many students in my class, assigned to think about a place that was important to them, used the assignment to go on a quest for something deeper than the place itself: a meaning, an idea, some sliver of the past. The result was that the class always had an unusually warm dynamic for a group of strangers. (Some classes even held reunions.) Every quest that a student embarked on found an echo in some search or yearning of our own. Moral: any time you can tell a story in the form of a quest or a pilgrimage you'll be ahead of the game. Readers bearing their own associations will do some of your work for you.

Intention is what we wish to accomplish with our writing. Call it the writer's soul. We can write to affirm and to celebrate, or we can write to debunk and to destroy; the choice is ours. Destruction has long been a journalistic mode, rewarding the snoop and the hatchet man (or woman) and the invader of privacy. But nobody can make us write what we don't want to write. We get to keep intention. Nonfiction writers often forget that they are not required to acquiesce in tawdry work, to carry the trash for magazine editors who have an agenda of their own—to sell a commercial product.

Writing is related to character. If your values are sound, your writing will be sound. It all begins with intention. Figure out what you want to do and how you want to do it, and work your way with humanity and integrity to the completed article. *Then* you'll have something to sell.

23

A Writer's
Decisions

This has been a book about decisions—the countless successive decisions that go into every act of writing. Some of the decisions are big ("What should I write about?") and some are as small as the smallest word. But all of them are important.

The previous chapter was about big decisions: matters of shape, structure, compression, focus and intention. This chapter is about little decisions: the hundreds of choices that go into organizing a long article. I thought it might be helpful to show how some of those decisions get made, using one of my own pieces as the specimen being dissected.

Learning how to organize a long article is just as important as learning how to write a clear and pleasing sentence. All your clear and pleasing sentences will fall apart if you don't keep remembering that writing is linear and sequential, that logic is the glue that holds it together, that tension must be maintained from one sentence to the next and from one paragraph to the next and from one section to the next, and that narrative—good old-fashioned storytelling—is what should pull your readers along without their noticing the tug. The only thing they should notice is that you have made a sensible plan for your journey. Every step should seem inevitable.

My article, called "The News From Timbuktu," which ran in *Condé Nast Traveler*, is one writer's solution to one problem, but it illustrates issues that apply to all extended tasks of nonfiction. I've annotated the piece, explaining the decisions I made along the way.

The hardest decision about any article is how to begin it. The lead must grab the reader with a provocative idea and continue with each paragraph to hold him or her in a tight grip, gradually adding information. The point of the information is to get readers so interested that they will stick around for the whole trip. The lead can be as short as one paragraph and as long as it needs to be. You'll know it's over when all the necessary work has been done and you can take a more relaxed tone and get on with your narrative. Here the first paragraph gives readers an arresting notion to think about—one that I hope has never occured to them before.

> What struck me most powerfully when I got to Timbuktu was that the streets were of sand. I suddenly realized that sand is very different from dirt. Every town starts with dirt streets that eventually get paved as the inhabitants prosper and subdue their environment. But sand represents defeat. A city with streets of sand is a city at the edge.

Notice how simple those five sentences are: plain declarative sentences, not a comma in sight. Each sentence contains one thought—and only one. Readers can process only one idea at a time, and they do it in linear sequence. Much of the trouble that writers get into comes from trying to make one sentence do too much work. Never be afraid to break a long sentence into two short ones, or even three.

That, of course, is why I was there: Timbuktu is the ultimate destination for edge-seekers. Of the half-dozen places that have always lured travelers with the mere sound of their name—Bali and Tahiti, Samarkand and Fez, Mombasa and Macao—none can match Timbuktu for the remoteness it conveys. I was surprised by how many people, hearing of my trip, didn't think Timbuktu was a real place, or, if it was, couldn't think where in the world it might be. They knew it well as a word—the most vivid of all synonyms for the almost-unreachable, a God-given toy for songwriters stuck for an "oo" rhyme and a metaphor for how far a lovestruck boy would go to win the unwinnable girl. But as an actual place—surely Timbuktu was one of those "long-lost" African kingdoms like King Solomon's Mines that turned out not to exist when the Victorian explorers went looking for them.

The first sentence of that paragraph grows out of the last sentence of the previous paragraph; the reader is given no chance to squirm away. After that the paragraph has one purpose: it acknowledges what the reader already knows—or half knows—about Timbuktu. It thereby welcomes him as a fellow traveler, someone who brings the same emotions to the trip as the writer himself. It also adds a certain kind of information—not hard facts, but enjoyable lore.

The following paragraph gets down to hard work—work that can't be put off any longer. Notice how much information is crammed into these three sentences:

The long-lost Timbuktu, however, got found, though the men who finally found it after terrible ordeals—the Scotsman

Gordon Laing in 1826 and the Frenchman René Caillié in 1828—must have felt cruelly mocked for their efforts. The legendary city of 100,000 people described by the 16th-century traveler Leo Africanus—a center of learning with 20,000 students and 180 Koranic schools—was a desolate settlement of mud buildings, its glory and its population long gone, surviving only because of its unique location as the junction of important camel caravan routes across the Sahara. Much of what got traded in Africa, especially salt from the north and gold from the south, got traded in Timbuktu.

So much for the history of Timbuktu and the reason for its fame. It's all that a magazine reader needs to know about the city's past and its significance. Don't give readers of a magazine piece more information than they require; if you want to tell more, write a book or write for a scholarly journal.

Now, what do your readers want to know next? Ask yourself that question after every sentence. Here what they want to know is: why did *I* go to Timbuktu? What was the purpose of my trip? The following paragraph gets right to it—again, keeping the thread of the previous sentence taut:

It was to watch the arrival of one of those caravans that I had come to Timbuktu. I was one of six men and women bright enough or dumb enough—we didn't yet know which—to sign up for a two-week tour we had seen announced in the Sunday *New York Times,* run by a small travel agency of French origins that specializes in West Africa. (Timbuktu is in Mali, the former French Sudan.) The agency's office is in New York, and I had gone there first thing Monday morning to beat the crowd; I asked the usual questions and got the usual answers—yellow fever shots, cholera shots, malaria pills, don't drink the water—and was given a brochure.

Besides explaining the genesis of the trip, that paragraph does one other job: it establishes the writer's personality and voice. In travel writing you should never forget that you are the guide. It's not enough just to take your readers on a trip; you must take them on *your* trip. Make them identify with you—with your hopes and apprehensions. This means giving them some idea of who you are. The phrase "bright enough or dumb enough" calls up a familiar figure in travel literature: the tourist as a possible patsy or buffoon. Another throwaway phrase is the line about beating the crowd. I put it in just to amuse myself. Strictly, that fourth paragraph is too late to say where Timbuktu is. But I couldn't find a way to mention it earlier without pulling apart the fabric of the lead.

Here's paragraph five:

"It's your opportunity to participate in a once-in-a-lifetime extravaganza—the annual Azalai Salt Caravan to Timbuktu!" the brochure began. "Picture this: Hundreds of camels carrying huge slabs of precious salt ('white gold' to the natives of land-locked West Africa) make their triumphant entry into Timbuktu, an ancient and mystical part desert/part city of some 7,000 inhabitants. The colorful nomads who drive the caravans have traveled 1,000 miles across the Sahara to celebrate the end of their trek with outdoor feasts and traditional tribal dances. Spend the night in a desert tent as guest of the tribal chief."

That's a typical example of how a writer can get other people to do helpful work for him—in their words, which are usually more revealing than the writer's words. In this case the brochure not only tells the reader what kind of trip has been promised; its language is an amusement in itself and a window into the grandiosity of the promoters. Be on the watch for funny or self-serving quotes and use them with gratitude. Here's the last paragraph of the lead:

Well, that's my kind of trip, if not necessarily my kind of prose, and it also turned out to be my wife's kind of trip and four other people's kind of trip. In years we ranged from late middle age to Medicare. Five of us were from mid-Manhattan, one was a widow from Maryland, and all of us had made a lifelong habit of traveling to places on the edge. Names like Venice and Versailles didn't bob up in our accounts of earlier trips, or even Marrakech or Luxor or Chiang Mai. The talk was of Bhutan and Borneo, Tibet and Yemen and the Moluccas. Now—praise Allah!—we had made it to Timbuktu. Our camel caravan was about to come in.

✻

That concludes the lead. Those six paragraphs took as long to write as the entire remainder of the piece. But when I finally wrestled them into place I felt confidently launched. Maybe someone else could write a better lead for that story, but *I* couldn't. I felt that readers who were still with me would stay to the end.

No less important than decisions about structure are decisions about individual words. Banality is the enemy of good writing; the challenge is to not write like everybody else. One fact that had to be stated in the lead was how old the six of us were. Initially I wrote something serviceable like "we were in our fifties and sixties." But the merely serviceable is a drag. Was there any way to state the fact with freshness? There didn't seem to be. At last a merciful muse gave me Medicare—and thus the phrase "from late middle age to Medicare." If you look long enough you can usually find a proper name or a metaphor that will bring those dull but necessary facts to life.

Even more time went into the sentence about Venice and

Versailles. Originally I wrote, "Names like London and Paris didn't turn up in our accounts of earlier trips." Not much fun there. I tried to think of other popular capitals. Rome and Cairo? Athens and Bangkok? No better. Maybe alliteration would help—readers enjoy any effort to gratify their sense of rhythm and cadence. Madrid and Moscow? Tel Aviv and Tokyo? Too tricky. I stopped thinking of capitals and tried to think of tourist-infested cities. Venice popped into my head and I was glad to see it; everybody goes to Venice. Did any other cities begin with V? Only Vienna, which was too close to Venice in several respects. Finally I shifted my thinking from tourist cities to tourist sites, mentally fanning out from the major capitals, and it was on one of those excursions that I hit Versailles. It made my day.

Next I needed a fresher verb than "turn up." I wanted an active verb that conveyed an image. None of the usual synonyms was quite right. Finally I thought of "bob"—a three-letter word, ludicrously simple. Yet it was the perfect word: it paints a picture of an object periodically rising to the surface of the water. That left just one decision: what slightly offbeat tourist sites would seem commonplace to six travelers who had signed up for Timbuktu? The three that I finally chose—Luxor, Marrakech and Chiang Mai—were quite exotic in the 1950s, when I first visited them. Today they're not; the age of jet travel has made them almost as popular as London and Paris.

Altogether, the sentence took almost an hour. But I didn't begrudge a minute of it. On the contrary, seeing it fall into place gave me great pleasure. No writing decision is too small to be worth a large expenditure of time. Both you and the reader know it when your finicky labor is rewarded by a sentence coming out right.

Notice that there's an asterisk at the end of the lead. (It could also be a blank space.) That asterisk is a signpost. It announces to the reader that you have organized your article in a certain way and that a new phase is about to begin—perhaps a change of chronology, such as a flashback, or a change of subject, or emphasis, or tone. Here, after a highly compressed lead, the asterisk enables the writer to take a deep breath and start over, this time at the more leisurely gait of a storyteller:

We got to Timbuktu by flying from New York to Abidjan, capital of the Ivory Coast, and taking a plane from there to Bamako, capital of Mali, its neighbor to the north. Unlike the verdant Ivory Coast, Mali is dry, its southern half nourished mainly by the Niger River, its upper half pure desert; Timbuktu is literally the last stop for travelers going north across the Sahara, or the first stop for travelers coming south—a coveted speck on the horizon after weeks of heat and thirst.

None of us on the tour knew much about Mali or what to expect of it—our thoughts were fixed on our rendezvous with the salt caravan at Timbuktu, not on the country we would cross to get there. What we didn't expect was that we would be so instantly taken with it. Mali was an immersion in color: handsome people wearing fabrics of intoxicating design, markets bright with fruits and vegetables, children whose smile was a routine miracle. Desperately poor, Mali was people-rich. The tree-lined city of Bamako delighted us with its energy and confidence.

Up early the next morning, we drove for ten hours in a van that had seen better days, but not much better days, to reach the holy city of Djenné, a medieval center of trade and Islamic scholarship on the Niger that predated Timbuktu and rivaled it in luster. Today Djenné can only be reached by a small ferry, and as we bounced over unspeakable roads, hurrying to arrive before dark, the spires and turrets of its great clay mosque, looking like a distant sandcastle, taunted us by seeming to recede. When we finally got there the mosque still looked like a sandcastle—an elegant fortress that might have been built by children on a beach. Architecturally (I later learned) it was in the Sudanese style; all these years, children on beaches have been building in the Sudanese style. To linger in Djenné's ancient square at dusk was a high moment of our trip.

The next two days were no less rich. One was spent driving into—and back out of—Dogon country. The Dogon, who live on an escarpment not easily reached by outsiders, are prized by anthropologists for their animist culture and cosmology and by art collectors for their masks and statues, and the few hours that we spent climbing around their villages and watching a masked dance gave us too brief a glimpse of a society that was far from simple. The second day was spent in Mopte, a vibrant market town on the Niger that we liked enormously and also left too soon. But we had a date in Timbuktu and a chartered plane to take us there.

Obviously there's far more to say about Mali than is jammed into those four paragraphs—many scholarly books have been written about the Dogon culture and the Niger River peoples. But this wasn't an article about Mali; it was about a quest for a camel caravan. Therefore a decision had to made about the larger shape of the piece. My decision was to get across Mali as fast as possible—to explain in the barest number of sentences what route we took and what was important about the places where we stopped.

At such moments I ask myself one very helpful question: "What is the piece *really* about?" (Not just "What is the piece about?") Fondness for material you've gone to a lot of trouble to gather isn't a good enough reason to include it if it's not central to the story you've chosen to tell. Self-discipline bordering on masochism is required. The only consolation for the loss of so much material is that it isn't totally lost; it remains in your writing as an intangible that the reader can sense. Readers should always feel that you know more about your subject than you've put in writing.

Back to "But we had a date in Timbuktu":

> The exactness of that date was what had worried me most when I visited the travel agency. I asked the head of the agency how she could be so sure the salt caravan would arrive on December 2; nomads leading camels aren't my idea of people operating on a timetable. My wife, who isn't cursed with my optimism about such life forces as camels and travel agents, was certain we would be told at Timbuktu that the salt caravan had come and gone, or, more probably, hadn't been heard from at all. The travel agent scoffed at my question.
>
> "We're in close touch with the caravan," she said. "We send scouts into the desert. If they tell us the caravan is going to be a few days late we can juggle your itinerary in Mali." That made sense to me—optimists can make sense of anything—and now I was in a plane not much bigger than Lindbergh's, flying north toward Timbuktu over terrain so barren that I saw no sign of human habitation below. Simultaneously, however, hundreds of camels carrying huge slabs of salt were moving south to meet me. Even now tribal chiefs were turning their thoughts to how to entertain me in their desert tent.

Both of the preceding paragraphs contain touches of humor—tiny jokes. Again, they are efforts to keep myself amused. But they are also a deliberate attempt to maintain a persona. One of the oldest strains in travel writing and humor writing is the eternal credulity of the narrator. Used in moderation, making yourself gullible—or downright stupid—gives the reader the enormous pleasure of feeling superior.

> Our pilot circled over Timbuktu to give us an aerial view of the city we had traveled so far to see. It was a large sprawl

of mud buildings that looked long abandoned, as dead as Fort
Zinderneuf at the end of *Beau Geste;* surely nobody was alive
down there. The Sahara in its steady encroachment, which
has created the drought belt across central Africa known as
the Sahel, had long since pushed past Timbuktu and left it
marooned. I felt a tremor of fear; I didn't want to be put
down in such a forsaken place.

The reference to *Beau Geste* is an effort to tap into associations that readers bring to the story. Much of what makes Timbuktu legendary was put there by Hollywood. By invoking the
fate of Fort Zinderneuf—Brian Donlevy played a sadistic
French Foreign Legion commandant who propped the dead
bodies of his soldiers back into the niches of the fort—I'm
revealing my own fondness for the genre and striking a bond
with fellow movie buffs. What I'm after is resonance; it can do a
great deal of emotional work that writers can't achieve on their
own.

Two words—"tremor" and "forsaken"—took a while to find.
When I found "forsaken" in my *Roget's Thesaurus* I was quite
sure I had never used it before. I was glad to see it there among
the synonyms. As one of Jesus's last words (speaking of resonance), it could hardly convey more loneliness and abandonment.

At the airport we were met by our local guide, a Tuareg
named Mohammed Ali. For a travel buff he was a consoling
sight—if anybody can be said to own this part of the Sahara, it
is the Tuareg, a race of proud Berbers who wouldn't submit to
the Arabs or the later French colonials who swept into North
Africa, withdrawing instead into the desert and making it
their preserve. Mohammed Ali, who was wearing the traditional blue robe of Tuareg men, had a dark, intelligent face,
somewhat Arabic in the angularity of its features, and he
moved with an assurance that was obviously part of his char-

acter. As a teen-ager, it turned out, he had gone with his father on the *haj* to Mecca (many Tuareg eventually converted to Islam) and had stayed for seven years in Arabia and Egypt to study English, French and Arabic. The Tuareg have a language of their own, with a complex written alphabet, called Tamashek.

Mohammed Ali said he had to take us first to the police station in Timbuktu to have our passports checked. I've seen too many movies to feel comfortable in this kind of interview situation, and as we sat in a dungeon-like room being interrogated by two armed policemen, not far from a jail cell where we could see a man and a boy sleeping, I had another flashback—this one to *The Four Feathers* and the scene of the British soldiers long imprisoned at Omdurman. The oppressiveness stayed with me when we got back out and Mohammed Ali walked us through the forlorn city, dutifully showing us its few "points of interest": the Grand Mosque, the market, and three dilapidated houses, commemorated by plaques, where Laing, Caillié and the German explorer Heinrich Barth lived. We didn't see any other tourists.

❖

Again, the *Four Feathers* allusion, like the mention of *Beau Geste*, will bring a chill of recognition to anyone who knows the movie. The fact that the movie was based on a real campaign—Kitchener's expedition up the Nile to avenge the Mahdi's defeat of General Gordon—gives the sentence an edge of fear. Obviously Arab justice in outposts of the Sahara is still far from merciful.

Once more the asterisk announces a change of mood. It says, in effect: "So much for Timbuktu itself. Now we're going to get down to the real business of the story: looking for a camel caravan." Making these divisions in a long and complex article not only helps the reader to follow your road map. It also takes some of the anxiety out of the act of writing, enabling you to break your material into manageable chunks and to take one chunk at a time. The total task seems less formidable, and panic is staved off.

At the Azalai Hotel, where we appeared to be the only guests, we asked Mohammed Ali how many tourists were in Timbuktu to greet the salt caravan.

"Six," he said. "The six of you."

"But . . ." Something in me didn't want to finish the sentence. I took a different approach. "I don't understand what this word 'Azalai' means. Why is it called the Azalai Salt Caravan?"

"That's the word the French used," he said, "when they organized the caravan and all the camels made the trip together once a year, around the beginning of December."

"What do they do now?" several voices asked.

"Well, when Mali got its independence they decided to let the traders bring their salt caravans to Timbuktu whenever they wanted to."

Mali got its independence in 1960. We were in Timbuktu for an event that hadn't been held in 27 years.

The last sentence is a small bomb dropped into the story. But it is allowed to speak for itself—just the facts, please—without comment. I didn't add an exclamation point to notify readers that it was an amazing moment. That would have spoiled their own pleasure of discovery. Trust your material.

My wife, among others, was not surprised. We took the news calmly: old travel hands who have faith that they will find their camel caravan one way or another. Mainly our reaction was one of amazement that the canons of truth-in-advertising had been so brazenly disregarded. Mohammed Ali knew nothing about the gaudy promises tendered by the brochure. He only knew he had been hired to take us to meet a salt caravan, and he told us that in the morning we would go looking for one and would spend the night in the Sahara. Early December, he said, was the usual time for caravans to start arriving. He didn't say anything about a chieftain's tent.

More carefully chosen words: "canons," "brazenly," "gaudy," "tendered." They're vivid and precise, but not long or fancy. Best of all, they are words that readers probably weren't expecting and that they therefore welcome. The sentence about the chieftain's tent, referring back to a phrase in the brochure, is another tiny joke. These "snappers" at the end of a paragraph propel readers into the next paragraph and keep them in a good mood.

In the morning my wife—a voice of reason at the edge of infinity—said she wouldn't go into the Sahara unless we went in two vehicles. I was therefore glad to see two Land Rovers awaiting us outside the hotel. One of them was having its front tire pumped up by a boy with a bicycle pump. Four of us squeezed into the back seat of one Land Rover; Mohammed Ali sat in front, next to the driver. The second Land Rover took our other two tour members and two boys who were described as "apprentices." Nobody said what they were apprenticing for.

Another startling fact that needs no embellishment—the tire-pumping—and another small joke at the end.

We drove straight out into the Sahara. The desert was a brown blanket without any end and with no tracks of any kind; the next big town was Algiers. That was the moment when I felt most at the edge, when a small voice said, "This is crazy. Why are you doing this?" But I knew why; I was on a quest that I could trace back to my first encounters with the books by Britain's "desert eccentrics"—solitaries such as Charles Doughty, Sir Richard Burton, T. E. Lawrence and Wilfred Thesiger, who lived among the Bedouin. I had always wondered what that austere existence was like. What was its hold over those obsessed Englishmen?

More resonance. The reference to Doughty and his compatriots is a reminder that the desert has a written literature no less powerful than its movie literature. It adds one more item to the emotional baggage that I was carrying and that the reader was entitled to know about.

The following sentence pursues the question that ended the previous paragraph:

Now I was starting to find out. As we drove over the sand, Mohammed Ali gave the driver an occasional gesture: a little more to the right, a little more to the left. We asked how he knew where he was going. He said he could tell by the dunes. The dunes, however, all looked alike. We asked how long we would have to drive to find a salt caravan. Mohammed Ali said he hoped it wouldn't be more than three or four hours. We kept driving. To my object-oriented eye there was almost nothing to see. But after a while the almost-nothingness became an object in itself—the entire point of the desert. I tried to get that fact into my metabolism. It lulled me into a certain acceptance and I totally forgot why we were out there.

Suddenly the driver made a sharp left and came to a stop. "Camels," he said. I strained my urban eyes and didn't see anything. Then it came into focus, far away: a caravan of forty camels moving at a stately gait toward Timbuktu, as camel caravans have for a thousand years, bringing salt from the mines at Taoudenni, twenty days to the north. We drove to within a hundred yards of the caravan—no nearer, Mohammed Ali explained, because camels are nervous creatures, easily panicked by anything "strange." (We were undeniably strange.) He said that the camels are always brought into Timbuktu to unload the salt late at night, when the city is empty of people. So much for the "triumphant entry."

It was a thrilling sight, far more dramatic than an organized march would have been. The aloneness of the caravan was the aloneness of every caravan that had ever crossed the Sahara. The camels were hitched to each other and seemed to be walking in unison, as precise as Rockettes in their undulating rhythm. Each camel had two slabs of salt roped to each side. The salt looked like dirty white marble. The slabs (which I subsequently measured in the Timbuktu market) are 3½ feet long, 1½ feet high, and ¾ inch thick—the maximum size and weight, presumably, that can be loaded onto a camel. We sat on the sand and watched the caravan until the last camel disappeared over a dune.

The tone has now settled into straight narrative—one declarative sentence after another. The only hard decision involved "aloneness," which is not my kind of word—it's too "poetic." But I finally decided that there was no other word that could do the same job, and I reluctantly stayed with it.

By now it was midday and the sun was fiercely hot. We climbed back in our Land Rovers and drove farther into the desert until Mohammed Ali found a tree that cast a shadow just big enough for five New Yorkers and a widow from Maryland, and there we stayed until about 4, having a picnic lunch, gazing at the bleached-out landscape, dozing, moving our blanket periodically as our shadow moved with the sun. The two drivers spent the entire siesta tinkering with and seeming to dismantle the engine of one of the Land Rovers. A nomad appeared from nowhere and stopped to ask if we had any quinine. Another nomad appeared from nowhere and stopped briefly to talk. Later we saw two men walking toward us across the desert and beyond them... was it our first mirage? It was another salt caravan, this one fifty camels long, silhouetted against the sky. Spotting us from God knows how far away, the two men had left the caravan to come over for a visit. One of them was an old man, full of laughter. They sat down with Mohammed Ali and got the latest news of Timbuktu.

The hardest sentence there was the one about the drivers tinkering with the Land Rover. I wanted it to be as simple as all the other sentences and yet have a small surprise tucked into it—a wry touch of humor. Otherwise my purpose at this point was to tell the remainder of the story as simply as possible:

So the four hours passed before we knew they were gone, as if we had slipped into a different time zone, Sahara time, and in the late afternoon, when the sun's heat had begun to ebb, we got back into our Land Rovers, which, to my surprise, still worked, and set out across the Sahara for what Mohammed Ali called our "encampment." I pictured, if not a chieftain's tent, at least a tent—something that announced itself as an encampment. When we finally did stop, it was at a spot that looked strikingly similar to what we had been driving over all day. It did, however, have one small tree. Some Bedouin women were crouched under it—black-garbed figures, their faces veiled—and Mohammed Ali put us down on the desert next to them.

The women shrank back at the sight of us—white aliens dumped abruptly in their midst. They were huddled so close together that they looked like a frieze. Obviously Mohammed Ali had just stopped at the first sight of "local color" that he happened to find for his tourists, counting on us to manage for ourselves after that. We could only sit and try to look friendly. But we were very conscious of being intruders, and we probably looked as uncomfortable as we felt. Only after we had sat there for a while did the black frieze slowly come apart and turn into four women, three children and two naked babies. Mohammed Ali had gone off somewhere, seemingly not wanting to have anything to do with the Bedouin; perhaps as a Tuareg he considered them desert riffraff.

But it was the Bedouin who had the grace to put us at ease. One of the women, lowering her veil and revealing a movie star's smile—white teeth and shining black eyes in a beautiful face—rummaged in her belongings, pulled out a blanket and a straw mat, and brought them over for us to sit on. I remembered from all those books that in the desert there's no such thing as an intruder; anyone who turns up is somehow expected. Soon after that, two Bedouin men came in from the desert, completing the family unit, which, we now saw, consisted of two men, two wives for each man, and their various children. The older husband, who had a strong and handsome face, greeted both of his wives with a gentle tap on the head, somewhat like a blessing, and then sat down not far from me. One of the women brought him his dinner—some millet in a bowl. He immediately offered the bowl to me. I declined, but the offer is one I won't forget. We sat in companionable silence while he ate. The children came over to get acquainted. The sun went down and a full moon came up over the Sahara.

Meanwhile our drivers had spread some blankets next to the two Land Rovers and started a fire with desert wood. We regrouped on our own blankets, watched the stars coming out in the desert sky, had some kind of chicken for dinner, and got ready to turn in. Bathroom facilities were ad hoc—to each his

own. We had been warned that Sahara nights were cold and
had brought sweaters along. I put on my sweater, rolled up in
a blanket, which slightly softened the hardness of the desert,
and fell asleep surrounded by an immense stillness. An hour
later I was awakened by an equally immense racket—our
Bedouin family had brought in their herd of goats and their
camels for the night. Then all was quiet again.

In the morning I noticed paw prints in the sand next to
my blanket. Mohammed Ali said that a jackal had come by to
clean up the leftovers from our dinner—of which, as I
recalled the chicken, there must have been quite a few. But I
didn't hear a thing. I was too busy dreaming that I was
Lawrence of Arabia.

[END]

A crucial decision about a piece of writing is where to end it.
Often the story will tell you where it wants to stop. This ending
was not the one I originally had in mind. Because the goal of our
trip was to find a salt caravan I assumed that I would have to
complete the ancient cycle of trade: to describe how we
returned to Timbuktu and saw the salt being unloaded and
bought and sold in the market. But the nearer I got to writing
that final section, the more I didn't want to write it. It loomed as
drudgery, no fun for me or for the reader.

Suddenly I remembered that I was under no obligation to
the actual shape of our trip. I didn't have to reconstruct *everything*. The real climax of my story was not finding the salt caravan; it was finding the timeless hospitality of the people who live
in the Sahara. Not many moments in my life have matched the
one when a family of nomads with almost no possessions offered
to share their dinner. Nor could any other moment distill more
vividly what I had come to the desert to find and what all those
Englishmen had written about—the nobility of living on the
edge.

When you get such a message from your material—when your story tells you it's over, regardless of what subsequently happened—look for the door. I got out fast, pausing only long enough to make sure that the unities were intact: that the writer-guide who started the trip was the same person who was ending it. The playful reference to Lawrence preserves the persona, wraps up a multitude of associations and brings the journey full circle. The realization that I could just stop was a terrific feeling, not only because my labors were over—the jigsaw puzzle solved—but because the ending felt right. It was the correct decision.

As a postscript, there's one last decision I'd like to mention. It has to do with the nonfiction writer's need to make his or her own luck. An exhortation I often use to keep myself going is "Get on the plane." Two of the most emotional moments of my life came as a result of getting on the plane in connection with my book *Willie and Dwike*. First I went to Shanghai with the musicians Willie Ruff and Dwike Mitchell when they introduced jazz to China at the Shanghai Conservatory of Music. A year later I went to Venice with Ruff to hear him play Gregorian chants on his French horn in St. Mark's basilica at night, when nobody else was there, to test its unique acoustics. In both cases Ruff had no assurance that he would be allowed to play; I might have wasted my time and money by deciding to go along. But I got on the plane, and those two long pieces, which originally ran in *The New Yorker*, are probably my two best articles. I got on the plane to Timbuktu to look for a camel caravan that was an even bet not to materialize, and I got on the plane to Bradenton for spring training not knowing whether I would be welcomed or rebuffed. My book *Writing to Learn* was born because of one phone call from a stranger. It raised an educational idea so interesting that I got on the plane to Minnesota to pursue it.

Getting on the plane has taken me to unusual stories all over the world and all over America, and it still does. That isn't to say

I'm not nervous when I leave for the airport; I always am—that's part of the deal. (A little nervousness gives writing an edge.) But I'm always replenished when I get back home.

As a nonfiction writer you must get on the plane. If a subject interests you, go after it, even if it's in the next county or the next state or the next country. It's not going to come looking for you.

Decide what you want to do. Then decide to do it. Then do it.

2 4

Write as Well as You Can

I'm occasionally asked if I can recall the moment when I knew I wanted to be a writer. No such blinding flash occurred; I only knew that I thought I would like to work for a newspaper. But I can point to a set of attitudes that I inherited early in life and that have guided me ever since. They came from both sides of my family, by different routes.

My mother loved good writing, and she found it as often in newspapers as she did in books. She regularly clipped columns and articles out of the paper that delighted her with their graceful use of language, or their wit, or their original vision of life. Because of her I knew at an early age that good writing can appear anywhere, even in the lowly newspaper, and that what matters is the writing itself, not the medium where it's published. Therefore I've always tried to write as well as I could by my own standards; I've never changed my style to fit the size or the presumed education of the audience I was writing for. My mother was also a woman of humor and optimism. These are lubricants in writing, as they are in life, and a writer lucky enough to have them in his baggage will start the day with an extra round of confidence.

Originally I wasn't meant to be a writer. My father was a businessman. His grandfather had come from Germany in the great immigration of 1848 with a formula for making shellac. He built a small house and factory in a rocky field far uptown in Manhattan—at what is now 59th Street and Tenth Avenue—and started a business called William Zinsser & Company. I still have a photograph of that pastoral scene; the land slopes down toward the Hudson River, and the only living creature is a goat. The firm stayed at that location until 1973, when it moved to New Jersey.

For a business to remain in the same family on the same Manhattan block for more than a century is rare, and as a boy I couldn't escape the naggings of continuity, for I was the fourth William Zinsser and the only son; my father's fate was to have three daughters first. In those Dark Ages the idea that daughters could run a business as well as sons, or better, was still two decades off. My father was a man who loved his business. When he talked about it I never felt that he regarded it as a venture for making money; it was an art, to be practiced with imagination and only the best materials. He had a passion for quality and had no patience with the second-rate; he never went into a store looking for a bargain. He charged more for his product because he made it with the best ingredients, and his company prospered. It was a ready-made future for me, and my father looked forward to the day when I would join him.

But inevitably a different day arrived, and not long after I came home from the war I went to work for the *New York Herald Tribune* and had to tell my father I wasn't going to carry on the family business. He accepted the news with his usual generosity and wished me well in my chosen field. No boy could receive a finer gift. I was liberated from having to fulfill somebody else's expectations, which were not the right ones for me. I was free to succeed or fail on my own terms.

Only later did I realize that I took along on my journey another gift from my father: a bone-deep belief that quality is its own reward. I, too, have never gone into a store looking for a bargain. Although my mother was the literary one in our family—magpie collector of books, lover of the English language, writer of dazzling letters—it was from the world of business that I absorbed my craftsman's ethic, and over the years, when I found myself endlessly rewriting what I had endlessly rewritten, determined to write better than everybody who was competing for the same space, the inner voice I was hearing was the voice of my father talking about shellac.

Besides wanting to write as well as possible, I wanted to write as entertainingly as possible. When I tell aspiring writers that they should think of themselves as part entertainer, they don't like to hear it—the word smacks of carnivals and jugglers and clowns. But to succeed you must make your piece jump out of a newspaper or a magazine by being more diverting than everyone else's piece. You must find some way to elevate your act of writing into an entertainment. Usually this means giving the reader an enjoyable surprise. Any number of devices will do the job: humor, anecdote, paradox, an unexpected quotation, a powerful fact, an outlandish detail, a circuitous approach, an elegant arrangement of words. These seeming amusements in fact become your "style." When we say we like a writer's style, what we mean is that we like his personality as he expresses it on paper. Given a choice between two traveling companions—and a writer is someone who asks us to travel with him—we usually choose the one who we think will make an effort to brighten the trip.

Unlike medicine or the other sciences, writing has no new discoveries to spring on us. We're in no danger of reading in our morning newspaper that a breakthrough has been made in how to write a clear English sentence—that information has been around since the King James Bible. We know that verbs have more vigor than nouns, that active verbs are better than passive verbs, that short words and sentences are easier to read than long ones, that concrete details are easier to process than vague abstractions.

Obviously the rules have often been bent. Victorian writers had a taste for the ornate and didn't consider brevity a virtue, and many modern writers, like Tom Wolfe, have broken out of the cage, turning a headlong exuberance of language into a source of positive energy. Such skillful acrobats, however, are rare; most nonfiction writers will do well to cling to the ropes of simplicity and clarity. We may be given new technologies like the word processor to ease the burdens of composition, but on the whole we know what we need to know. We're all working with the same words and the same principles.

Where, then, is the edge? Ninety percent of the answer lies in the hard work of mastering the tools discussed in this book. Add a few points for such natural gifts as a good musical ear, a sense of rhythm and a feeling for words. But the final advantage is the same one that applies in every other competitive venture. If you would like to write better than everybody else, you have to *want* to write better than everybody else. You must take an obsessive pride in the smallest details of your craft. And you must be willing to defend what you've written against the various middlemen—editors, agents and publishers—whose sights may be different from yours, whose standards not as high. Too many writers are browbeaten into settling for less than their best.

I've always felt that my "style"—the careful projection onto paper of who I think I am—is my main marketable asset, the only possession that might set me apart from other writers. Therefore I've never wanted anyone to tinker with it, and after I submit an article I protect it fiercely. Several magazine editors have told me that I'm the only writer they know who cares what happens to his piece after he gets paid for it. Most writers won't argue with an editor because they don't want to upset him; they're so grateful to be published that they agree to having their style—in other words, their personality—violated in public.

Yet to defend what you've written is a sign that you are alive. I'm a known crank on this issue—I fight over every semicolon. But editors put up with me because they can see that I'm serious. In fact, my crankiness has brought me more work than it has driven away. Editors with an unusual assignment often thought of me because they knew I would do it with unusual care. They also knew they would get the article on time and that it would be accurate. Remember that the craft of nonfiction writing involves more than writing. It also means being reliable. Editors will properly drop a writer they can't count on.

Which brings us to editors. Are they friends or enemies—gods who save us from our sins or bums who trample on our poetic souls? Like the rest of creation, they come in all varieties. I think with gratitude of a half-dozen editors who sharpened my writing by changing its focus or emphasis, or questioning its tone, or detecting weaknesses of logic or structure, or suggesting a different lead, or letting me talk a problem through with them when I couldn't decide between several routes, or cutting various forms of excess. Twice I threw out an entire chapter of a book because editors told me it was unnecessary. But above all I remember those good editors for their generosity. They had an enthusiasm for whatever project we were trying to bring off together as writer and editor. Their confidence that I could make it work kept me going.

What a good editor brings to a piece of writing is an objective eye that the writer has long since lost, and there is no end of ways in which an editor can improve a manuscript: pruning, shaping, clarifying, tidying a hundred inconsistencies of tense and pronoun and location and tone, noticing all the sentences that could be read in two different ways, dividing awkward long sentences into short ones, putting the writer back on the main road if he has strayed down a side path, building bridges where the writer has lost the reader by not paying attention to his transitions, questioning matters of judgment and taste. An editor's hand must also be invisible. Whatever he adds in his own words shouldn't sound like his own words; they should sound like the writer's words.

For all these acts of salvation, editors can't be thanked fervently enough. Unfortunately, they can also do considerable harm. In general the damage takes two forms: altering style and altering content. Let's look at style first.

A good editor likes nothing better than a piece of copy he hardly has to touch. A bad editor has a compulsion to tinker, proving with busywork that he hasn't forgotten the minutiae of grammar and usage. He is a literal fellow, catching cracks in the road but not enjoying the scenery. Very often it simply doesn't occur to him that a writer is writing by ear, trying to achieve a particular sound or cadence, or playing with words just for the pleasures of wordplay. One of the bleakest moments for writers is the one when they realize that their editor has missed the point of what they are trying to do.

I remember many such dismal revelations. A minor one that comes to mind involved an article I wrote about a program called Visiting Artists, which brought artists and musicians to a group of economically depressed Midwestern cities. Describing them, I wrote: "They don't look like cities that get visited by many visiting artists." When the galleys came back the sentence said: "They don't look like cities that are on the itinerary of many visiting artists." A small point? Not to me. I had used repetition because it's a device I like—it takes readers by surprise and refreshes them in midsentence. But the editor remembered the rule about substituting synonyms for words that are repeated, and he corrected my error. When I called to protest, he was amazed. We argued for a long time, neither of us yielding. Finally he said, "You really feel strongly about this, don't you?" I feel strongly that one such erosion leads to another and that the writer must take a stand. I've even bought articles back from magazines that made changes I wouldn't accept. If you allow your distinctiveness to be edited out, you will lose one of your main virtues. You will also lose your virtue.

Ideally the relationship between a writer and an editor should be one of negotiation and trust. Frequently an editor will make a change to clarify a muddy sentence and will inadvertently lose an important point—a fact or a nuance that the writer included for reasons the editor didn't know about. In such cases the writer should ask to have his point back. The editor, if he agrees, should oblige. But he should also insist on his right to fix whatever had been unclear. Clarity is what every editor owes the reader. An editor should never allow something to get into print that he doesn't understand. If *he* doesn't understand it, at least one other person won't, and that's one too many. The process, in short, is one in which the writer and the editor proceed through the manuscript together, finding for every problem the solution that best serves the finished article.

It's a process that can be done just as well over the phone as in person. Don't let editors use distance or their own disarray as an excuse for altering your work without your consent. "We were on deadline," "we were already late," "the person who usually deals with you was out sick," "we had a big shake-up here last week," "our new publisher has just come on board," "it got put in the wrong pile," "the editor's on vacation"—these dreary phrases cloak a multitude of inefficiencies and sins. One unpleasant change in the publishing profession has been the erosion of courtesies that were once routine. Magazine editors, especially, have become cavalier about a whole series of procedures that should be automatic: notifying the writer that the piece has arrived, reading it with reasonable speed, telling the writer whether it's O.K., returning it immediately if it's not, working supportively with the writer if the piece needs changes, sending the writer galley proofs, seeing that the writer gets paid promptly. Writers are vulnerable enough without being put through the repeated indignities of calling to learn the status of their article and to beg for their money.

The prevailing notion is that such "courtesies" are merely frills and can therefore be dismissed. On the contrary, they are organic to the craft. They are the code of honor that anchors the whole enterprise, and editors who forget them are toying with nothing less than the writer's fundamental rights.

This arrogance is at its most injurious when an editor goes beyond changes of style or structure and enters the sacred realm of content. I often hear freelance writers say, "When I got the magazine I looked for my article and I didn't even recognize it. They had written a whole new lead and had me saying things that aren't what I believe." That's the cardinal sin—tampering with a writer's opinions. But editors will do what writers allow them to do, especially if time is short. Writers conspire in their own humiliation, allowing their piece to be rewritten by an editor to serve his own purposes. With every surrender they remind editors that they can be treated like hired help.

But finally the purposes that writers serve must be their own. What you write is yours and nobody else's. Take your talent as far as you can and guard it with your life. Only you know how far that is; no editor knows. Writing well means believing in your writing and believing in yourself, taking risks, daring to be different, pushing yourself to excel. You will write only as well as you make yourself write.

My favorite definition of a careful writer comes from Joe DiMaggio, though he didn't know that was what he was defining. DiMaggio was the greatest player I ever saw, and nobody looked more relaxed. He covered vast distances in the outfield, moving in graceful strides, always arriving ahead of the ball, making the hardest catch look routine, and even when he was at bat, hitting the ball with tremendous power, he didn't appear to be exerting himself. I marveled at how effortless he looked because what he did could only be achieved by great daily effort. A reporter once asked him how he managed to play so well so consistently, and he said: "I always thought that there was at least one person in the stands who had never seen me play, and I didn't want to let him down."

SOURCES

Most of the material that I have quoted in these pages was first written for a magazine or a newspaper and was subsequently reprinted in a book. In general the source cited below is for the original hardcover edition of the book. Many of those editions are now out of print but are available in public libraries. In many other cases the book has been reprinted in paperback and is quite easy to obtain.

PAGE

27–28   Preface by E. B. White to *A Basic Chicken Guide,* by Roy E. Jones. Copyright 1944 by Roy E. Jones. Reprinted by permission of William Morrow & Co. Also appears in *The Second Tree From the Corner.* Harper & Bros., 1954.

28–29   "The Hills of Zion," by H. L. Mencken. From *The Vintage Mencken,* gathered by Alistair Cooke. Vintage Books (paperback), 1955.

30–31   *How to Survive in Your Native Land,* by James Herndon. Simon & Schuster, 1971. Reprinted by permission of Simon & Schuster, a division of Gulf & Western Corporation.

57–58   *The Lunacy Boom,* by William Zinsser. Harper & Row, 1970.

60–61   *Slouching Toward Bethlehem,* by Joan Didion. Farrar, Straus & Giroux, 1968. Copyright 1966 by Joan Didion. Reprinted by permission of the publisher.

62–63   *The Dead Sea Scrolls, 1947–1969,* by Edmund Wilson. Renewal copyright 1983 by Helen Miranda Wilson. Reprinted by permission of Farrar, Straus & Giroux, Inc.

66   "Coolidge," by H. L. Mencken. From *The Vintage Mencken*.

67   *Pop Goes America*, by William Zinsser. Harper & Row, 1966.

91–92   *Spring Training*, by William Zinsser. Harper & Row, 1989.

113–14   *The Bottom of the Harbor*, by Joseph Mitchell. Little, Brown
            and Company, 1960. Reprinted by permission of Harold Ober
            Associates, Inc. Copyright 1960 by Joseph Mitchell. Repub-
            lished in a Modern Library edition (Random House), 1994.

119–20   *Slouching Toward Bethlehem*.

121–22   *Coming Into the Country*, by John McPhee. Farrar, Straus &
            Giroux, 1977.

122–23   "Mississippi Water," by Jonathan Raban. Copyright 1993 by
            Jonathan Raban. Reprinted with the permission of Aitken &
            Stone Ltd. The full text of the piece first appeared in *Granta*,
            issue #45, Autumn 1993.

124   "Halfway to Dick and Jane: A Puerto Rican Pilgrimage," by
            Jack Agueros. From *The Immigrant Experience*, edited by
            Thomas Wheeler. Doubleday, 1971.

125   "The South of East Texas," by Prudence Mackintosh. From
            Texas Monthly, October 1989.

125–26   *The Right Stuff*, by Tom Wolfe. Copyright 1979 by Tom
            Wolfe. Reprinted by permission of Farrar, Straus & Giroux,
            Inc.

127–28   *The Offensive Traveler*, by V. S. Pritchett. Alfred A. Knopf,
            1964.

129   *The Fire Next Time*, by James Baldwin. Copyright 1962, 1963
            by James Baldwin. Copyright renewed. Published by Vintage
            Books. Reprinted with permission of the James Baldwin
            estate.

131   *American Places*, by William Zinsser. HarperCollins, 1992.

137–38   *One Writer's Beginnings*, by Eudora Welty. Copyright 1983,
            1984 by Eudora Welty. Reprinted by permission of the pub-
            lishers, Harvard University Press, Cambridge, Mass.

139–40   *A Walker in the City*, by Alfred Kazin. Harcourt, Brace, 1951.

140–42   "Back to Bachimba," by Enrique Hank Lopez. From *Hori-
            zon*, Winter 1967. American Heritage Publishing Co., Inc.

142–43   *The Woman Warrior*, by Maxine Hong Kingston. Copyright

1975, 1976 by Maxine Hong Kingston. Reprinted with permission of Alfred A. Knopf, Inc.

144–45   "For My Indian Daughter," by Lewis P. Johnson. From *Newsweek,* Sept. 5, 1983.

145–46   *Clinging to the Wreckage,* by John Mortimer. Penguin Books, 1984.

146–47   "Ornament and Silence," by Kennedy Fraser. Originally in *The New Yorker,* Nov. 6, 1989. Copyright 1989 by Kennedy Fraser. Reprinted by permission. Subsequently included in *Ornament and Silence: Essays on Women's Lives,* by Kennedy Fraser. Alfred A. Knopf, 1996.

151–53   "Brain Signals in Test Foretell Action," by Harold M. Schmeck, Jr. From *The New York Times,* Feb. 13, 1971. Copyright 1971 by The New York Times Company. Reprinted by permission.

153–54   "The Mystery of Memory," by Will Bradbury. From *Life,* Nov. 12, 1971. Copyright 1971 by Time Inc. Reprinted by permission.

154–55   *Eleven Blue Men and Other Narratives of Medical Detection,* by Berton Roueché. Little, Brown and Company, 1954.

155–56   *Beyond Habitat,* by Moshe Safdie. The M.I.T. Press, 1970.

157–58   "Bats," by Diane Ackerman. From *The New Yorker,* Feb. 28, 1988.

158   *The Immense Journey,* by Loren Eiseley. Random House, 1957.

159   *Lives of a Cell: Notes of a Biology Watcher,* by Lewis Thomas. Copyright 1971 by Lewis Thomas. Originally appeared in *The New England Journal of Medicine.* Reprinted by permission of Viking Penguin, a division of Penguin Books USA Inc.

160   "The Future of the Transistor," by Robert W. Keyes. From *Scientific American,* June 1993.

162–65   "How Iraq Reverse-Engineered the Bomb," by Glenn Zorpette. From *I.E.E.E. Spectrum,* April 1992. Copyright 1992 by I.E.E.E.

167   "Politics and the English Language," by George Orwell.

183–84   "Hub Fans Bid Kid Adieu," by John Updike. From *Assorted Prose,* by John Updike. Alfred A. Knopf, Inc., 1965.

188–90   *Confessions of a Fast Woman,* by Lesley Hazleton. Copyright 1992 by Lesley Hazleton. Reprinted by permission of Addison-Wesley Publishing Co., Inc.

190–91   "Breaking Away," by Janice Kaplan. From *Vogue,* January 1984.

191–92   "Politics of Sports," by Janice Kaplan. From *Vogue,* July 1984.

192–93   *Life on the Run,* by Bill Bradley. Quadrangle/The New York Times Book Co., 1976.

199–200 "Deep Streep," by Molly Haskell. From *Ms.,* December 1988. Copyright 1988 by Molly Haskell.

201–2   *Living-Room War,* by Michael J. Arlen. Viking Press, 1969.

203   *The Musical Scene,* by Virgil Thomson. Alfred A. Knopf, 1945.

204   Review by John Leonard. From *The New York Times,* Nov. 14, 1980. Copyright 1980 by The New York Times Company. Reprinted by permission.

205–6   "T. S. Eliot at 101," by Cynthia Ozick. *The New Yorker,* Nov. 20, 1989. Copyright 1989 by Cynthia Ozick. Reprinted by permission of Cynthia Ozick and her agents, Raines & Raines, 71 Park Ave., New York, N.Y. 10016.

210–11   *The Haircurl Papers,* by William Zinsser. Harper & Row, 1964.

216–17   *The America of George Ade,* edited and with an introduction by Jean Shepherd. G. P. Putnam's Sons, 1961.

218   *Archy and Mehitabel,* by Don Marquis. Doubleday & Co., 1927.

219   *Benchley—or Else!,* by Robert Benchley. Harper & Bros., 1947.

220–21   *Strictly From Hunger,* by S. J. Perelman. Random House, 1937. Also in *The Most of S. J. Perelman.* Simon & Schuster, 1958.

221   *Getting Even,* by Woody Allen. Random House, 1971.

222   "Trump Solo," by Mark Singer. From *The New Yorker*, May 19, 1997. Reprinted by permission; copyright 1997 by Mark Singer. Originally in *The New Yorker.* All rights reserved.

223   "End of the Trail," by Garrison Keillor. Originally in *The New Yorker.* Copyright 1984 by Garrison Keillor. Published in *We Are Still Married,* by Garrison Keillor. Viking Penguin, Inc., 1989. Reprinted by permission of Garrison Keillor.

223–24   "How the Savings and Loans Were Saved," by Garrison Keillor. Originally in *The New Yorker.* Copyright 1989 by Garrison Keillor. Published in *We Are Still Married.* Reprinted by permission of Garrison Keillor.

225   *Dating Your Mom,* by Ian Frazier. Farrar, Straus & Giroux, 1986.

226–27   "Glad Rags," by John Updike. From *The New Yorker,* March 1993.

234–35   "Death of a Pig" from *The Second Tree from the Corner* by E. B. White. Harper & Bros. 1953.

266–83   "The News From Timbuktu," by William Zinsser. From *Condé Nast Traveler,* October 1988.

INDEX